SUTTON HOO

The Excavation of a Royal Ship-Burial

SUTTON HOO

THE EXCAVATION OF
A ROYAL SHIP-BURIAL

Charles Green

MERLIN PRESS *LONDON*

FIRST PUBLISHED IN ENGLAND 1963 BY
Merlin Press Limited
112 WHITFIELD STREET LONDON WI

COPYRIGHT © 1963 BY *Charles Green*

DESIGNED BY *Robin Collomb*

PRINTED IN ENGLAND BY
Camelot Press Limited
LONDON AND SOUTHAMPTON

TO IDA

for her patience

CONTENTS

LIST OF ILLUSTRATIONS   9

INTRODUCTION   13

I   PRELIMINARY ACTIVITY AT SUTTON HOO   21

II   THE SHIP-BARROW EXCAVATION   33

III   THE SHIP AND SOME OTHERS   48

IV   THE GRAVE-GOODS: I   66

V   THE GRAVE-GOODS: II   78

VI   THE KING-BURIAL: WHICH KING?   92

VII   NORTH SEA CROSSINGS   103

VIII   THE BEGINNINGS OF EAST ANGLIA   114

IX   THE SETTLEMENT OF THE SANDLINGS   127

X   THE CONSOLIDATION OF THE KINGDOM   140

BIBLIOGRAPHICAL SUMMARY   148

INDEX   155

ILLUSTRATIONS

FIGURES IN TEXT

1. Map of tribal distributions 16
2. General map of East Anglia 22
3. Map of the surroundings of the barrows 23
4. Plan of the barrow group 24
5. Squat jar of glass from the boat-burial in Barrow No. 2 28
6. Plan of ship-barrow 34
7. Sections of ship-barrow 35
8. Section of the burial-chamber roof 36
9. Plan of the funeral-deposit 37
10. General arrangement of the objects under the great silver dish 39
11. Lines of the Sutton Hoo ship 48
12. Some midship cross-sections 50
13. Suggested restoration of gunwale and upper strakes seen from the inside 53
14. Various kinds of clench-nail used in the Sutton Hoo ship 53
15. Section of stem of Nydam ship showing method of attachment of strake ends 55
16. Sutton Hoo boat No. 2 56
17. Stem and stern fastenings of the Snape boat, reconstructed according to Davidson's description of the clench-nails and end-bolts 58
18. Plan of the Snape boat 59
19. Some claw-shaped tholes 61
20. Iron standard with bronze stag 67
21. Iron grill from standard, seen in plan 67
22. Designs from silver mounts of drinking horns 74

9

23. Design of ornament on pyramids from sword-knot 82

24. Gilded bronze "ring" from the pommel of a ring-sword 82

25. Interlace motives in cloisonné-work where the beaded cloison is used:
a, Sutton Hoo rectangular strap-mount; b, Faversham, Kent,
composite disc-brooch 85

26. Examples of the "simple" and "two-stepped" mushroom-cell designs:
a, b, c, Sutton Hoo; d, Tongres; e, Wilton cross; f, Egbert shrine,
Trier 86

27. The Sutton brooch, showing true and bungled mushroom-cells 87

28. The Wuffing family tree 91

29. Chart of the North Sea, showing coastwise routes 113

30. Some East Anglian place-names 123

31. East Anglian cemeteries and other sites 128

32. Map of Denmark and south Sweden 133

ILLUSTRATIONS

PLATES

(appearing between pages 80–81)

Frontispiece: The Purse-lid.

    I (*a*).   The great silver dish, bronze cauldrons and other objects when first exposed.

    (*b*).   View after lifting the silver dish.

    II (*a*).   Bronze bowls, angons and spearheads, when exposed.

    (*b*).   The drinking-horn complex when first exposed.

    III (*a*).   The Nydam ship.

    (*b*).   The Gokstad ship.

    IV.   The Oseberg ship.

    V.   The Sutton Hoo ship: (*a*) looking forward, (*b*) looking aft.

    VI.   The Sutton Hoo ship: (*a*) extra nailing and other details on the port side.

    (*b*) the thole, showing the iron spikes.

    VII (*a*).   The Utrecht boat.

    (*b*).   The Kvalsund boat.

    VIII.   The bronze stag and iron ring from the top of the standard.

    IX (*a, b*).   The Sutton Hoo ceremonial whetstone.

    (*c*).   The Hough-on-the-Hill whetstone.

    X.   The Sutton Hoo helmet: (*a*) front view, (*b*) side view.

    XI.   The Sutton Hoo shield: front view.

    XII.   The Sutton Hoo shield: back view.

    XIII (*a*).   The Coptic bowl.

    (*b, c*).   The gourd-cups.

    (*d*).   The pottery bottle.

    XIV (*a*).   The large hanging-bowl.

    (*b*).   Enamelled bronze fish on internal escutcheon.

    (*c*).   The silver patch with bird's head decoration.

    (*d*).   Bronze animal mask from beneath an escutcheon.

II

XV. Escutcheons from the large hanging-bowl, decorated with red and green enamel and millefiori glass: (*a*) for suspension, (*b*) intermediate, (*c*) from below the bowl, (*d*) from inside the bowl.

XVI (*a*). The harp.

(*b*). A square-headed brooch of Leeds' 'Kenninghall' (Bi) type from Ipswich.

XVII. The great silver dish: (*a*) top view, (*b*) side view, (*c, d*) the control stamps of the Emperor Anastasius.

XVIII (*a, b*). Two of the nest of silver bowls.

(*c*). The fluted silver bowl.

XIX (*a*). The silver cup.

(*b*). The bowl of the ladle.

(*c*). The silver spoons inscribed SAVLOS and PAVLOS.

(*d*). A side view of one of the spoons.

XX. The great gold buckle.

XXI. The Merovingian gold coins and billets found with the purse.

XXII (*a-g*). Gold and jewelled buckles and mounts.

XXIII (*a-f*). Gold and jewelled buckles and mounts.

(*g, h*). Panels (reconstructed) from the Sutton Hoo helmet.

XXIV (*a*). The Sutton Hoo sword.

(*b*). Details of the sword-hilt and scabbard-mounts.

XXV. One of the jewelled clasps.

INTRODUCTION

I T IS a commonplace that in the veins of most modern Englishmen there runs the blood of many ancestral peoples. We may turn for example to Daniel Defoe who, in 1703, gave us 'The True-born Englishman', in which he descanted on the mixed descent and summarised it with

> 'The Western Angles all the rest subdued,
> A bloody nation, barbarous and rude,
> Who by the tenure of the sword possessed
> One part of Britain, and subdued the rest.
> And as great things denominate the small,
> The conquering part gave title to the whole;
> The Scot, Pict, Briton, Roman, Dane, submit,
> And with the English-Saxon all unite.'

And then he goes on to satirise at greater length the Norman strain in the hotch-potch.

But this mongrelism, as it is often called, can be and often is somewhat exaggerated. For Angles, Saxons, Frisians, Jutes, Danes and Norsemen were little more than tribal names of folk of closely-related stocks, of cognate speech and culture. Normans too were transplanted Norsemen somewhat modified by admixture with Saxons and Franks, another northern tribal group. And though the ancient British element, itself compounded of many strains, has modified the 'Nordic' mixture, it has still to be shown that its proportion is considerable in the English amalgam.

Many attempts have been made to prove this: to show, as one writer put it, that in 'those dark and anarchic centuries when, as we conjecture, a certain (probably small) number of North Sea pirates and revolted German mercenaries achieved a measure of political power and perhaps a certain infusion of new blood in the deserted province of Britain. Nay, it actually became a part of English patriotism to prefer this dingy and unattractive origin for our nation to the grandeur of a highly civilized part of the Roman Empire.'

But no competent student of the Dark Ages holds this extreme view. And as modern Dark Age studies progress, the mixed Anglo-Saxon and Scandinavian origin of a large proportion of the English nation becomes ever clearer. It must be noted too that from the first, the settlers commmonly called themselves English. Alfred the king, himself a West Saxon, always calls his language 'English' and the peoples of the Heptarchy the 'English-kin', never the 'Saxon-kin'. Oddly at variance with this is the use by Anglian monks of the name 'Saxons' for the English, but this seems only to be when writing in Latin, in which language earlier writers of the continent had used the name.

Great advances have been made this century in linguistic and historical studies of the Dark Ages. The results of research by physical anthropologists who attempted in the latter part of last century to define the physical types of the various strains, fell under suspicion as modern genetic studies revealed the uncertain foundations on which these racial conclusions were erected. But new techniques, in accordance with the greater complexities of their task, are now being devised and practised and in due course should clarify many obscure points. Most significant of all has been the progress in archaeological studies, which for long lagged behind those of the pre-historic and Romano-British periods.

In earlier centuries, remains found in pagan Anglo-Saxon graves were commonly attributed to the Romans. It was not until the latter part of the eighteenth century that the Rev. James Douglas, who excavated a series of Kentish graves, recognised the true origin of his finds. During the nineteenth century many cemeteries were discovered and either excavated or destroyed and from them large quantities of grave-goods came into the hands of museums and private collectors. Still more, particularly the handmade cremation urns, were broken and lost. J. Y. Akerman, Charles Roach Smith and others strove hard to record the best of them, but little attempt was made to study critically this mass of material. And, it must be noted, these earlier evidences were all from graves. It was not until after the Great War of 1914-1918 that the first early Anglo-Saxon dwelling site was recorded.

We owe to three men the great advances in our knowledge which began to be made in the present century. These were Reginald A. Smith of the British Museum, Professor G. Baldwin Brown and, most notable of all, Edward Thurlow Leeds of the Ashmolean Museum, Oxford. They for the first time classified and described this material by comparative methods. The distribution-patterns of the various types of objects were mapped and the sources of these objects were sought, in conjunction with European scholars, in the old Anglo-Saxon homeland. And immediately difficulties began to accrue.

In a famous passage in his *Ecclesiastical History of the English Nation*, Bede (A.D. 672-735), the monk of Jarrow, says: 'Those who came over were of the three most powerful nations of Germany—Saxons, Angles and

Jutes. From the Jutes are descended the people of Kent and of the Isle of Wight, and those also in the province of the West Saxons who are to this day called Jutes, seated opposite to the Isle of Wight. From the Saxons, that is, the country which is now called Old Saxony, came the East Saxons, the South Saxons, and the West Saxons. From the Angles, that is, the country which is called *Angulus*, and which is said, from that time, to remain desert to this day, between the provinces of the Jutes and Saxons, are descended the East Angles, the Middle Angles, Mercians, all the race of the Northumbrians, that is, of the nations that dwell on the north side of the river Humber, and the other nations of the English.'

With this passage must be considered another by Procopius, a writer of the early sixth century in the Eastern Roman Empire, that Britain was peopled by the Angles, Frisians and Britons. This cannot be summarily dismissed as the mere hearsay of a man living at the other end of the Roman world for, as will later be seen, it is curiously supported in some ways by the archaeological evidence.

The late H. M. Chadwick in his *Origin of the English Nation* (1907) made the classic analysis of all the evidence given by the earlier authors, such as Tacitus, Ptolemy and Orosius, whose works hold references to the North German tribes in the centuries before the Anglo-Saxon migration. From his work and that of later scholars, it seems clear that shortly before the Migration Period began, the continental Saxons inhabited what we now call Holstein, the province between the rivers Eider and Elbe, and East Friesland, the coastal strip of Hanover from the Elbe to the Ems. The Angles were seated to the north of them in what is now Schleswig though, in the century before they came to Britain, many had been moving southward into eastern Holstein, where their characteristic pottery is found side by side with that of Saxon type. The position of the Jutish homeland has occasioned much controversy, but it seems to have lain originally in what is now known as Jutland, the mainland province of Denmark, though many of the Jutes may well have left this province to settle in Saxo-Frisian areas before they came to Britain. And this broad distribution seems to be in general accord with the statements of Bede. Other peoples not mentioned by Bede include the Frisians, who occupied a broad coastal belt in what is now Holland, from the Ems to the Rhine. To the south of them were Frankish tribes. The Swaefe—or Swabians— of whom traces can be found in East Anglia, had by the beginning of the *Adventus Saxonum*, moved to the Middle Rhine, but a remnant of the tribe is believed to have stayed in Schleswig where they occupied a belt of country to the west of the Angles.

When, however, the archaeologists and particularly Thurlow Leeds, pursued their analyses, it became clear that though in some ways these tended to confirm the geographical and cultural divisions of Bede, in others

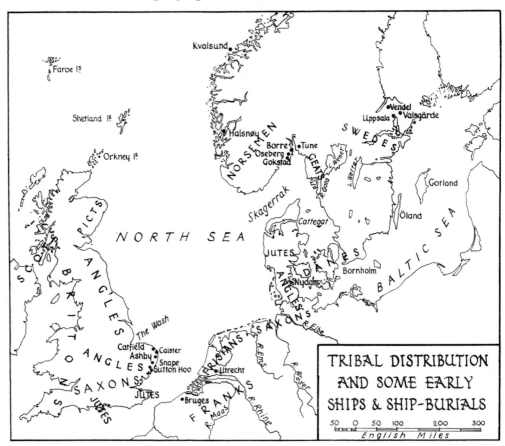

FIG. 1

they were curiously confused and, indeed, reversed. In particular, it is certain that though the various English areas may broadly be either Anglian or Saxon, there were mixed elements in each. This was most pronounced in Middle Anglia, the country immediately to the south and west of, and including most of, the Fenland. Furthermore, though in origin the 'Men of Kent'—i.e. east of the Medway—may be Jutish, yet there are features both in their institutions and particularly in their personal ornaments which point strongly to a source in the Rhineland.

By 1930, Mr. T. D. Kendrick, later to be Sir Thomas Kendrick, Director of the British Museum, had begun to publish a series of studies in books and periodicals, in which he offered startling alternative interpretations to what were now orthodox conclusions drawn from this funerary material. Controversy waxed and was further excited by the discoveries of Mr. T. C. Lethbridge, who worked mainly near the Fenland border of East Anglia. It was then, also, that Dr. J. N. L. Myres began that close and careful study of the pagan cremation urns from which he is now drawing far-reaching conclusions.

Much of the controversy centred on the reliability or otherwise of the early settlement history given in the *Anglo-Saxon Chronicle* and the writings of such men as the British Gildas who, in his *De Excidio et Conquesto Britanniae*, a polemic aimed at the native British leaders and written in the second quarter of the sixth century, described somewhat luridly though vaguely the horrors of the Saxon conquest. It cannot be said that these disagreements are yet resolved, but the sudden appearance of a mass of new evidence has enabled, and will further enable, fresh light to be thrown on many of the more doubtful and controversial points, though its discovery has also raised many new questions which are by no means yet fully answered.

It was the late spring of 1939 which saw 'the most remarkable archaeological discovery ever made in England' as Sir Thomas Kendrick was to describe it. This discovery, that of a ship-burial with a wealth of gold, silver, jewellery and other grave-furniture, generally believed to be that of a member of the ancient East Anglian royal house, led to a unique team of archaeologists being drawn together for its complete excavation. For a full realisation of the importance of the find it was unfortunate that, as the investigation progressed, European political tension was increasing and justly had pride of place in the national press. Then, a few days after the last stages of the work were completed, England went to war, the greatest war in her long history.

It is true that some preliminary newspaper reports appeared as the rich finds were brought to light and, as will be described below, these finds came almost at once into the hands of the British Museum. But for the duration of the war, after hasty preliminary treatment, they had necessarily to be deposited in safety from air-raid and other enemy action, so that their full and proper study and publication were much delayed.

Since the end of the war in 1945, work on these finds by the staff of the British Museum has gone steadily forward, notably by Mr. R. L. S. Bruce-Mitford, now Keeper of British and Medieval Antiquities. A vital part was also played by the members of the Laboratory staff under Dr. H. J. Plenderleith and his successor, Dr. A. E. Werner. In this they were assisted by Mr. Herbert Maryon, whose special knowledge of metals and their treatment led to his help being enlisted. As the treatment in the laboratory progressed, many of the objects became available for exhibition. To introduce them to visitors, the British Museum produced in 1947 a well-illustrated *Provisional Guide* which described both the excavation and the grave-goods. This was written by Mr. Bruce-Mitford and has been reprinted several times. He and other scholars, both British and continental, have also published many specialised papers dealing with various aspects of this great discovery. Among these are valuable descriptions by Mr. Maryon of the most important individual objects which have received his particular attention. More yet has to be done and it may be that the final word will not be written for many years to come.

But it has seemed that, so far as the non-specialist reader is concerned, the long break of the wartime years has meant that the full importance and interest of the story has perhaps not been savoured. This book has therefore been written to give a full account of the Sutton Hoo grave: an account comprising the story of the discovery, the details of the excavation, a description of the grave-goods, with the best pieces illustrated in colour and finally, a discussion of the considerable changes brought about in our views of both Early English settlement and political history, and of Early English craftsmanship and artistic accomplishment. In all these ways our enlightenment has been considerable and our evaluation of our Anglo-Saxon forebears greatly enhanced.

This book, then, is not primarily designed for archaeological specialists but for that increasing number of enlightened laymen who are interested both in the realities of the past and in the archaeological activities and techniques which are revealing them to us. It is of necessity greatly indebted to the published papers of specialists, particularly of Mr. C. W. Phillips, now Archaeology Officer to the Ordnance Survey, who directed the major excavation and to those of Mr. R. L. S. Bruce-Mitford. I am also personally indebted to them both for other help.

But in addition to this purely descriptive narrative, I have attempted to do more. In Chapter III I have reviewed the whole troubled question of the design and capabilities of early Anglo-Saxon ships. Our understanding of these vessels has been bedevilled in the past by the occurrence of an odd, apparently square-sterned, boat at Snape in Suffolk, not far from Sutton Hoo, which also contained a seventh-century inhumation burial. However, a careful analysis of the evidence has made it possible to show that this vessel did not depart from the general design inherent in the others, and so to clear up many misunderstandings and uncertainties.

Introduction

By establishing a 'norm' for ships of the period, it has been made possible to discuss more closely in Chapter VII the problem of the crossing from the continent to Britain and to assess the resulting settlement pattern. In Chapters VIII, IX and X I have in consequence looked anew at that of East Anglia and tried to relate the 'Sutton Hoo community' to the rest of the province. In this the picture, as in Chapter III, has been amplified by the results of my own fieldwork, and has also greatly benefited from the survey I made for the *Making of the Broads* (1960). In these last chapters, I am alone responsible for opinions expressed unless their author is clearly stated. At the same time, the statements in this book have not been documented in detail. But the bibliographical list at the end is fairly full. It includes the more important literature of the subject published in English, as well as a few other works. For those who may wish to follow up some part of the story in greater detail, the books and papers in this list, together with their appended bibliographies of works both in English and other languages, will make this easily possible.

ACKNOWLEDGEMENTS

As I have already said, this book could not have been written without the active assistance of Mr. R. L. S. Bruce-Mitford, to whom and to the Trustees of the British Museum I am also grateful for permission to publish many photographs. The Society of Antiquaries of London and Mr. C. W. Phillips have permitted the reproduction of several illustrations from the first account of the excavations. My friend Mr. Norman Smedley, Curator of the Ipswich Museums, has given great help in many ways and to him and to the Museums Committee my thanks are due for permission to publish extracts from their original unpublished records. Those consulted included all Mr. Brown's original field-plans and section-drawings with contemporary annotations by Mr. Guy Maynard. Both Mr. H. E. P. Spencer and Mr. B. J. W. Brown, now or formerly members of the Museum staff, have been most helpful, notably in amplifying detail of the happenings of 1938 and 1939.

At my request, my friend Dr. Calvin Wells undertook the first examination of the cremated bones from Barrow No. 3 and, when he recognised the presence of domestic animal bones, also arranged the supplementary examination by Miss Judith King of the British Museum (Natural History). My friends Mr. and Mrs. J. N. Hutchinson gave great help in the selection and acquisition of Viking-ship photographs from the University Museum of Oslo. I am indebted to Dr. H. Jankuhn of Göttingen University and to Professor Kersten and Dr. Raddatz of the Schleswig-Holsteinisches Landesmuseum für Vor- und Frühgeschichte for photographs of the Nydam ship. For many details of the Utrecht boat, which has not been published in an easily accessible form, I am very grateful to Dr. M. Elisabeth Houtzager, Director of the Centraal Museum der Gemeente, Utrecht. Mr. F. T. Baker, Director of the City and County Museum, Lincoln, has generously given me a photograph of the Hough-on-the-Hill whetstone and I am grateful to him and his Committee for permission to publish it.

I am grateful to the Ministry of Works, for whom some of my own fieldwork was done, for permission to use some of my results here. My friend Mr. R. Rainbird Clarke, Curator of the Norwich Museums, has both discussed some of the problems with me and provided several new ideas in his own recently-published archaeological survey, *East Anglia* (1960). Both he and my daughter Barbara Green have read my text and clarified many of my ambiguities. To my friends Mr. J. L. Plummer and Messrs. Joseph, John and David Woodhouse, all of the Caister lifeboat crew, past or present, I am greatly indebted for discussing with me at length a variety of technical points. My friend Mr. R. H. Haylett has also given great help in the examination and solution of North Sea problems.

The quoted translations from Anglo-Saxon poetry are taken by permission from Professor R. K. Gordon's *Anglo-Saxon Poetry* (1954), published by Messrs. J. M. Dent and Sons Ltd., in their Everyman Library. Those from Bede's *Ecclesiastical History* are from the same publisher's 1910 Everyman edition. I am also grateful to the editor of *Antiquity* for permission to quote from several articles which have appeared in that magazine and which are listed in the bibliography.

Acknowledgement to the undermentioned is due for permission to reproduce the following illustrations: *British Museum:* Figs. 4, 6, 7, 9, 13, 20, 21, 22, 23, 24, 25, 26, Plates I, II, V, VIII, IX (*a*) and (*b*), X, XI, XII, XIII, XIV, XV, XVI (*a*), XVII, XVIII, XIX, XX, XXI, XXII, XXIII, XXIV, XXV, and frontispiece. *Society of Antiquaries:* Figs. 3, 8, 10, 14. *Science Museum, London:* Fig. 11. *Lincoln Museum:* Plate IX (*c*). *Ipswich Museum:* Plate XVI (*b*). *Miss M. K. Lack:* Plate VI (*a*). *Miss B. Wagstaff:* Plate VI (*b*). Fig. 15 is after *C. W. Phillips, Esq. Museum of Prehistory, Schleswig:* Plate III (*a*). *University Museum, Oslo:* Plates III (*b*), IV, VII (*b*). *Centraal Museum, Utrecht:* Plate VII (*a*).

I

PRELIMINARY ACTIVITY AT

SUTTON HOO

Fᴿᴼᴹ ᴛʜᴇ Waveney to the Stour, the coastline of Suffolk is broken by several long estuaries, and of these, that of the river Deben is perhaps the most pleasant. Near its head on the west bank, some ten miles upstream from the open coast, stands the small town of Woodbridge and across the river lies the parish of Sutton. Here, on a broad sandy tract of heath known as Sutton Walks, some 100 feet or more above sea-level, stands a group of eleven barrows or burial mounds of different sizes. In Britain, barrows of this general type most commonly cover the graves of Bronze Age people of the second millennium B.C. In the succeeding Early Iron Age and Roman periods they were much rarer and in the early Anglo-Saxon period they were uncommon though in some parts of England, pagan Anglo-Saxon burials are not infrequently found as later intrusive burials in the barrows of the Bronze Age.

This barrow-group, known as 'Sutton Mounts', though today concealed from Woodbridge and the river by a nineteenth-century plantation, must formerly have stood boldly outlined on the skyline near the edge of the scarp which slopes down to the water's edge. It lies, too, close to the head of a small combe which provides an easily-sloping access up the scarp. Seven of the barrows are roughly on an almost north-south line, while the remaining four are grouped a little to the west near the southern end of the line. They fall into several rather clearly-defined sub-groups which may yet prove to be of some significance. The smallest, No. 11 (for the numbering, see Fig. 4) has a diameter of some 50 feet and stands 2½ feet high. Nos. 4, 6, 8 and 9 are about 65 feet in diameter by some 3-4 feet high. Larger still are Nos. 3, 5, 7 and 10, with a diameter of 85 feet and a height of 5-7 feet, though today No. 5 has been almost levelled to a flat platform less than a foot above the surrounding surface. Still larger is No. 2, nearly 100 feet across by 7 feet high. No. 1, an oval barrow, today no more than 75 feet by 65 feet across, stands about 9 feet high. But, as is

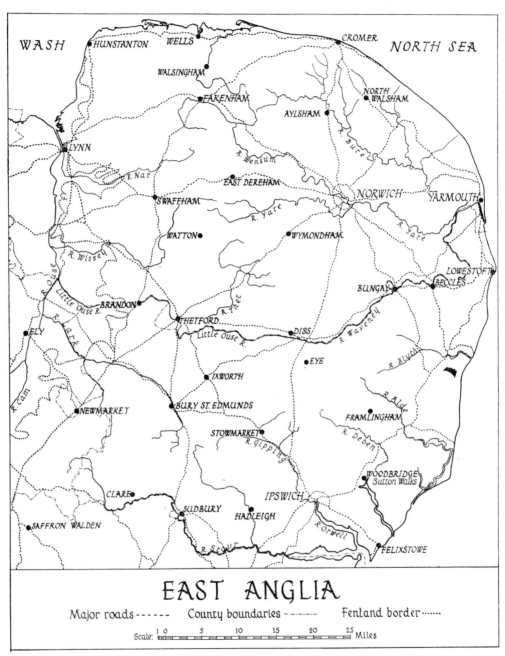

FIG. 2

described below, this originally was much larger, its diameters being estimated to have been some 120 feet by 75 feet. The reduction in size appears to have been partly due to ploughing, which removed a considerable portion of the north-western end and also, from time to time, the barrow has been robbed of its material for use elsewhere. Those numbered 7 and 10 show distinct signs of having been trenched from east to west in the past; it is not impossible however, that these depressions may be due to

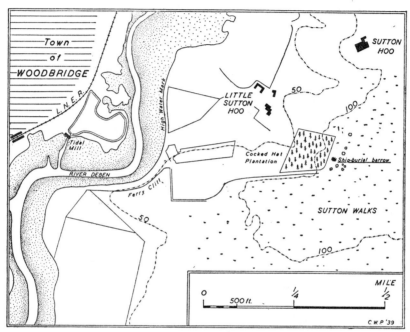

FIG. 3.   Map of the surroundings of the barrows

internal collapse over a long trench in the underlying natural surface. If so, they may point to other boat-burials, though this is perhaps unlikely. Furthermore, all the barrows in some degree showed evidence of disturbance from burrowing by rabbits.

The gravel and sand subsoil, in Anglo-Saxon times as today, was ill able to carry a heavy vegetation, and so the 'Walks' must have been an open heath as, indeed, an analysis of turfy remnants from the barrows has confirmed. The subsoil is described as 'yellow, but as it becomes humified towards the surface it grows much darker'. This indeed was to prove of great value to the excavators, for the colour-changes made it easy for them to recognise the distinction between untouched and disturbed sand.

23

SUTTON HOO SHIP-BURIAL

In 1938, ten of the barrows lay just within the estate of the late Mrs. E. M. Pretty, J.P., the other (No. 11) being over the boundary of an estate belonging to the Duke of Rutland. Mrs. Pretty had frequently

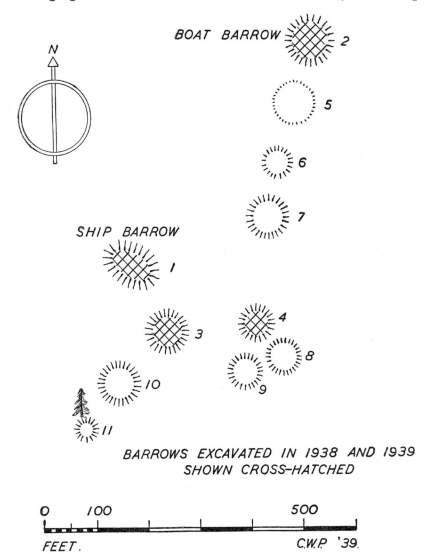

FIG. 4.   Plan of the barrow group

expressed her curiosity about the contents of these barrows and at last arranged with Mr. Guy Maynard, at that time Curator of the Ipswich Museum, to have some of them opened. On Mr. Maynard's staff was

Mr. B. J. W. Brown, whose primary duties were field reconnaissance and test-digging in the county. To Mr. Brown, therefore, fell the privilege of testing these barrows by excavation. Visits were also paid from time to time by Mr. H. E. P. Spencer, now geologist in the museum, who also kept certain records in addition to those made from day to day by Mr. Brown.

During that year, three of the barrows, Nos. 2, 3 and 4, were opened. Mrs. Pretty had at first expressed a wish for work to begin on No. 1, the highest of all. But wisely and most fortunately as it transpired, Mr. Maynard dissuaded her by pointing out that some evidence of their date and structural method should first be obtained from some of the smaller—and presumably less important—members of the group. In consequence, work was begun on No. 4, one of the 65-foot sub-group. As a fully detailed account of these first barrow-excavations and their results has yet to be published and will shortly appear from the pen of Mr. Bruce-Mitford, a summary only can be given here. It should also be mentioned that Mr. Brown, though of acute perception and wide experience, had not been trained in the most modern techniques of excavation and his methods, judged by those standards, were sometimes unorthodox.

Barrow No. 4, a broad rather flattened mound, was marked at its centre by a funnel-shaped hollow which penetrated almost to the original surface-level. A 5-foot trench was cut to the centre of the mound where a 14-foot square exposed the central grave dug into the original surface. This grave, a long oval pit some 14 feet by 4½ feet, with its long axis almost due east and west, contained at its eastern end a heap of cremated bone fragments covering an area some 3 feet by 2 feet. There was also a thin scatter of bone fragments over much of the grave-base. With the bones at the east end were many small fragments of thin bronze sheeting which, it was thought, were the remains of a bronze bowl largely destroyed by corrosion. Some of these fragments carried traces, impressed in the corroded surface, of finely-woven fabric.

Mr. Brown's exposed sections made it fairly clear that the funnel-shaped hollow in the overlying mound had been left in the past by barrow-robbers who had dropped a central shaft into the original grave. It is possible, though not certain, that the scatter of bones was due to their disturbance. What is more, it seems probable that grave-furniture, other than the corroded bronze bowl, was removed by them, though of the nature and extent of this hypothetical loot there was no trace. It was also noted that the barrow had originally been surrounded by a ditch.

The second barrow to be investigated was No. 3, a member of the 85-foot sub-group. This also was surrounded by a shallow ditch and showed an oval hollow in the centre of the mound. A superficial examination might have led to this being taken for a robber-pit, but excavation showed this not to be true. Though the pit had been dug to a point a little below the original surface-level, it had not penetrated deeply into the grave. Its base proved to be lined with a fine black silty deposit, which led to the suggestion that it had been constructed as a dewpond. But whatever its precise use, it had certainly contained water at one time and had not been dug to expose the grave.

Trenches were first dug to the centre from the north, west and south sides. A square with 12-foot sides was then opened over the central grave and a further T-shaped trench exposed sections in the east end of the pond. The grave-pit had a broad oval shape some $12\frac{1}{2}$ feet by 10 feet in plan, the longer dimension lying almost due east and west. Its base was some 5 feet below the original surface and, below the accumulated silt of the pond, it was filled with reddish sand and stones. This sandy filling was divided horizontally by a thin layer of clay which reached almost to the sides of the pit and thus effectively sealed the base of the grave. Here there lay a long rectangular tray-like object of wood. Its corners were not sharply angular, but slightly rounded. The substance of the wood had long been destroyed by decay and so the tray could not be lifted. But its essential structure was fairly clear and adequate measurements could be taken. Its overall length was $5\frac{1}{2}$ feet and its breadth some 2 feet 4 inches. All round ran a raised rim, some 3 inches broad, and the whole shape showed that this tray was a great slab of timber with its upper surface hollowed. It was, in effect, a very shallow dugout coffin without a lid.

At the west end of the tray, just inside the raised lip, lay a heap of cremated bones which also contained a large fragment of pottery, a bronze object and fragments of what appeared to have been a bone comb. Close by was another potsherd and a small bronze object. Near the east end of the tray, but on the grave floor, lay another heap of cremated bones, also with a sherd of pottery. Another fragment of bronze lay close by, near the tray. It was the two large potsherds, each with cremated bones, which determined immediately the period of the burial. Each came from a large handmade urn of pagan Anglo-Saxon type. One—that at the east end—was devoid of decoration, but the other bore characteristic incised patterns. And the dating of these two sherds was further confirmed by the presence of a very rusted axe-head which lay on the floor of the grave close to the south-western corner of the tray. This axe-head was of the so-called bearded type which developed from the Frankish throwing-axe, the 'francisca' and which later, in an enlarged form, was to become a favourite axe-type of the early Viking period. The socket still held a fragment of its wooden haft which was sheathed in iron. With it were traces of a leather holster which had doubtless held the axe. Unfortunately, this axe has since disappeared and only a photograph of it in its rusted condition, together with sketches made at the time, remain for its study. Axes of this type, however, are known in Germany from the middle of the sixth century and so the date of the pottery is confirmed. The burial in fact may well fall between A.D. 550 and 600.

Many if not all of the calcined bone fragments were preserved and have more recently been fully assessed by competent persons. Unfortunately the remains, as they are now preserved, cannot be assigned to one or the other of the two deposits and may probably have been mixed. Many are so badly crushed that their identification is quite impossible. Others, however, may be determined with some precision. These include some skeletal fragments of an adult human being and some fragments of the skeleton of a young horse. Still more are so damaged that their precise specific determination is uncertain, but their size shows them to have been of pig or sheep and possibly even dog. This careful scrutiny of the bones also brought to light a small plano-convex gaming-piece or counter and a scrap of metallic slag. The gaming-piece was about three-quarters of an inch in diameter and showed some warping by fire. It is probably of bone but just possibly is of ivory.

Barrow No. 2, the largest in obvious diameter, was the third to be excavated in 1938. This was recorded by Mr. Brown as some 90 feet in diameter and 7 feet high, and again a shallow ditch was found to have surrounded the mound. A broad trench was driven to the centre where it was expanded in a rectangular shape some 18 feet by 24 feet. This clearance exposed a long pointed-oval grave-area which when emptied, proved to be a grave-pit containing the decayed remains of a boat. The wood itself of the boat had long ago decayed, but its presence was shown by a dark smear in the sand-filling of the pit. Present also were the rusty nodules which had once been the clench-nails of a clinker-built vessel. This immediately confirmed the post-Roman date of the interment and its contents, when examined, pointed to a date not before the early years of the seventh century.

Scattered in the bottom of the boat were the remains of a blue-glass 'squat jar' with moulded lattice decoration, an iron ring and other iron fragments. There were also a number of bronze objects including a broken buckle, a fragment of decorated strip, a decorated disc and a stud or button. The bronze of the last three is gilded and this gilding still retains its original lustre and surface.

The digging of this barrow also made certain what had before been suspected, that the area had been occupied during the Bronze Age some 2,000 years earlier. In the substance of the barrow were found scraps of Bronze Age pottery which had been gathered up with the surface soil to

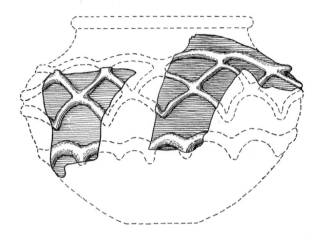

FIG. 5. Squat jar of glass from the boat-burial in Barrow No. 2 ($\frac{1}{2}$)

make the mound. Also, of greater archaeological importance, was a small tubular segmented bead of faience, of a type commoner in Wiltshire than East Anglia and dating to about 1450 B.C. or a little later and therefore of no significance in dating the boat.

The pit which had been dug to take the boat had been nicely judged for size and, except at the stern which touched the end of the pit, showed a gap of about 1 foot all round at the presumed gunwale level. It is probable, however, that the stemhead of the boat had projected above the original surface and had been destroyed either before or during the preliminary uncovering. There were other significant finds relating to this boat. As the first trench was being dug towards the centre of the mound, a patch of red burnt sand covered by a layer of ash, some 2 feet by 1 foot, was noted at about 20 feet from the edge of the mound. Close to this there was a scatter of clench-nails lying on the old surface. It was also noted that, after the boat-grave had been refilled, the surplus yellow sand from the original digging of the grave-pit had been spread in a broad oval layer some 30 feet wide over the grave and its surrounding natural surface. This appeared to be unbroken over the boat. If so, the grave-furniture was intact and had not been robbed in the past. In the sand filling of the pit round the ship and in this sand spread over the grave, were many sherds of Anglo-Saxon pottery. Most of these were fragments of handmade pots of pagan type but there was also present a single rim-fragment of that Middle Saxon type known as 'Ipswich ware', of great importance when the dating of these burials comes to be discussed.

All the finds which were made during the season's digging were given by Mrs. Pretty to the Ipswich Museum. To an archaeologist who specialised in the period the discoveries, particularly of what seemed to be a cremation burial in a boat and the cremation burials with the tray, were of great interest and importance and seemed to point to new possibilities in the study of Anglo-Saxon times. But the loose finds transferred to the museum were not very spectacular and the other results had not been widely publicised, so that their real significance was at that time hardly suspected.

Mrs. Pretty, however, was determined to know more about the contents of her barrows. She held further discussions with Mr. Maynard and, in Mr. Brown's own words,[1] 'On April 4, 1939, I received a letter from Mr. Guy Maynard containing the following: "If you would like another spell at Sutton Hoo, Mrs. Pretty is willing to resume work on the barrows." On Monday, May 8, I arrived at Sutton Hoo and had an interview with Mrs. E. M. Pretty, during which arrangements were made regarding personnel and equipment for the excavation. We then went to the barrows and upon my asking Mrs. Pretty which mound she would like opened, she pointed to the largest of the group (Tumulus 1) and said: "What about this?" and I replied that it would be quite all right for me. After a preliminary survey of the mound, work was commenced in the afternoon and the technique decided upon was similar to that adopted for dealing with the tumuli explored in 1938.' So simply and almost casually was the decision made which led to the dramatic finding of the unique treasure-ship.

The story may now be continued in Mr. Brown's own words. 'The original form of the barrow had been greatly altered by various disturbances; on the west many tons of material had been removed and had it not been prevented by the late Colonel Frank Pretty, who turned down a proposal to use material from the mound to make up the farmyards, more would have gone, while on the east material had also been taken for bunkers of a private golf course. Also, evidence was forthcoming from a gamekeeper who had dug into the mound at the request of a former owner of the estate in the hope of finding treasure. Lastly there was damage from the rabbits which had burrowed into the mound for centuries. The mound

[1] I am grateful to the Committee and Curator of the Ipswich Museum who gave me access to their files and permitted me to make extracts from notes prepared at the time of the excavation.

which before excavation presented a hogback appearance, especially when observed from the west, was in plan an elongated oval. . . .

'An initial or exploratory trench 6 feet wide was cut east to west across the mound down to the old ground surface, care being taken to note any inequality in the level of the sand which might serve to indicate a grave beneath and also for ship-nails in view of the data obtained from the 1938 excavations. On May 11, I was able to deduce with certainty the existence of a pit or grave below the old ground surface and explained the indications to Mrs. Pretty and that our trench was practically following the same alignment. I proceeded to widen our exploratory trench to 12 feet to admit of clearing the grave pit.

'The first find was a loose ship-nail and then five others in position. We were definitely at one end of a ship which was protruding a little above the old ground surface which here had been much disturbed by rabbits, fortunately without destroying the end or displacing the iron nails which remained in their original places. It was at first thought that this was the stern end of the ship and that its bow would be pointing to the Deben, but it was not until the vessel had been almost completely excavated that this point was elucidated and that her bow was known to point to the east.

'From now on extreme care had to be practised and the ship's interior was gradually cleared, frame by frame, with small tools and bare hands, the spoil being removed with the kitchen dustpan from Little Sutton. As soon as the rust of a ship's nail showed in the sand or the black and grey dust from wood decomposition, these features were left. As work progressed and the ship gradually opened out, drastic cut-backs were made and timbering with terraces became necessary to avoid landslides; the cutting through the mound proper assumed a width of 40 feet. It now became evident from the indications that a larger craft than the Snape ship was to be expected with a strong possibility of a length of at least 70 feet.

'While I worked at clearing the vessel's interior, the men were engaged in clearing the top layers and cutting away the mound-content, section by section, towards the west and widening the cutting. A careful lookout was kept for anything of interest which might turn up, but the only finds were Bronze Age sherds and part of a stone axe.'

On May 30, Mr. Brown found, at about the old surface-level, the remains of a fire of sticks, a broken piece of animal bone and a part of a tiger-ware jug. A later analysis of the exposed section showed that this barrow, too, had been sampled in the past by other barrow-robbers than Mr. Brown's gamekeeper. A shaft had been dropped to the original surface level and these remains lay at its bottom, suggesting that the robbers had lunched there before they refilled their shaft. It was indeed the ancient mutilation of the mound which led to this assault on the barrow being fruitless. For they had dropped their shaft in what they thought was the centre of the mound but, owing to its mutilation, they were well to one side of the original centre-point and so failed to find the underlying burial-chamber (see Fig. 7).

The tiger-ware vessel shows that this attempt was probably made late in the sixteenth or early in the seventeenth century. The rather daring suggestion has been made that it could have been the work of Dr. John Dee, a well-known alchemist and astrologer of Elizabethan days. Though the evidence is rather vague, he appears to have been commissioned to search for gold on behalf of the queen and a record of an attempt he made to find gold at Beeleigh in Essex is preserved in the Maldon Corporation Records. But, whether official or private in origin, the search failed and the grave-goods remained intact.

By June 11, Mr. Brown had cleared to the eleventh frame of the ship. Here traces of a former timber barrier began to show, together with pieces of bronze and iron. From this it began to be inferred, as was later shown to be true, that in the central portion of the ship a burial-chamber had been constructed. Though it was anticipated that this could hardly have survived intact, the remains already seen showed that something at least was there and the very difficult problem of dealing with this part of the ship began to be considered.

It was just at this time that Mr. C. W. Phillips paid a short visit to the site. Mr. Phillips, then a lecturer at Selwyn College, Cambridge, and an archaeologist of considerable standing, quickly realised the potentialities and difficulties of the task before the excavators and strongly advised a halt while the British Museum and Office of Works were consulted. This advice was wisely followed and the discussions took place. Finally it was agreed that the work should be finished by the Office of Works (as it then was) and Mr. Phillips was invited by them to take charge on their behalf. For a detailed survey of the ship when it should be possible, the Science Museum agreed to provide a specialist for the purpose. And so we have Mr. Brown's note that 'On July 8, Mr. C. W. Phillips arrived. He would, I was informed, now supervise the work on behalf of the Office of Works, etc., while I would act as his assistant, Mrs. Pretty consenting to the arrangement.'

The problems which now confronted Mr. Phillips were of some magnitude. Had he directed the excavations from the beginning, he would probably have adopted a rather different method of dissecting the mound. But the work had progressed too far for any significant change to be practicable, and he could only continue to drive a broad trench through the body of the mound, leaving ample space on either side both for safety and as a working platform. Mr. Brown's good workmanship and care had made this possible and all that was required here was further extension to meet the increased complexity of the task. But it was not just a matter of exposing and emptying the ship. Before the central overburden could be fully removed it had so to be analysed that as full a picture as possible of the ruined burial-chamber could be obtained. Furthermore, the previous excavations had shown that the condition of the deposits in the ship would probably not be good. To work out their full story, specialist treatment would be required.

When it became clear that the chamber did, in fact, contain an untouched deposit which would need the best available skill and experience for its removal, other leading archaeologists came forward to give their services. Much of the work of removing the grave-goods was done by Mr. W. F. Grimes, who is now Professor of Prehistoric Archaeology and Director of the Institute of Archaeology in the University of London. Other important work was done by Mr. Stuart Piggott, now Abercromby Professor of Prehistory in the University of Edinburgh, and his wife. The late Mr. O. G. S. Crawford, then Archaeology Officer to the Ordnance Survey and Editor of *Antiquity*, made a complete photographic record of the emptying of the burial chamber; other valuable photographic work was done by Miss M. K. Lack and Miss B. Wagstaff. Many other workers of standing, including members of the British Museum staff, gave help at critical moments; they included Professor F. E. Zeuner of the Institute of Archaeology, who analysed the soils and substance of the barrow. It is fair to say that never before in the history of archaeology had there been such a team of specialists working together in the field.

Mr. Phillips bore another responsibility which rarely falls to an archaeologist in the field. This stemmed from the bullion value of many of the finds. With quantities of gold, silver and jewellery still in the ground, the working team endeavoured to observe a discreet reticence about their findings. But of course it was impossible to prevent some rumour of their quality spreading. And so, to prevent unauthorised raiding, a police-guard had to be provided. This surprising variant of normal police work was ably organised by Mr. G. E. Staunton, O.B.E., Chief Constable of East Suffolk; his men of the Woodbridge Division, like the dragon in Northern story, guarded the hoard of gold.

II

THE SHIP-BARROW EXCAVATION

WHEN MR. PHILLIPS took over the direction of the excavation, Mr. Brown and his team had just cleared from the bows of the ship to the eleventh frame, where they had seen what appeared to be a timber partition across the interior of the vessel. From this it had been inferred, as has been said, that the central part had contained some sort of burial-chamber, built to protect the body and its accompanying grave-goods. This inference was later shown to be true but, as what evidently had been a substantial timber partition now showed merely as a 'slight dark discoloration in the sand not more than a quarter of an inch thick . . . only the most careful watch made it possible to get any idea of what had formerly existed'.

In order to ascertain the structural detail of this chamber, a different method of clearance was adopted. The sides of the cutting in the mound were further cut back and the central area, for a length of some 25 feet, was cut away horizontally. This was done with long-handled coal shovels with which the sand could be shaved away in very thin slices. Any trace of discoloration in the area could then be noted and, as successive slices were removed, could be followed downward in whatever direction it might trend. By some trick of the packing or of the collapse, one fragment of wood, apparently from this structure, had not been disintegrated by decay. This carbonised oak was left in position on a supporting pillar of sand and so provided a 'control section' for the rest of the chamber. It also showed that the roof of the chamber had been covered with turf, though whether this was a special covering or just a part of the ordinary structure of the overlying mound was not quite clear. Mr. Phillips thought that the first explanation might well be true.

Excavation by this careful shaving-method was soon to be rewarded for, some $17\frac{1}{2}$ feet to the west of the first cross-partition, the second was exposed, again as a slight stain in the sand. The extent of the chamber having now been defined, the clearance progressed more confidently and quickly gave further results. On the south side of the chamber, another line of decayed wood appeared, this time running parallel to the ship's

c

side. When followed downward, this was seen to slope outward towards the side of the ship. A column of filling, containing this sloping line, was left standing for a time until the rest of the clearance had been finished. It could then be seen that, when the sloping roof of the chamber had collapsed, a small part on the south side had remained in position. From

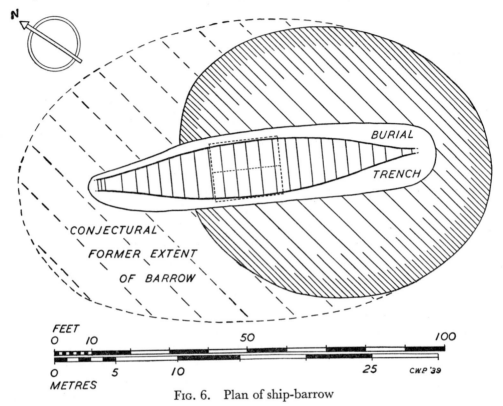

FIG. 6.   Plan of ship-barrow

this, of course, it was possible with some confidence to calculate the pitch and, from that, the height of the roof. This section is illustrated in Fig. 8 and the reconstructed line of the roof in Fig. 7. The two ends of the chamber, therefore, were gabled, the peak standing some 12 feet above the keel-plank, with the eaves of the roof resting on the ship's gunwale.

At a later stage of the work, the grave-goods were seen to be overlain in places by decayed planking, apparently fallen fragments of the roof. These remnants lay pointing in two directions at right angles to each other. From this it was inferred that the roof itself was of double thickness, one layer of planks running from gable to gable, the other from eaves to ridge. No trace of a door could be discerned at either end and nothing could be

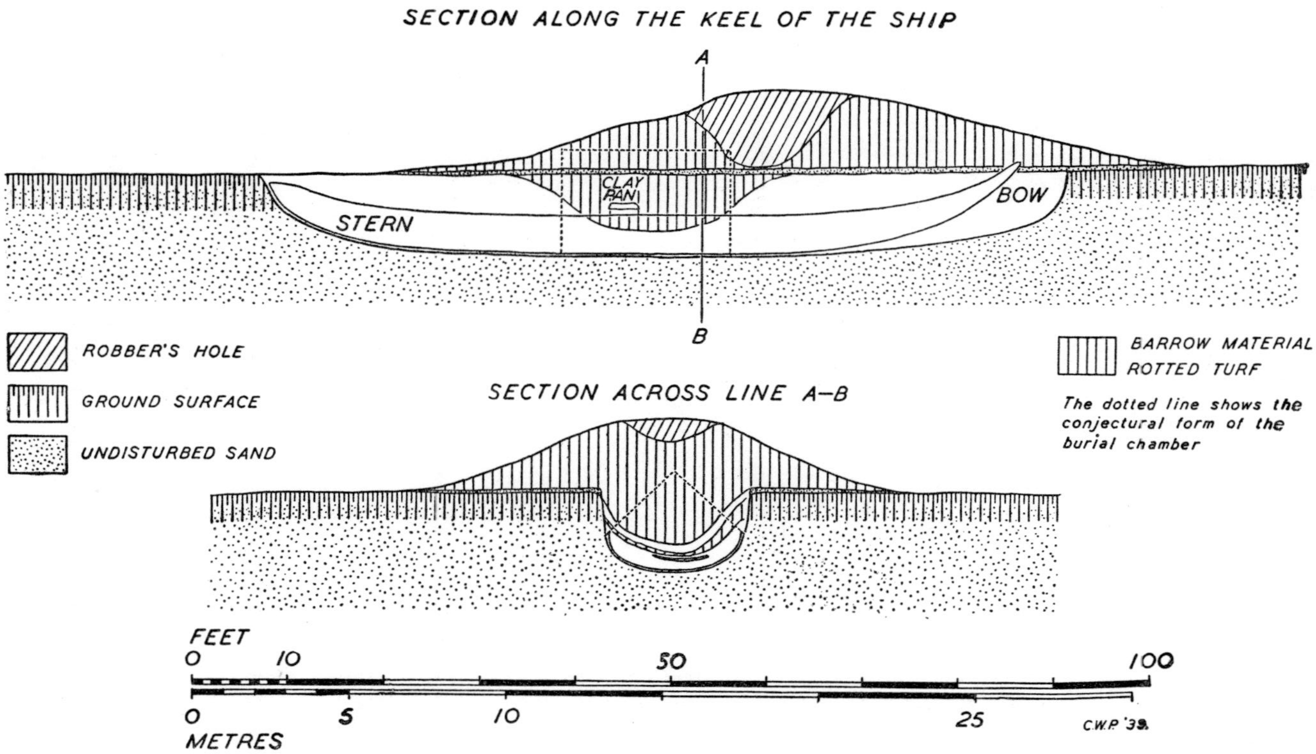

SECTION ALONG THE KEEL OF THE SHIP

BOW

STERN

CLAY PAN

A

B

SECTION ACROSS LINE A–B

BARROW MATERIAL

ROTTED TURF

The dotted line shows the conjectural form of the burial chamber

ROBBER'S HOLE

GROUND SURFACE

UNDISTURBED SAND

FEET

10   5   10   25   50   100

METRES

CWP '39.

FIG. 7. Sections of ship-barrow

inferred of the timber framework which must have supported the planked ends and roof. At one end, however, a rusted angle-iron was found; this probably had a place in the structure. And later, when the burial deposits had been cleared, a number of metal cleats forming a line on either side of the ship's floor was seen; they may also have served some structural purpose in this hut. Sawn-off scraps of planking were also found on the flooring; these, it was thought, were fallen pieces left by the chamber-builders. When the mound had been constructed over the chamber, the latter of course had not been filled with sand. The filling removed by the excavators was that which had fallen in after the collapse of the roof which seems not to have happened until many years after the burial. Outside the chamber, however, the ends of the ship had been completely filled at an early stage in the erection of the mound.

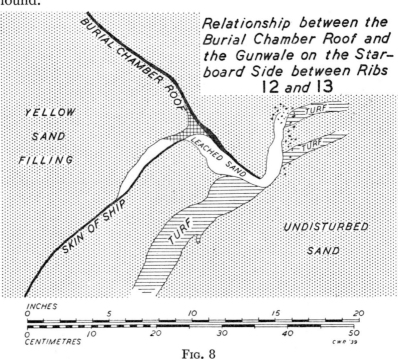

Relationship between the Burial Chamber Roof and the Gunwale on the Star-board Side between Ribs 12 and 13

Fig. 8

Above the grave-goods in this collapsed chamber-filling was found a curious clay structure. This was an oval slab of clay with a saucer-shaped hollow in its upper surface. The slab was about 36 inches by 18 inches by 5 inches deep and showed no traces of fire, so that it could not have been used as a hearth. It was, therefore, suggested that after the lower part of the mound had been built around and over the chamber, this receptacle had been laid above the roof where, perhaps, it received libations as a part of the burial ceremony. No exact parallel for this clay-pan is known. It will, however, be remembered that, in Barrow No. 3, the upper filling of the grave-pit contained a slightly concave clay layer though, as our record of this is inadequate, a close comparison cannot be made.

The emptying of the lower part of the burial-chamber now proceeded rapidly and soon the first objects began to show above the damp sandy filling. In Fig. 9 will be seen a plan of their distribution; it appears, as Mr. Phillips has said, 'in the form of a large letter H, with crossbar of exaggerated length'. The work now demanded even greater care and fore-thought than before. Gold, as is well known, is little subject to chemical corrosion and the objects of gold in the hoard were in essentially good condition. But the other objects, whether of silver, bronze, iron, or leather and woven fabric, were in parlous condition, partly due to the corrosion of the damp sand and partly to the pressure of the overlying collapsed roof and mound.

The method of clearing now had to be changed and the long-handled shovel gave place to paint-brush and packing needle. With these new tools, the topmost layer of sand on and around each object was removed, exposing the damper sand below. This soon dried in the hot sun and was then removed in similar fashion until the object was completely exposed and undercut as far as was possible. Such precise treatment, with its resulting slow pro-gress, was very necessary as, in their flimsy and corroded condition, the slightest adhesive contact of wet sand increased the strains on the thin and distorted metals and so lessened the chances of removing each object without further damage.

But some of the objects could not be allowed to dry in this way. Leather, the gourds and fabrics, as well as other things, began to distort and crumble as they dried and so these were frequently removed in a block and, wrapped carefully in damp coverings often of moss, were then transported to be individually cleaned and sorted when they had reached the laboratory. Though this meant that the precise nature of each object was not recog-nised at the time and the very existence of some was not suspected, the true shapes and relationships were better able to be worked out in the more suitable environment of the laboratory, where also were the resources required for the rapid treatment which sometimes was so urgently needed during the unpacking.

Not only in the uncovering and packing was this care exercised; equally important was the record-making as the objects emerged. For, grouped and disintegrated as they were, it was frequently difficult or impossible to be sure to which object a detached fragment might belong. For example, during the uncovering of the group under the great silver dish, a fluted bowl lay by the remains of a leather bag. This bag was equipped with a 'strap fitted with bronze buckle and slider to pass round it for support when full' and to this bag was also attributed a pair of silver handles. But later, in the laboratory, it was seen that the silver handles were, in fact, a part of the fluted bowl, from which they had become detached. And so, stage by stage and detail by detail, sketches and descriptive notes were multiplied. In this work the camera also proved its importance. While this part of the clearance was in progress Mr. O. G. S. Crawford made his very full photographic record, capturing each group as, little by little, they were exposed and so supplementing the notes with a permanent pictorial record of the precise position of each fragment. In the subsequent work of restoration all this was to prove invaluable.

Much of the work of removing the objects from the chamber, as has been said, was done by Mr. W. F. Grimes. In 1940 he published a description of that work, so that we may now follow him into the excavated pit and see what he saw. He says that 'the dominant feature in my first view of the ship was a great three-foot purple-grey disk; the silver dish, beneath which the lip of at least one other vessel was promise of more treasure to come. Other things there were already exposed—especially the two bronze bowls at the southwest corner of the burial deposit. But the urgent interest was centred on the dish and on the problem of whether it could be lifted entire, or whether steps should be taken by means of drawings and photographs to record its complete character before the hazardous work of lifting it began.'

Now this dish was lying right way up and it could be seen that it bore a complicated engraved ornament (see Pl. XVII and Chapter IV) so that, to record it fully, all this ornament would have had to be drawn and photographed in detail, a task of great difficulty. Fortunately, so much preliminary work was judged to be unnecessary as 'the metal was thick and seemed to be strong, in spite of a crack along one side'. The dish was safely lifted on July 26 and, as Mr. Grimes says, 'Beneath it was an assortment of articles, most of them in a fragile and parlous state, the recording, removal, and packing of which took the undivided attention of all working on the site.'

In the fluted bowl, for example, were several small cups with metal mounts; the cups themselves at first were thought to be of wood, though later it was realised that they were hollowed gourds. Warped and damaged as they were, no delay in their treatment could be allowed, sun-drying in

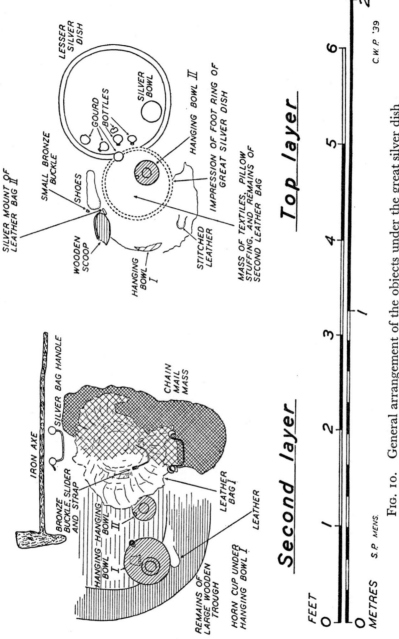

FIG. 10. General arrangement of the objects under the great silver dish

particular being the greatest danger. Into boxes they went at once, tightly packed in damp moss, which served to maintain their condition until laboratory treatment made them safe. Immediately under the great dish and around the fluted bowl were masses of leather and woven textile fabrics; the leather objects included bags and shoes. All these were decayed, the cloth being very rotten; to permit them to dry would have meant their complete loss. They were accordingly placed at once in bowls of water where they were kept until they could be properly packed for travelling. Also here were a small silver cup and what later proved to be a silver ladle, a small ivory gamespiece and two badly decayed bronze hanging-bowls.

When all these varied objects had been removed, it was seen that they had been resting on a great wooden tray, a part only of which remained. On this, protected by the cloth and leather, were found an iron axe and a mass of rusted iron chain-mail. The tray fragment, some at least of which was still in condition to be lifted, was finally dealt with. As so much of the wood in the ship and chamber had completely decayed, it was rather surprising that a part of this tray had, comparatively speaking, survived; it is thought that this was due largely to the protection given by the leather and cloth over which lay the great dish.

The greatest concentration of grave-goods was certainly that at the west end of the chamber; they lay packed close to the wooden wall. The first to be found was a giant whetstone with carved and bronze-decorated ends. This, of course, was in sound condition and was lifted with ease. But soon, more complex objects began to be exposed. Still closer to the wall lay a mass of rusted iron which, as it was cleared, was revealed as a long iron rod with various structural attachments. Though so heavily rusted, this 'lamp-stand' as it was named, was by no means destroyed and, when completely cleared of sand, was quite strong enough to be lifted by three persons on to a plank; on this it was suitably supported by packing and made fast. Near the upper part of this stand there lay an iron ring on which was a beautifully-modelled image in bronze of an antlered stag. It was at the time thought perhaps to be a helmet-crest.

On the other side of the stand was the collapsed ruin of a large wooden bucket with iron mountings. But sufficient of this was left to make its removal as a unit worth while. When the sand was cleared away, the remnants of the bucket were swathed in strong webbing. By slow degrees a thin iron plate was then slipped beneath, space for it being cleared by trowelling. It was now realised that the plate was too thin to carry the weight without bending, so the whole complex of plate and swaddled bucket was picked up on a spade and lifted on to a strong wooden base where it was made secure without any of its parts having suffered serious disturbance.

To the south of this bucket lay a complex group composed apparently of two bronze bowls, one inside the other, and a number of spear and angon heads of iron. The latter were even resting in one of the handles of the outer bowl and were rusted both to the handle and the body of the bowl with which they were in contact. Accordingly, the whole group was lifted as a single unit, to be treated and disengaged in the laboratory. Later, at a little distance, the iron ferrules from the butts of the spear-shafts were also found; from the position of heads and ferrules, of course, the overall length of the weapons could be approximately calculated; the spears were in fact some 9 feet long.

To the east of the bucket lay, in Mr. Grimes' words, 'a smudge of purple indicating silver, of which we had been conscious for some time. It was roughly circular in shape and near it was what appeared to be the end of a slender moulded bar.' Cleaning this silver was perhaps one of the most difficult tasks undertaken by Mr. Grimes. It proved finally to be a nest of inverted silver bowls and the silver rod was the handle of a spoon, below which lay another similar spoon. One of the bowls had slipped from the pile and was completely disintegrated, so that a photographic record only was possible. The remainder were lifted *en bloc* on an iron plate similar to that under the bucket and packed to be isolated in the laboratory. At first it was thought that this pack contained eight bowls, but later analysis proved that it held nine, six only of which were in good condition. Altogether therefore a stack of no less than ten of these bowls was deposited in the grave.

Near the north end of the stand was what Mr. Grimes himself claimed was 'perhaps the most intricate piece of cleaning: that of the remains of the shield', though this task, which took almost a whole day, he dismissed in comparatively few words. 'The central feature was the massive boss, which was solid and unlikely to cause trouble. But radiating irregularly from it were several richly decorated bronze mounts: some of almost paper thinness, some face upwards, some reversed, at all angles and presenting a picture of complete confusion. . . . To add to the difficulties this complex was partly covered with the remains of a fine wooden object ornamented with gold leaf. None of the material of the shield itself appeared to remain. The *umbo* was lifted without difficulty, but freeing the various adhesions of the mounts was a slow and tedious business. Each was lifted separately on two or more trowels after it had been drawn in on the plan.' In this very brief account, slight mention only is made of what was thought to be a thin wooden 'tray' with gilt gesso edging and animal-head decoration, which seemed to overlie the heavier mountings of the shield. It was not until the whole complex began to be analysed and studied in the British Museum that these, too, were seen to be a part of the shield itself.

To the east of the shield lay what was called the 'nucleus' of a helmet. It is not certain where this helmet was originally placed, for fragments of it were scattered over a much larger area, and it seems that it must have been damaged and dispersed by the fall of the roof. To the present writer it seems not unlikely that it may have hung on the gabled west wall of the chamber, to be flung down and broken when the first fall happened. But sufficient remained to make its unusual character evident and the description of the gathered fragments, made when they were unpacked (see p. 69), and the final reconstruction, serve to show its magnificence.

Close to the silver bowls and just to the south of the centre-line of the ship, were an iron blade and a sword. The blade was heavily rusted and appeared to be a scramasax, a characteristic weapon of the times, best described as a small cutlass. The sword itself had been a magnificent weapon, but it had been seriously damaged by the fall of the roof, as well as by rusting. It apparently had a wooden scabbard, bound with fabric at the lower end. Its hilt was decorated with gold and garnets.

Both over the sword and between it and the 'helmet nucleus' were scattered the gold and jewelled objects which formed the most costly part of the deposit; they were described by Mr. Phillips as 'the finest collection of Anglo-Saxon jewellery yet known'. These pieces comprised buckles, purse, clasps and small mounts of various types which, it seems, must have been attached to a complex leather harness made to be worn by a man, though its disposition was not what it would have been if worn by a body at the time of the burial. As Mr. Phillips records, most of these pieces lay face downward and he suggests that the harness may originally have been hanging up in the chamber, to be thrown down at the time of the collapse. The beautifully jewelled purse contained a number of Merovingian (Frankish) gold coins and two small gold ingots. These coins, as we shall see, were to provide a fairly close date for the burial.

Immediately to the east of the jewellery lay another complex which again, owing to its sadly decayed condition, was lifted *en bloc* to be treated and analysed in the laboratory. This complex had probably been in part protected by a layer of roof-planking, but at the time of the fall, the wood must have pressed the underlying objects flat. These very puzzling objects were finally seen to be a collection of drinking-horns with silver-gilt mounts. In two only was any of the original horn preserved. The others showed merely as flat triangles like the 'rays' of a starfish and there was some indication that these horns had originally been wrapped in cloth. The metal itself of the mounts had been converted to a salt of the element, but enough remained for the designs, or some of them, to be recorded, though permanent preservation was not possible.

On the south side of the chamber, a single object lay outside the H-pattern made by the others. This was a second iron-bound wooden bucket, generally similar to that lifted from the west end. And, near to the east end, close to the great silver dish, lay a wheel-turned pottery bottle and a small iron lamp. Finally, across the eastern end lay a further group of large objects. These comprised three bronze cauldrons of different sizes, a large iron-bound wooden bucket or tub and a mass of iron chainwork and bars. Of the wooden bucket nothing remained but the very rusty binding. The largest of the three cauldrons was much crushed, but the metal was still in fairly good condition, giving some hope of its future restoration. But the smaller cauldrons were so crushed and corroded that the thin sheet bronze of which they were made had fallen away into 'hundreds of small pieces', leaving little hope of a successful reconstruction.

Now in the layout of these grave-goods, the 'place of honour' would seem to have been on the central line towards the west end, below the gold and jewelled harness-fittings. Here the buried body would be expected to lie. But neither here nor, indeed, anywhere in the chamber could the slightest trace of a body be discovered. It is well known that, in some sandy soils, the acid moisture destroys bone. But even had this happened in the ship the teeth, or some of them, would be expected to have survived. Even had the body been toothless and so left no bony trace at all, there would have been its outline or at least the blank space it had occupied, surrounded by the weapons, personal articles such as finger-rings and armlets, and the small metal fittings of the clothing, to mark its position. Of this there was no evidence at all. Later, it may be said, further tests were carried out in the British Museum laboratory. These were designed to reveal, if indeed they existed, traces of a decayed body left on the remaining grave-goods. All these tests have failed to produce the slightest positive evidence. It is, therefore, now certain that an unburnt body never lay in this burial-chamber. The other possibility, that of a cremated body, is equally negatived. Calcined bone might be destroyed in the same way by soil acids; the presence of cremated bones in two of the other excavated barrows confirms that it has not happened here. Not a single receptacle in the chamber contained the smallest fragment of burnt bone nor was any found lying in the filling of the chamber. It is therefore generally agreed that this burial is a memorial, or *cenotaph*, burial for a person, clearly a man, whose body for one reason or another lay elsewhere.

The burial-chamber was now empty, but work did not cease as the remaining third of the boat, aft of the chamber, had still to be emptied of its filling of sand. Here the work was lightened, for most of the mound in this area had already disappeared. This clearance was completed without other significant finds being made and it was now possible to make a detailed survey of what remained of the ship itself. Though the woodwork was represented only by a discoloration of the sand, the rusted nodules which contained the original clench-nails were all in position and from these the lines and dimensions of the ship could be taken with a high degree of accuracy. Added to this, a detailed photographic survey of every part was made by Miss Lack and Miss Wagstaff, so that all its features can still be studied at leisure. The last details were recorded, the last objects were removed and, on August 26, the excavation which had begun with Mr. Brown's first cutting on May 8, came to a close.

At this point we may review the problem of how the ship was transported from the river and placed in the grave-pit. Though the steep sandy scarp was a poor approach up which to drag so large a vessel, the northern fork of the small combe which runs down the scarp from near the ship-barrow would have provided a fairly simple approach. Between the two map-contours of 50 and 100 feet, the horizontal distance is about 450 feet, so that the gradient in this steepest part is about 1 in 9—the overall average being about 1 in 22—and, with the aid of rollers, a strong party could have taken up the ship without undue difficulty. It is to be noted also that the barrow lies much closer to the head of the combe than does Barrow No. 2, where also a boat was buried. Now, as will later be seen, this smaller vessel was probably buried some 30 years before the great ship, so that the problem of its transport was still a living memory when the later burial had to be planned and doubtless due allowance was made for the larger vessel's much greater weight and bulk.

The second major problem was the placing of the ship in the pit. As will be seen from Fig. 7, it is certain that, though the grave was roughly shaped to fit the profile of the vessel, there was no long sloping ramp at the bow end, down which it could have been rolled. Mr. Phillips accordingly formed the opinion that the ship must have been lowered horizontally into the pit. He had already noted a thin irregular layer of excavated sand on the old ground surface below the mound. From this he inferred that the pit was first excavated and the spoil cleared from the site, this thin layer being sand spilt during the removal. Then, he inferred, poles were placed across the trench and the ship was laid over its final resting place. By means of a line of bollards on either side, ropes were stretched across below the ship, enabling it first to be slightly raised while the poles were withdrawn and then to be gently lowered to the bottom of the pit. To this Mr. Phillips adds: 'No actual evidence for this method was found, but it is difficult to see how the operation could have been performed otherwise.'

Now this solution, though feasible enough, does present some difficulties. The width of the grave-pit was some 16 feet and the bollards, in order not to pull from the sandy matrix would have to be placed some feet from the pit's edge. The length of the rope between each pair of bollards would then be more than 20 feet and, when carrying the weight of the ship, would certainly sag considerably. Bollards would accordingly be needed which stood 4 or 5 feet above the surface and would therefore have to be buried to at least the same depth, as well as being very stout logs. It is possible, though perhaps unlikely, that such bollard-pits would be untraceable in the ground; even more unlikely is the probability that the original grave-diggers undertook such a task as placing them if easier methods were available. It also seems unlikely that, if the ship were lowered in this fashion, it should fit so tightly to the grave-end at the stern, leaving a 6-foot gap at the bow. In fine, it is perhaps more probable that Mr. Phillips' first expectation of a sloping ramp down which the ship was drawn, is correct.

That this alternative is possible and may even fit the observed facts more satisfactorily, can be demonstrated. If the outlines of the grave were roughly marked out on the surface and the western end excavated approximately to fit the ship, leaving a long ramp to the east end, the ship could then have been drawn down tightly against the end where its weight would soon mould the roughly-cut sand to its shape. Without difficulty a few poles could then have been slipped under the stem and moved along to take the weight of the part still above ground-level. As most of the weight was already being taken by the sand below the stern, these poles need not have been unduly heavy. Then little by little the remainder of the pit could have been excavated, working below the ship from the west. From time to time as the ramp dwindled, the bearer-poles would be eased towards the east, so that the ship was kept well-supported by the sand. The last stages of the lowering of the ship could then easily have been accomplished by ropes or poles supported by the last cross-beam laid clear of the bow, or more probably by a pair of sheer-legs straddling the trench. By this means, no bollards would be needed, the very close fit at stern and sides, otherwise fraught with difficulty, was made easy and finally the 6-foot gap at the east end is explained. For here there would have had to be a space as the ship was gradually lowered to permit the diggers to remove their spoil and, finally, through which they themselves could climb out of the pit.

While these last stages of the excavation were progressing, other problems also exercised Mr. Phillips. The presence of gold and silver made necessary the holding of a coroner's inquest to decide the legal status of these pieces. Were they or were they not Treasure Trove? And so, on August 14, 1939, the inquest was held to determine the answer to this question. Now the law of Treasure Trove is difficult and perhaps obscure. But without going into its history and merely outlining the modern practice in its interpretation, a simple summary may be attempted. All objects of gold or silver—and these metals only—when found, are to be promptly handed by the finder to the police. A coroner's inquest on them is then held and it is the duty of the jury under the coroner's direction to make a decision. If the objects were *hidden* in the earth or in some other hiding-place such as a cavity in a wall resting on the earth, *with the intention at the time of their being reclaimed*, then the objects still belong to the owner or his legal heir. If the owner or his heir is unknown and cannot be ascertained, as must be the case when objects of antiquity are in question, the gold and silver are Treasure Trove and revert to the Crown. Where objects of archaeological interest are under consideration, the Crown is represented by the British Museum or its nominee—normally a suitable regional museum if the objects are not required for the national collection—and the antiquarian value is paid to the finder. The present purpose of this, of course, is not to confiscate for the financial value of the objects, but to preserve them where desirable for their scientific and artistic worth. If however the objects were 'dispersed', i.e. discarded or publicly disposed of with no intention of their being reclaimed, they are not Treasure Trove and so remain the property of landowner or finder according to the circumstances of their finding.

At this inquest it was made clear that the burial was a social function of its day, a religious ceremony carried out with a social sanction, when the grave-goods were placed in the grave in compliance with tradition. Some mention, it seems, was made of *Beowulf* and the funerals therein described. In fine, it was established that these grave-goods were *not hidden for safety* with any intention of their being reclaimed at a future date. The hoard therefore was adjudged not to be Treasure Trove and that, as landowner and finder—for she had initiated and controlled and, in its later stages authorised, the excavation for the purpose—they were the property of Mrs. Pretty.

And now followed an act of supreme generosity. The market value of the finds, not easily to be assessed, was vast. But Mrs. Pretty, realising that their true value lay in their unique archaeological importance, decided to forego any financial return for her efforts. On August 23, it was announced, the whole of the grave-goods of every kind had been given to the nation by Mrs. Pretty, as she deemed the British Museum to be the right and only suitable place for them to be housed. In this she was certainly right, but such insight and public spirit in the face of such great financial loss, are all too rare. And so the name of Edith May Pretty will always stand high in our list of national benefactors.

III

THE SHIP AND SOME OTHERS

THE CORRODING sand of the covering mound had not been kind to the fabric of the buried ship, for of its timbers there remained little more than a dark stain in the sand, with its ironwork a series of heavily-rusted nodules. But the skill of the excavators enabled the filling to be cleared without damage to these remnants of the vessel and it was possible to examine and record many of the details of its structure. For this difficult task, the excavators had the expert help of the late Lieutenant-Commander J. K. D. Hutchison, R.N., at that time on the staff of the Science Museum. In the first published description of the ship, given with Mr. Phillips' account of the excavation in 1940, insufficient allowance was made for the distortion brought about by pressure and suggestions were made about the stern of the vessel which are not tenable. But these in due course were corrected by R. C. Anderson and it is now possible to reconstruct this ship almost in its entirety.

To this end we are fortunate to have, in varying degree, detailed knowledge of other vessels of the same general type and period. From the East Anglian coast there are the smaller Sutton Hoo boat, the Snape boat and the Ashby Dell boat, all from sites in Suffolk. To these can be added the many boat-fragments from the Middle Saxon (i.e. *c.* A.D. 650-850) cemetery at Caister-on-Sea in Norfolk. But it is to the old continental home of the Angles that we must turn for the finest example for there, in the Schleswig-Holstein Museum of Prehistory, a complete ship of this type is still preserved. This ship, together with two others, was found lying in the peat of the Nydam Moss, Schleswig, in August 1863, when this province was still subject to the Danish crown. One was in parlous condition and could not be repaired; the second, built of fir, had to be left, but the third was duly extracted from its bed of peat. The Prusso-Danish war broke out, Schleswig and Holstein were incorporated in the Prussian kingdom and the ship was removed to the Kiel Museum, where it was restored and preserved. Here it survived the bombing of the Second World War and was then taken to its present home. This ship, a rowing-galley dating from about A.D. 400, represents well the type used both by the first Anglo-

48

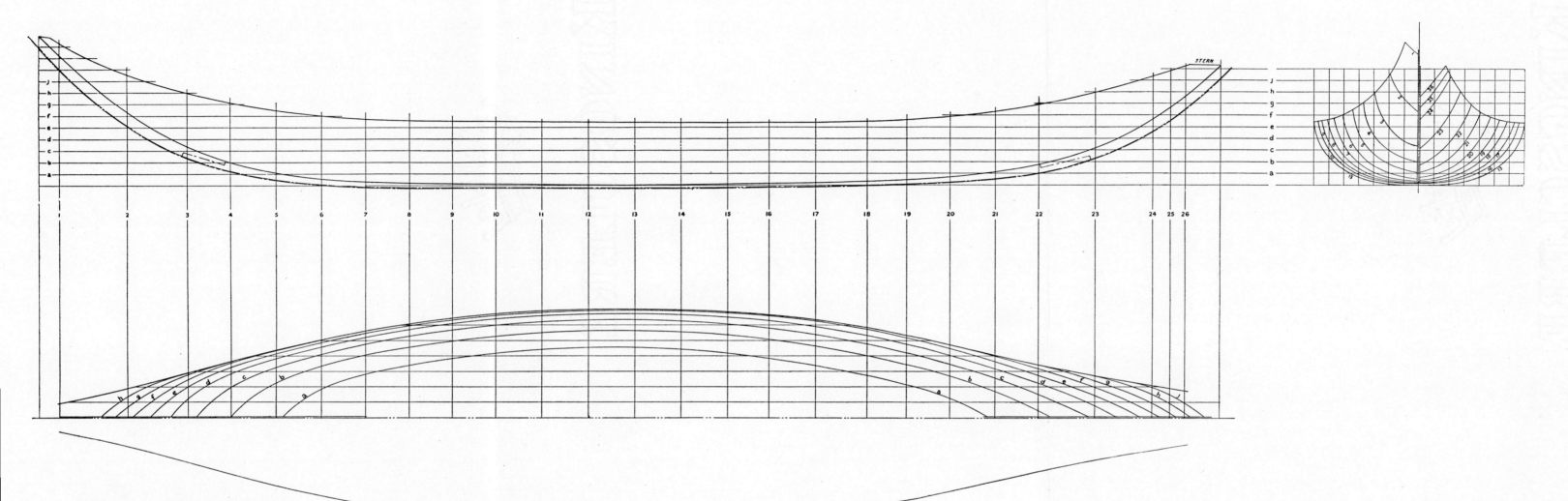

NOTE:—Lines were developed from measurements taken of
iron bolts found in position at excavation in sand,
and are incomplete at stem and stern.
Keel line is shown by dotted lines and was defined
by length of bolts found at scarf joints and by an
iron keel plate found at top of stem.

FIG. 11. THE LINES OF THE SUTTON HOO SHIP
Taken from the remains in the ground by the late Lt.-Commander J. K. D. Hutchison.

Saxons in their attacks on the Roman province of Britain, and by their descendants of the true Settlement Period who came to Britain in the fifth and sixth centuries. More recently a somewhat similar vessel—as it was at first considered—was found near Utrecht in Holland and is there preserved in the Centraal Museum.

Though ancestral to the later Viking ships, these earlier vessels were much more primitive in design and construction and their seafaring qualities were correspondingly limited. Sidonius, a fifth-century nobleman of Roman Gaul, who wrote to a friend about the warfare of the Saxons, says: 'When you see the rowers of that nation . . .' and again, 'to these men a shipwreck is capital practice rather than an object of terror. The dangers of the deep are to them, not casual acquaintances, but intimate friends. . . .' Historians have sometimes suggested that Sidonius exaggerated, but a study of these boats confirms that the risks of shipwreck must have been great.

Like the Viking ships, these Anglo-Saxon vessels were clench- or clinker-built, i.e. with the lower edge of each plank overlapping slightly the upper edge of the plank below and riveted to it at frequent intervals by clench-nails of iron, clenched on the inside over an iron washer, the rove. This technique is still used in the building of most of our smaller boats, such as dinghies and longshore fishing vessels, though nowadays the fastenings are generally of copper. Ancient vessels of this build, however, can readily be distinguished from modern clinker-built boats by the method used to fasten the clenched 'skin' to the frames or ribs. In both ancient and modern vessels of this type, the lower part of the planking is clenched first and the ribs inserted afterwards. A modern vessel has the planking riveted directly to the ribs, but ancient builders had a different practice. As the planks were adzed—not sawn—from split tree-trunks, raised strips were left at suitable intervals and when the ribs were later inserted, these raised strips were shaped to fit them. Then, through holes bored in these cleats, as they are known, fastenings of bast, withies or tough roots were passed and lashed round the frames, a method used both in the earlier Anglo-Saxon and the later Viking vessels. It is claimed that this method of attachment gave great elasticity to the boat in a seaway. This is doubtless true, though with the wear and tear of rough usage, the lashings must frequently have parted and that in moments of stress.

It was, however, in the structure of the wooden 'skin' that great advances were made by Viking times. For the keel, Viking ships had a stout 'plank-on-edge', which gave great longitudinal strength to the vessel, whereas the earlier boats had no true keel of this type, but merely a rather thicker plank than those adjoining it, set horizontally (Fig. 12). This gave a much less sturdy construction. Furthermore, the Viking shipwrights had learned to use narrow planks in comparatively short lengths, so that along the sides of the vessels there were frequent butt-joints where these short planks were pieced together. Each narrow plank carried only one cleat for attachment to each rib and the flexibility given by their use enabled well-rounded ships with high sheering ends to be built.

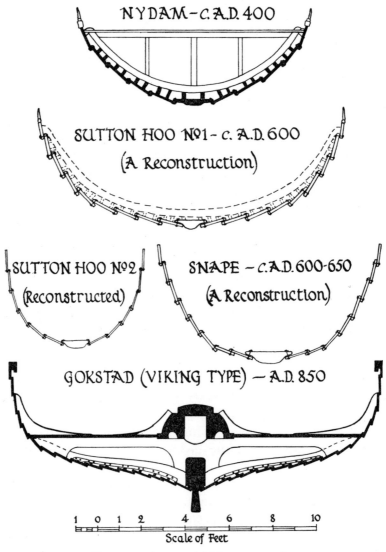

FIG. 12.   Some midship cross-sections

The earlier ships, however, were much simpler. That from Nydam was 73 feet 9 inches long overall. Each side was formed of six oak planks averaging 14 inches wide—excluding the gunwale—and carrying two cleats for each rib. Except for the uppermost strake—i.e. a line of planking from stem to stern—each strake was made of a single plank. Even the uppermost—gunwale—planks were pieced only once on each side, in the bows of the ship. So comparatively intractable were these great planks that the vessel had a broad shallow flat-floored cross-section amidships and, towards each end, a narrow almost straight-sided V-shaped section. This, of course, gave a much less seaworthy craft than those of the Vikings and it is easy to see why 'shipwreck' was 'capital practice rather than an object of terror', for seafaring in the short steep seas of the shallow North Sea must indeed have been fraught with hazard.

There were other differences. The external plank-on-edge keel of the Vikings made it possible for them to sail their ships and, as is well known their long passages were normally made under sail, with only occasional help from oars. But there is no evidence whatever that Anglo-Saxons of the Migration period had any sailing vessels at all. Certainly these flat-keeled ships would not have stood the strain of a single great sail. No trace of mast or rigging-fastening has been seen in any of those we know. And the reference by Sidonius to 'rowers' seems to confirm this conclusion.

The oblique evidence of contemporary literature also gives some confirmation. Bede in his *Ecclesiastical History*, includes a story told to him by Guthfrith, who later became abbot of Lindisfarne. Guthfrith and two of the brethren had gone by boat from Lindisfarne to Farne, some seven miles, to visit Ethelwald, the hermit successor of St. Cuthbert who died in 687. While returning to their own place, 'there ensued' in Guthfrith's own words, 'so great and dismal a tempest, that neither the sails nor oars were of any use to us, nor had we anything to expect but death'. By Ethelwald's prayers, however, the storm was stilled until they had reached land. Guthfrith then continues: 'When we had landed, and had dragged upon the shore the small vessel that brought us, the storm . . . immediately returned.' Here there seems to be good evidence of a sailing-boat in approximately the last decade of the seventh century, though it is also clear that a boat 'dragged upon the shore' by three men cannot have been a seagoing clinker-built ship. There is a possibility, indeed, that this small vessel may have been a skin-covered curragh—the modern descendants of which may still be seen on the west coast of Ireland—but if so, it does not in any way help a discussion of clinker-built boats.

There is an Anglo-Saxon poem *Andreas*, in which the hero makes a voyage. In it we read that 'the candle of the sky grew dark, the winds rose, the waves dashed, the floods were fierce, the cordage creaked, the sails were soaked. The terror of the tempest rose up with the might of hosts; the thanes were afraid; none looked to reach land alive'. No longer, it seems was shipwreck a capital practice rather than an object of terror. This poem, of the so-called Cynewulf school, was not written before the second half of the eighth century and, more probably, may be dated after A.D. 800. This seems to be almost the first certain reference to an Anglo-Saxon deep-sea sailing ship and is, of course, roughly contemporary with the opening of the Viking period, more than a century at least after the burial of the Sutton Hoo ship. The various references in the poem to 'the high-prowed vessel', 'the high-beaked vessel', also suggest a ship rather of Viking than of Nydam type.

There is one other reference which is somewhat earlier than the *Andreas*. This is in the epic poem *Beowulf*. In this poem, both the funeral ship of the mythical king, Scyld Scefing, and Beowulf's own ship which took him to and from the Danish kingdom, were sailing ships. But, though purporting to describe events which happened about the beginning of the sixth century, the poem in the form in which we have it was not composed until the eighth century and, with some degree of probability, near the middle of that century, if not a little later (see p. 138). We may, therefore, safely infer that it describes contemporary ships and not those of the earlier period. This is confirmed by descriptions of the ship, e.g. 'the boat with twisted prow', 'the ring-prowed vessel', so reminiscent of the prow of the Viking ship from Oseberg (Pl. IV). Again this gives a date at least a century after the date of the Sutton Hoo burial, thus tending to confirm that clinker-built sailing ships in Anglo-Saxon England began first to make their appearance after A.D. 700, though small sailing-boats may perhaps have been in use from a slightly earlier date.

The inferred construction of the Sutton Hoo ship agrees generally, even closely, with that of the Nydam ship and the occasional differences arise from two centuries' more of experience in the shipwright's craft. Its overall length, as seen, was some 80 feet, but as the uppermost part of both stempost and sternpost had been lost, it must originally have been 85 feet or even a little more. Its greatest beam was some 14 feet and its depth amidships 5 feet. Its draught, when lightly laden, would have been some 2 feet. Its keel appeared not to be of plank-on-edge type, but a horizontal plank of the Nydam type. This was probably rounded on its lower side, giving a slight external projection of some $2\frac{1}{2}$ inches (Fig. 12).

Of clinker build, it had nine planks a side, including the gunwale

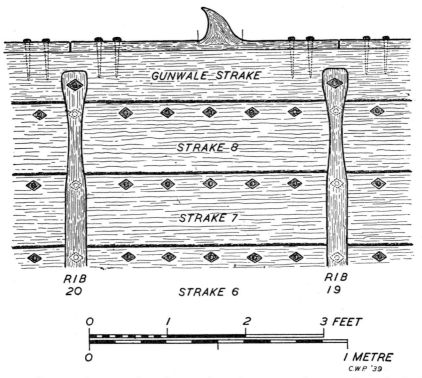

GUNWALE STRAKE

STRAKE 8

STRAKE 7

RIB 20   STRAKE 6   RIB 19

0   1   2   3 FEET

0   1 METRE
C.W.P. '39

FIG. 13. Suggested restoration of gunwale and upper strakes seen from the inside

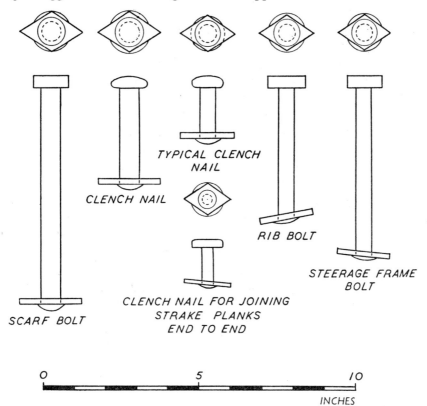

TYPICAL CLENCH
NAIL

CLENCH NAIL

RIB BOLT

STEERAGE FRAME
BOLT

SCARF BOLT

CLENCH NAIL FOR JOINING
STRAKE PLANKS
END TO END

0   5   10

INCHES

FIG. 14. Various kinds of clench-nail used in the Sutton Hoo ship

plank. Amidships, these planks were about 15 inches broad and were clenched at intervals of about 7 inches, by clench-nails over diamond-shaped roves. It was noted that these roves were all carefully set so that their long axes were horizontal (Fig. 13). This would have required very careful workmanship in their setting and is perhaps rather unusual. The clench nails from the twelve boat-fragments at Caister all show, more or less, the line of the wood-grain in their rusty surface, and it is possible to say that these, which more probably belong to average boats of the period, are not set with any care as to their direction, though they have a similar diamond shape.

As this normal clenching continued under the ribs, it seems probable that these frames were fastened to cleats on the inner surface of the planking, but this could not be confirmed with certainty. The stem and stern posts were joined to the keel with a scarf-joint, i.e. a long oblique half-joint, each joint being reinforced by three iron nails, $6\frac{1}{4}$ inches long, clenched over normal roves. Here there was a small variation from the Nydam pattern, for the latter ship had its fore and aft scarf-joints secured by the stout wooden pegs known as treenails. An added refinement lay in an iron strip nailed to the outer edge of the stern post, a protective device not seen in the Nydam ship. The planking details, however, were not those of Nydam, for each strake was built up of five lengths of plank, with the ends joined by short clench-nails, indicating the presence of half-joints giving flush surfaces.

In the Nydam ship, the 19 pairs of ribs were further secured by cross-braces or thwarts, resting on upright stanchions. To these thwarts were fastened the rowers' seats. The 26 pairs of ribs in the Sutton Hoo ship showed no evidence whatever of seats or thwarts, but these must have been cut away to accommodate the burial chamber. The Nydam ship was propelled by 15 oars a side and the oar-fittings on the gunwale are of great interest. Each oar was pulled against a single claw-shaped thole, to which it was attached by a grommet or ring of rope or hide. This passed through a hole in the base of the thole. These tholes were worked from naturally-grown forks, the longer arm of which was straight, with grooves cut to hold the lashings which fixed it to the gunwale. In the Sutton Hoo ship there were probably 19 tholes a side of similar shape, but the base pieces, each about 3 feet long, were attached to the gunwale by two or more iron spikes at each end. These ends were in contact with their neighbours and so formed a continuous rail around the gunwale. There was no evidence to show how the grommets were attached. (Fig. 19)

One structural puzzle which the excavators could not resolve was how the shipwright had attached the planking to the stem and stern posts. In the Nydam ship, a groove or rebate had been cut on each side of the posts into which the ends of the planks snugly fitted (Fig. 15). This may well have been done at Sutton Hoo, but is not certain. The remains rather suggested that this may have been done with the ends fastened in pairs by bolts which went right through both planks and the post. The shortness of the bolts, however, rather tells against this interpretation. As will be seen below

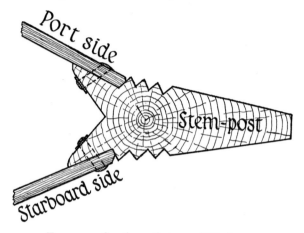

FIG. 15. Section of stem of Nydam ship showing method of attachment of strake ends

(p. 58), the strakes of the Snape boat were apparently fastened in this fashion.

The Nydam ship was steered by a large broad-bladed oar slung over the starboard quarter. At Sutton Hoo, no such steering-oar was seen, but the disposition of the ribs and their fastenings at this point, carefully designed to take the strain of the oar, showed that the steering mechanism was of Nydam type.

There was evidence that the Sutton Hoo ship was already old when it was buried. One seam amidships on the port side showed many additional clench-nails between the original ones. These had clearly been inserted in an attempt to tighten a strained and leaky joint. The stern scarf-joint, too, had been strengthened by additional nailing. Other slight abnormalities, however, probably belong to the deterioration and decay undergone by the ship after it was buried. There was evidence that the gunwale lines, both fore and aft, had sprung away from the stem and stern posts. This had at first given rise to the suggestion that the ship had a narrow square or rounded counter-stern. But Anderson showed that this shape would be assumed if the gunwale-ends had sprung from their fastenings and that, as would be expected, this ship was double-ended in the normal Northern fashion.

There had seemed at first to be some confirmatory evidence for this blunt-sterned variant in East Anglia. In Barrow No. 2 at Sutton Hoo, as has been described, a boat apparently about 18 feet long was found. In the absence of a competent boat specialist, this was less thoroughly surveyed and recorded than the great ship of 1939, but a plan was made by Mr. Brown, showing a boat with long pointed bow and a nearly square stern only a comparatively short distance aft of the greatest beam. From his notes made at the time, Mr. Maynard published a description of the constructional details of this stern, an article illustrated by sketches made by Mr. Spencer (Fig. 16). Careful study of this description makes it certain

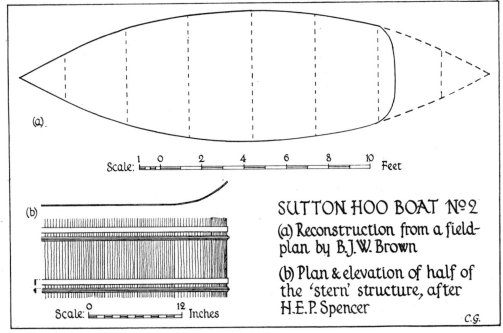

Scale: 1 0 2 4 6 8 10 Feet

(b)

SUTTON HOO BOAT № 2

(a) Reconstruction from a field-plan by B.J.W. Brown

(b) Plan & elevation of half of the 'stern' structure, after H.E.P. Spencer

Scale: 0 12 Inches

C.G.

FIG. 16

that this could not be a true stern at all, for it consisted only of short vertical boards held loosely together by iron strips without any nails, a quite impossible constructional method for a sea-going ship or, indeed, for any boat at all.

It will be remembered that the stern of this boat lay tightly against the end of the grave-pit, although the remainder of the boat had a gap of a foot all round. There were, too, on the original surface nearer the edge of the barrow, many loose clench-nails scattered around. It seems quite certain that one end of a normal double-ended boat—probably the stern, though this is by no means certain—was cut away and the larger portion was then lowered into the grave-trench. The vertical boards were then inserted along a curved line to the very end of the trench to prevent collapse of the containing sand, and the iron bands bent round to hold them in position. The part which was cut away was probably burnt on the patch of red sand and the fallen clench-nails were the indestructible remnants from this fire.

When reconstructed, assuming that the curve of the sides was accurately recorded, the boat shows an approximate overall length of 22 feet 6 inches, with a greatest beam of 6 feet. The removed portion, therefore, must have measured more than 5 feet in length. The trench-profile was rather roughly recorded and shows a greater midship depth than would be expected. As however, this drawing showed a horizontal gunwale, there must be some error, as a complete absence of sheer is virtually impossible. It is more likely indeed that the stemhead and the gunwale near it were originally above the surface and a normal sheer took the gunwale below the trench-lip amidships. If so, the midship-section (see Fig. 12) is too deep by at least one strake. This reduction would give an internal depth amidships of about 3 feet, a suitable dimension for a boat of this type and size.

It is possible to find some confirmation of this boat-cutting in the 'pseudo' boat-burials of seventh-century date found in the Middle Saxon cemetery at Caister. Here a number of graves were covered with sections, two, three or four strakes wide, cut from the sides of boats of from 20 to 40 feet long. These were set longitudinally with the outer convex curve uppermost. But a single grave had the body laid *in* such a fragment, as was shown by the clench-nails being under the skeleton with the roves above the heads of the nails. There is some reason to believe that this settlement was an outlier of the East Suffolk group and this odd method of burial has been tentatively interpreted as a 'poor man's' copy of the more magnificent ship-burials of their royal leaders.

Yet another East Suffolk square-sterned boat of the same period has been published in the past and seemed to support the validity of the Sutton Hoo square stern. This lay below a burial barrow half a mile east of Snape church and was excavated in 1862. Three primary accounts of this excavation were published, each by a man who took some part in it, and each contributed something not noted by the others. With two of these accounts appeared a plan, longitudinal elevation and cross-section of the boat, the plan and cross-section purporting to show the disposition of the clench-nails. When found, these were merely rough nodules of rusted iron and the woodwork of the boat was little more than a stain in the sandy filling of the grave. Mr. Bruce-Mitford, however, has published an X-ray photograph of one of these rusty fragments and the original shape of the characteristic clench-nail can be clearly seen inside the rust.

The drawings show the boat to have had a flat floor which made a sharp angle with the outward-curving sides. It also had a broad, slightly rounded stern. The published plan, however, immediately raises doubt of its accuracy. Seventeen rows of clench-nails are shown, six rows on either side and five on the flat floor, one of them running along the keel-line in the middle of the floor. Furthermore, the second from the port side stops several feet short of the stern. Even more remarkable is the disposition of the

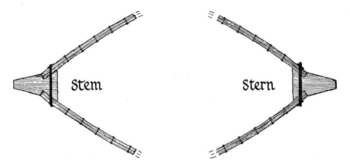

FIG. 17. Stem and stern fastenings of the Snape boat, reconstructed according to Davidson's description of the clench nails and end-bolts

clench-nails in the stern, for these are shown running right round the square stern in a quite impossible fashion. Of this plan Septimus Davidson, who was the leading excavator, says in a footnote: 'The plan, not having been made by a professional surveyor, may not be minutely accurate, especially as to the exact position of the rivets at the smaller end.' To this we may add with confidence that they are even less accurate—as shown— at the larger end, for no boat could ever have satisfactorily been built in this fashion. And this is fully confirmed by Davidson's own written description, for of the clench-nails he says: 'The rows were six in number on either side and *four or five* [my italics here and below] in number at the bottom of the boat. At the sides the rivets lay horizontally, at the bottom they rested vertically on the sand. *All the rows terminated in two rivets lying parallel with each other—the one at the stem, the other at the stern.*' This can mean only one thing. The parallel bolts at stem and stern held the ends of the two opposing strakes to the posts and this implies that there *must* have been a sharp-ended stern comparable in shape with the bow. The explanation of this surprising error in the plan would seem to lie in the method of its preparation. The rough notes and sketch-plans would have been handed to the draughtsman to prepare the engraving for Davidson's published account. The draughtsman, knowing nothing of early 'Nordic' boats, doubtless strove to make the details fit the shape of the nineteenth-century clinker-built transom-sterned boats he knew. And for a century his misconception has obscured the truth.

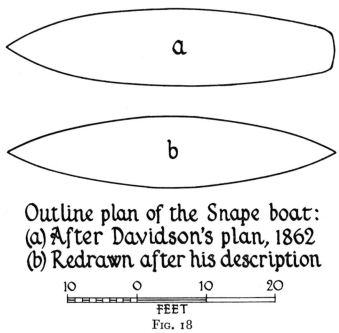

Outline plan of the Snape boat:
(a) After Davidson's plan, 1862
(b) Redrawn after his description

10   0   10   20
FEET

FIG. 18

Though the exact boat-shape shown in the cross-section is hardly credible as it stands, yet a reconstruction can be made (see Fig. 12). In this, the roves were carefully set on the recorded shape-line and the planking was restored, approximately as it must have lain, from these. It can thus be seen that this boat had not the broad shallow midship cross-section of either the Nydam or the Sutton Hoo ship (see Fig. 12). Taken in conjunction with the other illustrations, it would appear to have been a boat designed for use in estuarine or inshore waters and not for open-sea crossings. The comparatively sharp angle between strakes 2 and 3—numbered from the keel—would lead to the roves being set obliquely to the head. A similar arrangement was noted in some of the Caister clench-nails which suggests that these, too, may have been inshore vessels of this pattern, a suggestion perhaps supported by the comparatively large number of different boats there recorded.

To complete the tale of these Anglo-Saxon boats from Suffolk, that found in 1830 in Ashby Dell, in Lothingland, must be described. It is probable that this boat was exposed during excavations for the planting of trees. A full record, together with drawings, was made by a Mr. Keable, estate carpenter, who was also described as 'agent and draughtsman to H. Mussenden Leathes of Herringfleet Hall'. An abstract of this record, by Keable's great-nephew, Kenneth Luck, was published in a local newspaper in 1927. Luck died in 1933 and his papers were burned by his landlady, so that there is little hope of learning more of this extraordinarily interesting boat. Though neither uncle nor nephew was versed in the detail of ancient ships, both were carpenters by training and so may reasonably be trusted to have given accurate descriptions of joints. This, as will be seen, is an important point when the details are assessed. Luck evidently regarded this as a Viking ship, as did many of those present when it was exposed. But in 1830 Keable had noted at the end of his description that 'Mr. Ruskin thinks the ship a Batavian and pre-Danish, the squire that she belonged to the Priory of St. Olaff [sic]'. Whoever Mr. Ruskin may have been, it is certain that he was close to the truth as the following description shows.

The dimensions of the Ashby boat are a little difficult to understand. We are told that she was 54 feet long overall and 47 feet along the keel from stempost to sternpost, but that the upper parts of these posts had rotted away. As, however, the gunwale was present, very much cannot have been lost. If so, the boat cannot have had the long raking stem and stern seen in the Nydam and Sutton Hoo ships, but was in profile more like the smaller Sutton Hoo boat. On the other hand, the depth amidships was 6 feet and, from a line joining bow and stern, 9 feet. There was, then, a 3-foot sheer, which is almost exactly that of the Nydam ship, though the actual hull-depth of the Ashby boat is greater.

The stempost was scarfed to the keel in normal fashion, but the stern-post was morticed to the keel, which would seem to imply that this post was straight and not curved. Both joints were secured by treenails. The shape of the keel's cross-section is not recorded, but we are told that it was rebated to take the garboard—i.e., adjoining—strakes. This does not help in ascertaining the type of keel as, though rebating is essential with a plank-on-edge keel, both the Nydam and Sutton Hoo keels could be regarded as rebated by a man who did not understand their origin.

The planking is described as of 'riven larch . . . adzed . . . into form,' and each plank had two cleats for attachment to each frame. The cleats were slotted, with a hole on either side of the slot. The frames rested in these slots and were secured to the cleats by lashings passed through the holes. This is the technique employed in the Nydam ship and the double cleats show that the planks were wide, in the earlier style. One difference, however, may be noted. The cleats were not carved from the solid wood with the planks, but were made separately and affixed to the planks with treenails. The frames themselves were naturally-grown timbers and the cleats were 'eased or packed' where required to fit any irregularity.

The Nydam style is again seen in the tholes. These were claw-shaped, seven a side, and were lashed to the gunwale. Though there was provision

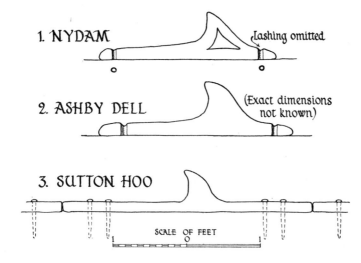

FIG. 19.   Some claw-shaped tholes

for seven oarsmen only a side, there were fourteen thwarts with seats, fixed to the frames and gunwale plank with both treenails and lashings, though the detail of this is not given. And oars must have been the only method of propulsion, as there was neither mast-step in the keel nor any mast-seating in a thwart. From the stempost to the first thwart was a short cross-piece along the midship line and this held loosely a rounded timber, 9 inches in diameter and 4 feet long. This had a horizontal hole bored right through it, apparently to take a small bar, and so led it to be regarded as a small capstan.

The most surprising feature of all appears to be that no iron was used in the boat's construction, all fastenings being either by treenails or by lashings through holes bored to receive them. If this is strictly true, the boat must have been clenched, not with iron rivets, but with lashings. Even this constructional method, primitive though it seems, is not without precedent for, in 1896, in a peat-moss at Halsnøy in Søndhordland, Norway, a boat clenched by just this method was found. It is described as generally of Nydam type, but with strakes still sewn by cords. It was dated to about A.D. 200 and was clearly an intermediate form between the ancestral elaborated canoe of Hjortspring type and the Nydam boat. There is evidence, also, that even as late as Viking times, some of the Nordland boats of North Norway were still sewn with sinews, at least in part.

The Hjortspring boat, found in the island of Als, Schleswig, in 1921, had a hull-length of 33 feet and a greatest width of 6 feet. There was a single bottom plank, slightly concave amidships, the concavity tapering in long narrow grooves which ran out in 'rams' projecting beyond the hull. Each side was made of two broad planks lapped clinker-fashion, but sewn with bast and caulked with resin. There were raised cleats, three to a plank, in each of ten rows, to which frames were lashed with bast cords. As there was neither mast nor thole, she must have been propelled by paddling. This vessel, clearly developed from a dugout canoe by the addition of raised sides, was dated to about 300 B.C.

In assessing the true position of the Ashby boat in this sequence of vessels, one other factor must be considered. The boat was not lying in a silted-up gutter, but had been deliberately buried, away from any water-course. Though there is no record of any grave-goods or body in the ship, it seems that this may perhaps have been another of the Anglo-Saxon burial series.[1]

The Ashby boat, therefore, may be seen to possess somewhat discrepant features. The seams clenched by lashings and not by iron nails—for treenails will not satisfactorily serve for this—are a primitive feature. The lashed claw-shaped tholes and double cleats to a strake-width are in true Nydam style, as is also the oar-propulsion. The considerable sheer and the scarfed stempost are also true to the same style, but the morticed stern-post and the relative proportions of overall and keel lengths are not. They rather suggest a Roman influence. Here it may be noted, Ashby Dell lies only a few miles from Belton Fen which, lying in the shelter of the Saxon Shore fort at Burgh Castle, has elsewhere been suggested as the possible local headquarters and dockyard of a detachment of the Roman fleet, the

---

[1] In 1956, Dr. J. M. Lambert and the writer made a series of borings around the approximate site of the boat in an attempt to determine if, indeed, it lay in the silt of a former creek. These borings showed no trace of open-water mud or estuarine clay, so that it must have been transported overland and buried.

Classis Britannica, in the fourth century. If so, it is possible—and no more—that this boat was built for an early Anglo-Saxon settler before the last traces of Roman influence had disappeared. But, as is discussed below, boat-burial can hardly have been introduced before the early years of the seventh century, which weakens the possibility.

The keel, stempost and sternpost were said to be of elm, which is credible. But the planking of 'riven larch' seems to be impossible. Larch does not appear to have been available at this time, either in Denmark or England. It is probable therefore that the timber was from another coniferous tree and its species was mistaken by Keable.

The tale of early Anglo-Saxon boats is now almost complete. From Catfield, a village lying close to the Norfolk coast, comes the story of a 'Viking ship' found about 1855 in a sandpit in the middle of the village.[1] The sandpit site suggests that this may have been yet another ship-burial, but as no detail of the ship's type has survived, it cannot contribute to the discussion of early ships.

A few others of doubtful type are known but these, too, can contribute little to the discussion. At Walthamstow, Essex, a clinker-built vessel was found in 1830 while excavating the East London Company's reservoirs. It was clinker-built, some 20 feet long, and between the lapped planks was a caulking-pad of a 'cement in which cowhair was used'. This feature suggests a date for the boat as late at least as the Viking period and, as other critical details are not recorded, it may here be disregarded.

In 1900, another clinker-built boat was found at Walthamstow. This, too, had some early-looking features, but as it was inverted over a burial of the Viking period and was clearly not a sea-going vessel, it may also be disregarded. Of another which still lies below King Street, Great Yarmouth, even less is known. That it had a pointed stem and was clinker-built with 2-inch clench-nails was recorded when it was first exposed in 1886, and again about 1911. But from what is now known of the growth of the bank on which Yarmouth stands, it is reasonably certain that this ship cannot be earlier than the Viking period and may possibly postdate the Norman Conquest. Other early clinker-built vessels from Britain belong to the Viking period or a later day, and so need not be considered here.

The Utrecht boat, though when first found it was dated as second

---

[1] Information about this discovery was given to the writer by the son of a former rector. When a small boy, he heard the parish clerk report the discovery to his father, the rector.

century A.D., may perhaps be likened to the second (1900) Walthamstow boat. It was found in 1930 in the sandy filling of an old channel of the river Vecht which, before about A.D. 860, was a main arm of the Rhine. Though primitive in some of its features and notably a flat keel-plank 47 feet long and 6 feet 7 inches (2 metres) broad amidships, it was certainly not a very early vessel (Pl. VII). A recent Carbon-14 test has given a date of A.D. 700 ±100 which, though possibly a little in error due to the remains having been creosoted, appears to make it later in date than the Anglo-Saxon settlement period. This boat was clenched with iron nails in the forward part but aft with treenails, a construction very ill-suited to a sea-going vessel. The method, however, is identical with that of the Walthamstow boat which also was clenched forward with iron and with treenails aft. The latter is generally regarded as a local river-barge used for the funeral of a Viking chief—to judge by his gold ornaments and sword—doubtless at a time when one of the party's own ships could ill be spared. There is some evidence that the Utrecht boat was fitted with a mast, though not in the normal Viking-ship fashion. Furthermore, double tholes for one pair only of oars were fitted and, as the boat is 54 feet 4 inches long and 13 feet 8 inches in beam, it is clear that it was not a normal rowing galley, but a river-craft of the eighth century or thereabouts.

From this survey, certain conclusions may be drawn. In spite of anomalous recording in the past, all early Northern clinker-built ships were double-ended and, before the end of the seventh century, on the English North Sea coast at least, were all oar-propelled. Of sailing ships in this period there is no real trace. Though the earlier Anglo-Saxon pirates must have been well-acquainted with Roman merchant vessels, which carried a large square sail and a small artemon, they did not themselves use such sails, probably because their craft lacked a strengthening plank-on-edge keel. This absence of sailing ships during the Settlement Period has, as is discussed below in Chapter VII, a very important bearing on the pattern of Anglo-Saxon settlement in eastern England, a bearing which justifies this somewhat close analysis, made possible by the discovery of the Sutton Hoo vessels. For this subject has not before been fully discussed and it will be seen not only to illuminate the origins of the 'Sutton Hoo group', but also the whole of the Anglo-Saxon migrations.

It is true that, in the past, the Anglo-Saxons' possession of sailing ships has been suggested on the evidence provided by the Galtabäck ship, and this must now be examined. This ship was found wrecked on the west coast of Sweden, south of Varberg. With an overall length of 42 feet, it was double-ended with flattish floor. It had an external plank-on-edge keel, to which the curved raking stem and stern posts were affixed by lapping joints which were not true scarfs. Its planks, ten strakes a side, were clenched, but were not attached to the frames by cleats and lashings, being clenched directly to the frames in more modern fashion. Furthermore, the frames were carefully-shaped timbers, not naturally-grown crooks and there was a carefully-constructed mast-step resting on the keel and a mast-seating in the after part of the appropriate thwart. Altogether the lines and structural detail are of a more modern type than either the earlier Migration or later Viking type of clinker-built vessel. By the analysis of the pollen-content of the containing peat-deposits, the Galtabäck ship has been attributed to the fourth or fifth century A.D., making it roughly of the same date as the Nydam ship. But this early date cannot be sustained for the lines, and particularly the constructional details, make it impossible, there being too many anachronistic features. The true date is probably more nearly a thousand years later.

There remains one other vessel to be mentioned. The Kvalsund boat, the larger of two found at Kvalsund, Herøy, in Sunmøre, Norway, was excavated in 1920. It was characteristically double-ended, clinker-built, with its fine ends upturned in a fashion approaching that of the later Viking ships (Pl. VII). Its overall length was 59 feet and its beam almost 10 feet. Its keel was a horizontally-set plank, but differed from the earlier keels by reason of a projecting rib which had been left along the centre-line of the outer side. The Norwegian ship-specialists, Dr. Brøgger and Professor Shetelig, considered this to be rather the first of the true Viking type than the last of the Migration type. Its rudder also was affixed to the boat's quarter in the more elaborate fashion, familiar from the Viking ships, required for a sailing vessel. This boat was tentatively dated by Professor Shetelig to about A.D. 600. But there is apparently no very cogent reason for so early a date and one at any time in the next century would seem to suit equally well. Even if the earlier date can be substantiated, this is after the close of the Anglo-Saxon Migration Period. In fine, with the Galtabäck ship discounted, there is no evidence whatever to suggest the presence of clinker-built sailing ships in England before the end of the seventh century and only the uncertain dating of the Kvalsund boat seems to preclude a similar statement for the Scandinavian North.

IV

THE GRAVE–GOODS: I

B EFORE ATTEMPTING to discuss the identity of the grave's subject, we must review in some detail the more important objects found in the burial-chamber and of these, pride of place should perhaps be given to the iron stand. In the 1940 report of the excavation it was shown on the plan as 'lamp stand' and, in the text, was called 'the flambeau'. It was described as an iron bar 5 feet 3 inches long with the lower end spiked and the upper end carrying an equal-armed cross set horizontally, the four arm-ends each carrying a stylised bull's-head ornament. Eleven inches below this was another horizontal fitting, a square gridded frame, also decorated at each corner with a similar bull's head. From these there had apparently once been thin stays running downward to a more closely-set third bracket on the rod though, when found, these stays had been largely destroyed by rust (Fig. 20). Nothing quite like this stand had been seen before and it was thought that, by the use of ignited oil-soaked rags twisted round the bars of the grid, it could have served as a portable lamp, the basal spike being set into the ground in any desired position. But when work began on these objects in the British Museum, it was soon realised that originally, the 4-inch ring bearing the cast bronze stag, was attached to the top of the stand. So delicate a crest, it was seen, could not have survived the flames from the burning rags and so the problem of its use was re-examined. And it soon became fairly clear that this elaborate structure was some kind of standard, perhaps that marking the authority of the Bretwalda.

Now 'Bretwalda' is a term the precise meaning of which is not known, though much ink has been spent in its discussion. Various suggestions have been 'ruler of Britain', 'ruler of the British', or 'the British leader'. From this it follows that, whatever its precise significance, the man who bore this title was in some way the most prominent of the English rulers at the time, for it was to one or other of the Anglo-Saxon kings that the title was accorded. By Bede we are given a list of them. In chronological order they were Aelle of the South Saxons, Ceawlin of the West Saxons, Ethelbert of Kent, Raedwald of East Anglia, Edwin of Northumbria and then Oswald and after him Oswy, both of Northumbria, Oswy being king when Bede

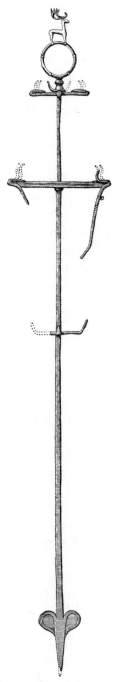

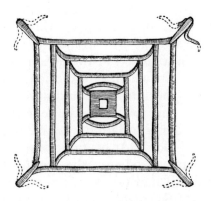

FIG. 21. Iron grill from standard,
seen in plan

FIG. 20. Iron standard with bronze stag

wrote his history. After describing the peace and prosperity enjoyed in Northumbria under Edwin's rule, Bede goes on to say: 'His dignity was so great throughout his dominions, that his banners were not only borne before him in battle, but even in time of peace, when he rode about his cities, towns or provinces with his officers, the standard-bearer was wont to go before him. Also, when he walked along the streets, that sort of banner which the Romans call *Tufa*, and the English, *Tuuf*, was in like manner borne before him.' Bede's original Latin has different words for the 'banner' or 'standard' of this translation. For the battle-banner he uses *vexillum*, which in the Roman army was the centurion's pennant, for the peace-time standard-bearer he has *signifer*, the bearer of the *signum* which was the official eagle-standard of the legion. Thirdly, the king's personal standard he calls *tufa*, for which no exact equivalent is known.

During the late sixth and seventh centuries, power in Northumbria passed from time to time to the representative of one or the other of the two established dynastic families based respectively on Bamburgh in Bernicia and York in Deira. At his father's death in about 605, Edwin's inheritance of Deira had passed into the hands of the Bernician king Ethelfrith and Edwin himself had taken refuge at the court of Raedwald of East Anglia. And in 617, Raedwald had led a great army northward to defeat Ethelfrith's hastily-gathered levies at the battle of the Idle river, where both Ethelfrith and Regenhere, Raedwald's eldest son, were slain. Until his death in 633, Edwin then ruled the whole of Northumbria. With this close association of Raedwald and Edwin in mind, it has been suggested with force that Edwin had become familiarised with the use by Raedwald of insignia to mark his Bretwaldaship and so, in later years, he continued their use in his own kingdom. This Sutton Hoo standard, buried as we shall see some forty years after Edwin's accession, may well have been that standard of Raedwald's which provided a model for the Northumbrian *signum* or *tufa* later mentioned by Bede. There is more than one reference in old Northern story to the stag, or hart, as an emblem of royalty and the stag-crest of this standard, it is suggested, had replaced the old Roman eagle in this modified version of the ancient legionary symbol. It was further noted that, in the burial-chamber, the symbols of power and inheritance, as distinct from the personal and domestic utilitarian objects, were grouped at the western end and this standard either stood or was laid in the most westerly position of all.

Closely associated with the standard is the decorated whetstone, a fraction only less than two feet long. It has been called a whetstone, but has never been used for sharpening any blade, nor is it a suitable implement for sharpening a sword. The whetstone has a square cross-section and is slightly tapered towards each end, the ends themselves being carved into a slightly lobed nearly globular shape, which had once been painted red. Attached to each end by an openwork cage of thin bronze strips was a shallow bronze saucer, one only of which now survives. Each face of both tapered ends bears a stylised bearded face carved in relief and set in a pointed oval frame; the beard-treatment differs slightly at each end. This stone is quite unlike any true functional hone found, as they not infrequently are, in any Northern tomb and it was soon recognised to have had a ceremonial function only. It has also been called 'sceptre' or 'mace' and, in 1939, Sir Thomas Kendrick was able to write that 'nothing like this monstrous stone exists anywhere else. It is a unique, savage thing; and inexplicable, except perhaps as a symbol, proper to the king himself, of the divinity and mystery which surrounded the smith and his tools in the northern world.' Since then this statement has had to be modified a little for, though they are smaller and less richly decorated, two whetstones with a carved head at one end of each, have come to light from the Celtic west, though they are probably of a later date. A third, a fragment only, has more recently been found at Hough-on-the-Hill, in Lincolnshire, though not in the early cremation cemetery in that parish (Pl. IX).

Towards the west end of the burial-chamber lay the remains of a helmet and its condition was such that the story of its restoration records a triumph of Mr. Maryon's skill and insight. In 1947 he wrote: 'When unpacked . . . the remains . . . covered a good-sized table. They appeared to consist of a gilded bronze nose and mouth piece, two gilded bronze dragon heads, parts of what once had been a silver crest, and three or four hundred fragments of sand-encrusted rusty iron. . . . Though almost all of the pieces were of iron they were so corroded that little metal remained. . . . Some were friable; others had become mineralized and, in fact, had been partially transformed into limonite—a hydrate of iron. Traces of ornament and mouldings showed upon them.' From this assemblage of scraps, Mr. Maryon was able to reconstruct the magnificent vizored helmet seen in Plate X. The Swedish professor, Sune Lindqvist, has offered minor criticism of some of the details of the reconstruction, but its substantial accuracy is undoubted; it provides one of the most certain 'Swedish' elements in this burial, the significance of which is discussed in Chapter IX.

The helmet was basically a hemispherical iron cap to which were attached vizor, cheek-pieces and neck-guard of iron. The cheek-pieces were hinged, but the front and back attachments were rigidly secured. Inside the cap there was space for padding and the head was further protected from weapon-blows by the tubular crest which ran from back to front. This was an iron tube encased in silver of about $\frac{1}{8}$-inch thickness and its ends carried gilt-bronze dragon heads. Other bronze fittings are the eyebrows, further decorated with silver wire and niello-inlay and edged below with garnets inset over gold foil. The eyebrows are further embellished with a gilt boar's head at each outer end. A single bronze casting also comprises the nose and mouth-piece of the vizor, again decorated with silver and niello-inlay. And to complete the adornment, the iron surfaces of the cap and its attachments were originally covered with very thin sheets of tinned bronze decorated with panels in relief and further bound at the helmet-edges by a rim of gilded bronze. Though the helmet looks dull enough to us after centuries of change and decay, how right was Mr. Maryon when he said: '. . . we have to imagine it in its original condition as an object of burnished silvery metal, set in a trellis-work of gold, surmounted by a crest of massive silver, and embellished with gilded ornaments, garnets and niello—in its way a magnificent thing and one of the outstanding masterpieces of barbaric art'.

The panels of relief-decoration fall into five groups. Two of these are varieties of interlace-ornament and three contain figure-groups. Of these, one bears a mounted warrior overriding a fallen foe, another has a pair of standing warriors, each with a crescentic-winged helmet; of the third practically nothing can be ascertained. The designs of these figure-groups are familiar from Swedish examples and confirm the close resemblance of this helmet to several found in seventh-century burials in the Uppland province of Sweden, though the Sutton Hoo specimen appears to be a finer and more elaborate example than those of the Swedish graves.

Between the helmet and the standard as they lay in the burial-chamber, were the remnants of a shield. Its wooden body had long since been reduced by decay, but the metal fittings and other embellishments were sufficiently intact to be treated and restored; they have enabled the whole shield to be reconstructed after a process of study and comparison similar to that given to the helmet. When this was done, the shield was seen to be circular, 33 inches in diameter and slightly concave on the inner side. The body of the shield was of wood, $\frac{5}{16}$-inch thick, protected on both sides by a thin covering of leather. As held on its owner's arm, the grain of the wood was horizontal. The edge, which was of thicker wood than the main part, was protected by a U-sectioned binding of bronze gilt. At equal distances round this raised rim were twelve dragon heads in gilt bronze, set radially. Of these, nine of the originals were missing and had been replaced in antiquity by copies in gilded gesso.

The great shield-boss, which covered the central hole where the back of the hand lay, was of iron, variously decorated with gilt bronze, tin, niello-inlay and garnets; some of this metal bore the form of dragon heads and other parts carried zoomorphic designs. This boss was held in position by five domed rivets, two of which, on the inner side, also held the bar of the hand-grip; this hand-grip is extended to an overall length of 25 inches by elaborate cast-bronze embellishments. On the outside also, set vertically in line, were two domed rivet-ends of gilt bronze; the rivets of these passed through the shield to hold the arm-strap of leather. To balance these domes, the face of the shield was further decorated with a long narrow panel of zoomorphic ornament in gold foil, held in position by a central gilt-bronze domed rivet. The upper and lower spaces of the shield held respectively a stylised bird and a dragon. The bird has a gilt bronze head inlaid with garnet, a leg of gilt and tinned bronze with more garnet inlay; the wing is of wood covered with decorated gold foil, the tail is of decorated gold foil and the body, of which traces only remained, has been conjecturally restored. The dragon is of gilt bronze with relief-decoration, further embellished with tinning, niello-work and garnet-inlay. At the time of the burial or earlier, this dragon had been found to be damaged and the missing parts, as on the rim, had been replaced with gilded gesso.

Of this shield, Professor Lindqvist has written: 'In my opinion, the reconstruction of the shield needs correction in several important details. If these corrections are made, the astonishing agreement with various parallels at Ulltuna, Vendel, Valsgärde and Vallstenarum becomes even more pronounced. The technique of manufacture is exactly the same. ... The Sutton Hoo shield is obviously made with greater care and more costly materials than any Swedish shields known as yet—that is to say, it was made for a more fastidious patron. Nevertheless I see no reason why it should not have been made on Swedish soil. If so, it was most likely made on Gotland or in Uppland. This possibility will be strengthened if it proves to be the case that not even any fragmentary remains of really similar shields occur on other English sites. ... Similar shields from Vallstenarum, and from Graves I and XII at Vendel, may perhaps provide dating evidence, although these too seem to have been of considerable age when buried in their respective graves. If one must give a date in years for the manufacture of the Sutton Hoo shield, I say about A.D. 600; but with reservations in favour of a possibly still earlier date.' To this question of date we shall later return.

An important group, also found close to the west end of the burial-chamber, comprised spear-heads, ferrules and angons, together with the bronze 'Coptic' bowl which held a bronze hanging-bowl. The 'Coptic' bowl has two looped drop-handles and a footstand. Inside the bowl, a line of engraved animals forms a zone of decoration; they are described as 'a camel, a donkey, a lion and another large feline'. Standing bowls of this type, though not very common, are well-enough known in a pagan Anglo-Saxon setting and are imports into England. They derive originally from the Near East, but some appear to have been copies made in the Rhineland workshops. It is thought that this example may have come from Alexandria.

The bronze hanging-bowl is a much more important piece than its container. Nearly a hundred of these bowls—some only in fragmentary form—are known and they pose one of the problems, still unsolved, of early Anglo-Saxon archaeology. In essentials, the Sutton Hoo bowl is typical of the series, but the quality and kind of its embellishments make it an outstanding piece. These hanging-bowls have rounded bases and loop handles designed for suspension. The loop handles are secured to the body of the bowl by hooks which are themselves appendages of broad medallions known as 'escutcheons'. The escutcheons are frequently decorated with enamel in the curvilinear patterns which characterise Late Celtic art; but it is a late phase of this art which not uncommonly shows the influence of Romano-British styles of decoration. The Sutton Hoo bowl has three such round escutcheons holding its suspension-hooks. The three intermediate spaces each hold a rectangular escutcheon—a less usual feature —and another round medallion or 'print' on the outside of the convex base. Finally, on the inside of the bowl, set on a stem springing from yet another round escutcheon, is a bronze fish decorated with enamel. This fish has been identified as a rainbow trout.

All the escutcheons on this bowl are richly enamelled and further decorated with millefiori glass fragments in the enamel. Millefiori glass originated in the Near East and is made by fusing together into a thicker single rod many thin rods of different colours. The thick rod is then cut across into thin slices, each of which shows a mosaic of the original colours. Another interesting feature of the bowl lay in its having been repaired; its surface showed several small silver patches riveted over holes in the original bronze. The largest of these patches is decorated internally with zoomorphic ornament similar to that on other pieces in the hoard; the repairs, it is clear, were carried out by an East Anglian goldsmith.

When found under controlled conditions and their associations made clear, these bowls are customarily seen to have been buried in pagan Anglo-Saxon graves. On occasion, indeed, they have occurred in use as cremation urns holding calcined bone fragments. Sometimes detached escutcheons only are noted and an escutcheon has been seen worn as a trinket. Yet the designs and workmanship, in particular the quality of the enamelling, are those of the Celtic West, where the techniques survived from Roman times. The place of their manufacture is not known, but it is generally thought that they must be sub-Roman British bowls looted during the early settlement period though some probably came, at a later date, into Anglo-Saxon hands by more legitimate channels. The problem of their original use is also unsolved; they may, it has been suggested, have served as lamps or water-containers in the sanctuary of a sub-Roman Christian church. But without much more definite evidence, the question of their original use cannot be answered.

In this bowl lay the fragments of another object of outstanding interest, a musical instrument. This was a harp, an instrument of Anglo-Saxon times well known from literary references. The harp has been reconstructed; it has six strings remarkable for their soft tone. Of it, Mr. Bruce-Mitford has said: 'Vibrant chords can be struck on it, and it is capable of simple harmonies and a fair melodic range.' This harp, it was ascertained, had been deposited in a bag of beaver-skin, which was doubtless its everyday case when not in use. This skin was probably of local origin, for it appears that the animal was still at that time to be found in the rivers of eastern England, though perhaps not in large numbers. It was, however, slowly being exterminated for in 1188, the year when Gerald de Barri—commonly known as Giraldus Cambrensis—made his tour of Wales, the Teifi was perhaps the only stream in which it certainly survived.

This mention of the occurrence of a now-extinct British animal leads immediately to that of another. Among the grave-goods were the remains of seven drinking horns. These horns carried silver-gilt mounts with stamped relief-ornament in characteristic zoomorphic patterns. Somewhat similar ornamented drinking horns were found many years ago in a richly-furnished barrow-burial of a seventh-century chieftain at Taplow in Buckinghamshire. But two of the Sutton Hoo horns differed from all the others by being horns of the great wild ox, the aurochs (*Bos primigenius*), known to us in Julius Caesar's writings as the Urus. These two horns greatly exceeded the others in size; measured along the curve they were some $3\frac{1}{2}$ feet long and each held six quarts. Such horns were used for drinking ale or mead in the king's hall and were passed from hand to hand. Now the aurochs, though its semi-fossilised remains are found in England in deposits dating from prehistoric times, is believed to have been extinct in this country before the beginning of Roman times. It may perhaps have lingered a little in the great Caledonian Forest of the Scottish Highlands, though this is doubtful, but it was certainly to be found in Central Europe until a later day, the last known of these animals being killed near Warsaw in 1627. These two Sutton Hoo horns, therefore, must have been brought into England and, with probability, came from the North German Forest.

Very different in origin was the great silver dish. This circular salver, some 2 feet 3 inches in diameter, has a slightly raised rim and a deep footstand. It is ornamented with engraved classical designs and, on its base, there is the equivalent of our modern hall-mark, four impressed stamps which are the imperial assay marks of the Byzantine (Eastern

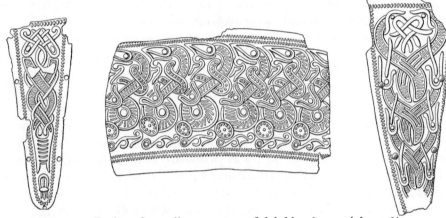

FIG. 22.   Designs from silver mounts of drinking horns (about $\frac{1}{1}$)

Roman) Empire. They are those of the Emperor Anastasius I, who reigned from A.D. 491 to 518, during which time this dish was tested and stamped. The survival of this dish for a century and a half before being buried is a pointer to the difficulty of dating a burial with precision by one item of its grave-furniture, unless corroborated by other evidence such as was found here. It shows, also, how wide was the field from which this East Anglian treasure was drawn.

Other silver dishes were also of classical origin. There were ten silver bowls, each 9 inches in diameter; six only of these bowls are in good condition, the others having barely survived complete decay. Each is decorated with a formalised geometric leaf-design set in a roundel which forms the centre of a four-armed cross, also with leaf-design; the arms of this cross extend to the rim of the bowl. A larger dish, some 15 inches in diameter, has a plain rim capping internally-fluted sides; on the inside of the base, within a band of formal design, there is in low relief, a crudely-executed female head in profile. The dish also has a pair of drop-handles attached to nearly circular escutcheons. It has been compared with the finer fluted bowl forming part of the 'Mildenhall Treasure', also in the British Museum. This remarkable hoard was found at Mildenhall in Suffolk during the last war and, in 1946, found its way to the museum as Treasure Trove. As it was discovered by accident, the circumstances of its concealment are obscure. It consists of twelve magnificently made and ornamented silver dishes and bowls, together with two goblets, five ladles and eight spoons, all of silver and elaborately designed.

All but one of these pieces were fairly certainly made in the fourth century and, though many of the finest undoubtedly came from a Mediterranean workshop, one or more may perhaps have been made in Britain where good, if not superb, workmanship was by no means uncommon. This group of vessels, apparently the plate of a wealthy Romano-British family, was probably buried for safety either late in the fourth or early in the fifth century and, by some misfortune, was never recovered. It is clear that such pieces could easily have fallen into the hands of Anglo-Saxon raiders and so eventually have appeared at the court of the East Anglian king. A vessel such as the Sutton Hoo fluted bowl might well have both been made and used in Britain in late Roman times though, of course, the Anastasius dish could not have reached Britain until a much later date, when sub-Roman Britons could not possibly have imported such classical silver for their own use. At the same time, it is the generally accepted view that all the Sutton Hoo silver came from Mediterranean workshops, and stress has been laid on the absence of such pieces from both continental and English Germanic graves of this period.

The Sutton Hoo silver also included a small plain cup and a decorated ladle, as well as two spoons. These spoons, with fig-shaped bowls and simple, slightly balustered stems, have proved to be two of the most debated items of the hoard. For each bears a simple inscription, one the name *SAULOS* and the other *PAULOS*, the Greek forms of SAUL and PAUL. These spoons are universally regarded as a pair of christening spoons, presented to a convert at his baptism, so that they hold a significant place in the discussion of the subject of the burial.

Other vessels found among the grave-goods are perhaps of less importance, though the tiny drinking vessels with silver-gilt mounts are, indeed, unique. These astonishing little cups are made from gourds and it has been suggested that they were for stronger liquor than the mead or ale drunk from the horns. This suggestion of the use of a distilled spirit, an early *aquavit* or, perhaps, a primitive whisky made from the barley more commonly used for brewing ale, throws further light on seventh-century life at a royal court.

The larger vessels were the normal possessions of a chieftain, those vessels needed for the communal life of a great hall. The three iron-mounted buckets, one large and two much smaller, need no special notice. Wooden buckets with iron or bronze mountings were not uncommon in pagan Anglo-Saxon times and many have been found in graves. One at least of their uses was to hold the supply of ale or mead, from which the drinking vessels could be refilled. In these examples, the wood itself was decayed. The large bucket, or possibly tub, had handles, collar and binding straps of iron, all heavily rusted; the smaller buckets were similarly decayed. But of the latter, one also carried decoration in the form of rectangular and circular bronze escutcheons, a less usual feature.

The three bronze cauldrons were all very badly broken and decayed. They were generally similar except in size; in this, they formed a graded series, large, medium and small. Made of thin sheet bronze, their rims were turned outward over strengthening iron collars. Large bronze cauldrons had been known in Celtic Britain for many centuries before the Anglo-Saxon invasions, though the earlier ones differed much in the detail of their structure; as the Irish legends tell, a chief's importance depended in part on the number of cauldrons he owned. For the life of the hall they were a necessity, as in them was seethed the flesh which formed the staple dishes at the daily feast; a great king would need to have many in his possession to feed his numerous retainers. The mass of chainwork and iron bars, grouped with the cauldrons in the burial-chamber, was so rusted when excavated that its purpose was not then clear. Examination in the British Museum, however, has led to its being interpreted as the equipment used to suspend the cauldrons over a fire while in use.

Two other true hanging-bowls were both smaller and of less importance than the fine 'fish-bowl' found in the west end of the chamber. Both of these were adorned with the normal enamelled escutcheons. The small iron 'lamp' was, in effect, a hemispherical cup on a short stem with spreading feet. Its provisional interpretation as a lamp was based on its internal divisions, believed to have held wicks; a rather similar one had been found many years ago in a grave at Broomfield in Essex. Laboratory examination, however, has shown these divisions not to be a part of the original structure, but rusty deposits developed after the object was buried; it is now not thought to be a lamp. The small silver cup had a footring and was about $3\frac{1}{2}$ inches in diameter. The silver ladle found below the large silver dish had lost its handle, but this lay close by and so the whole can be reconstructed. The remaining vessels include wooden cups and a horn cup, but of these little can be said.

Far more interesting and important is the mail-coat, corslet or byrnie, as they were generally known in the North. Unfortunately, this was rusted into a solid mass, so that it has not been possible to restore it, or even to determine its size and shape. Byrnies are well known from literary sources; for example—to choose among many references in *Beowulf*—we read that 'Beowulf spoke—on him his corslet shone, the shirt of mail sewn by the art of the smith', and again, 'The war corslet shone, firmly hand-locked, the gleaming iron rings sang in the armour as they [the armed band] came on their way in their trappings of war even to the hall.'

Known specimens of byrnies are less common. Fragments of one were found by Thomas Bateman in 1848 in a barrow at Benty Grange, near Monyash in Derbyshire. This was a primary Anglo-Saxon burial mound and contained an inhumation burial, with which were deposited a silver-mounted leather cup, personal ornaments and the iron framework of a helmet to which horn plates had once been pinned with silver rivets. This helmet was crested in bronze and iron with the likeness of a boar. The byrnie appears to have been a garment of cloth to which chains of short linked rods were sewn. But examples of true ring-mail have also been found. In a peat-moss at Thorsbjerg in Schleswig, a fine ring-mail corslet was excavated, as well as the remains of several more. Other fragments come from Vimose in the Danish island of Fyen and also from Vendel in Uppland, Sweden. These byrnies commonly belonged only to chiefs and leaders. So usual was this that, as Professor Whitelock points out, 'a legal treatise finds it necessary to state that to have a helmet, a coat of mail and a gold-plated sword, is not in itself enough to entitle a man to the status of a thegn. If he has not five hides of land, he remains a *ceorl*, for all this grand equipment.'

Of some interest too is the iron axe. This is a 'francisca' or throwing-axe, more commonly found on the continent where it was a weapon of the Franks. Such axes are however by no means unknown in England in the early Anglo-Saxon settlement area, though they are perhaps more common in Kent than elsewhere. Five others are recorded from Suffolk and three more from Cambridgeshire east of the Fens. The unusual feature of the Sutton Hoo axe lies in its iron handle for in general the francisca was fitted with a haft of wood. Little can be said of the leather bags and shoes, or of the silver shoe-buckles but the pillow, which was stuffed with goose feathers, is a foretaste of the 'new-wedded lord and a goose-feather bed'. A rusted iron scramasax—a long knife or short sword—sundry iron spear-ferrules, bone combs and the remains of textiles, complete the tale of the humbler finds, leaving only the gold-work and jewellery to be described.

V

THE GRAVE–GOODS: II

THE BODY-HARNESS which carried the gold and jewelled mountings has been described as a sword-belt and baldrick, together with a purse and the straps by which it was hung. It may broadly be likened to a British Army officer's 'Sam Browne' harness, which is essentially composed of waist-belt and shoulder-strap, to which are sometimes attached a sword-frog and pistol-holster. To point the likeness, we may count the metal fittings on this modern utilitarian harness. The belt carries one buckle, six rings or loops, one hook, one stud and six rivet-heads, all of brass. The slide is of leather. The shoulder-strap has one buckle and two studs, also of brass; in all there are eighteen visible brass fittings.

Sir Thomas Kendrick's catalogue of the Sutton Hoo fittings includes four buckles, nine strap-mounts and a tenth with a loop attachment, two hinged clasps with a chain-attached fastening pin and two filigree strips, one with a hoop-attachment. In addition there is the purse of which only the metal parts survive. These comprise the frame of the flap which has three hinged attachment-pieces and a sliding-clasp fastener, together with eleven ornamental plaques from the flap. This gives a total of seventeen harness fittings apart from the purse, though the clasps may perhaps have come from a garment and not from the strapping. From this it may be seen that, not counting the purse, the Sutton Hoo mountings are substantially the same in number as those of the modern equipment, the difference lying in their essential richness. The harness therefore need not be visualised as a functionless piece of ceremonial equipment, though it is true that the weight of the gold may well have been a handicap to its wearer in moments of stress. Of these pieces, all of which are of gold, three only are without the added enrichment of jewels. These are the great buckle, a looped strap-mount and a plain strap-end.

Excluding sheet-metal stampings and castings, Anglo-Saxon decoration on small objects of precious metal falls into four main groups. A smooth surface may be chased and the incisions sometimes emphasised, as in the great buckle, with niello-inlay. Niello may be described as a fine black paste which was used to fill the incised lines of a pattern and so to enhance the details by giving them a strong black outline. A surface may also be decorated by the application of filigree-work. Filigree is fine decorative lace-like units built up from delicate metal threads and nodules, the wire threads normally being twisted into slender cables. This type of decoration is rare in the Sutton Hoo jewellery, but as will later be seen is one of the most characteristic features of Kentish work. The other types of decoration differ by the presence of lapidary-work, the enrichment of surfaces by the application of gemstones, coloured glass, shell and perhaps enamel. There are two ways of doing this; the more usual is by the use of cloisonné work, the other by the champlevé technique.

Cloisonné-work involves the attachment by soldering to the plain surface of tiny cell-like cavities which are made by the jeweller from strips of metal bent into suitable shapes; into these cells—or cloisons as they are known—are inserted tiny pieces of the semi-precious stone—usually garnet—which are cut to fit them. The base of each cell is frequently further enhanced by the insertion of gold foil tooled in a diaper-pattern which shows through the translucent stone. An occasional variant is the so-called lidded-cloisonné work; in this some of the cells have a flat plate of gold laid over them instead of the usual garnet-filling and so presenting an alternation of surfaces such as appears in true champlevé. The fourth style is this champlevé, a much rarer technical method. It consists of decoration made by cutting hollows in the surface of the metal into which the jewel or enamel is introduced, so making a true inlay.

The great buckle, though without the red colour of garnet inlay, is a magnificent object over 5 inches long and weighing nearly 15 oz. (Pl. XX). The surface of this great piece is covered with an intricate interlace of conventionalised animal-patterns and the details are further embellished by a generous use of niello-inlay. The plate of the buckle was attached to the leather by three catches; the ends of the rivets are marked on the outside of the plate by three plain domes with beaded rims. The loop of the buckle bears two panels of complex interlace which has been likened in general style to that which was later to decorate so many of the northern Anglian cross-shafts. The tongue itself is a plain ridged bar, but its roundel-base has a close interlace of which two of the ends bear biting heads. Large bird-heads border the pair of domes near the tongue. Two more, this time biting the body-interlace, border the central lobe of the plate and another pair are just above the third dome, beyond which is a small crouching beast. Similar crouching beasts are known from mounts found in an Anglian barrow-burial at Caenby, Lincolnshire and Mr. Bruce-Mitford has stressed the 'characteristically Anglian rhythm' of the whole decorative scheme.

But in spite of this, both he and Sir Thomas Kendrick have also pointed out that, though it is undoubtedly of English origin, its interlace is very similar in style to that of some objects found in the Vendel (Swedish) boat-graves.

The jewelled pieces are in quite another artistic style and their finding has greatly widened our ideas of the development and practice of Anglo-Saxon lapidary-work. But this cannot be discussed until the pieces have been described. Of prime importance is the great purse-flap (see frontis.). The gold frame, some $7\frac{1}{2}$ inches long, is believed to have held a plate of ivory or bone into which the decorative plaques were sunk and fixed with small rivets. The straight top-bar carries three plain gold hinges which were riveted to the leather of the harness, possibly the belt itself. The frame is jewelled with rectangular cloisons holding small garnet panels sometimes interspersed with insets of blue and white mosaic (millefiori) glass and from the top bar there also project four jewelled tongues. The gracefully-curved lower part of the frame bears in addition a further enrichment of gold filigree-work on its outer edge.

The decorative plaques other than the upper central unit fall into pairs, to give a bilateral symmetry. The small roundels have a cloisonné garnet border with a mosaic glass centre, one of which survives. The upper central unit is an intricate animal-interlace in which the garnet filling is contrasted with the smooth gold of lidded cloisons. On either side of this is a hexagon with a complex geometric design in garnet and gold. The design includes a border of alternating 'mushroom-cells' and many more of these occur in the inner panels. This mushroom-cell is a cloison with a rounded 'top' and a simple rectangular 'stem' below. This cell-shape also occurs, as will later be seen, in a slightly more elaborate form with double-stepped stem; the design has prime importance in the discussion of origins. Centrally below, the paired units each display a hawk seizing a duck and in these the garnet infill is again accompanied by mosaic glass. Outside these are examples of what is called the 'Daniel in the Lion's Den' motif, a man between two upright biting animals, carried out in garnet and glass cloisonné.

The two clasps also have a special interest, for nothing quite like them is known elsewhere (Pl. XXV). Each clasp is in two parts which are joined centrally to form a hinged unit by the insertion of a pin; the pin is secured by a tiny chain to one of the half-units. Each half-unit has a central panel with stepped cloisons set diagonally; they contain either garnet or mosaic glass and form a diaper-pattern not before seen in Anglo-Saxon work of the pagan period. As Mr. Bruce-Mitford has pointed out, the nearest English parallels are found in Hiberno-Saxon manuscripts illuminated in Christian Northumbria in Bede's day. These panels are framed in an animal-interlace

(*a*) The great silver dish, bronze cauldrons and other objects when first exposed.

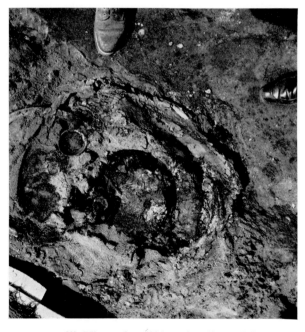

(*b*) View after lifting the silver dish.

PLATE I

(*a*) Bronze bowls, angons and spearheads, when exposed.

(*b*) The drinking-horn complex when first exposed.

PLATE II

(*a*) The Nydam ship.

(*b*) The Gokstad ship.

PLATE III

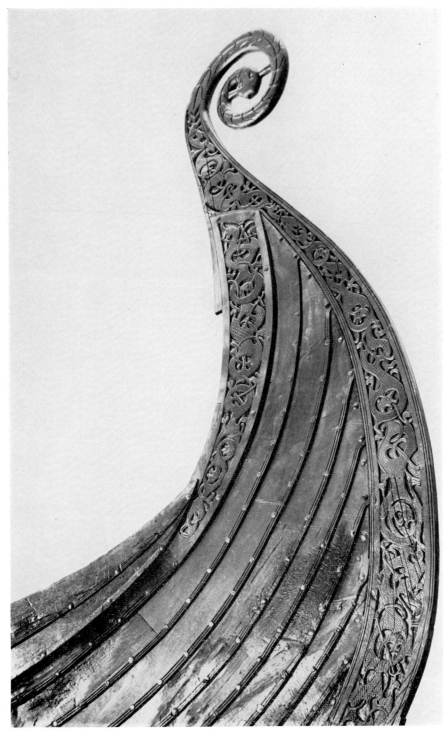

The Oseberg ship.

PLATE IV

The Sutton Hoo ship: (*a*) looking forward.

(*b*) looking aft.

PLATE V

The Sutton Hoo ship: (*a*) extra nailing and other details on the port side.

(*b*) the thole, showing the iron spikes.

PLATE VI

(*a*) The Utrecht boat.

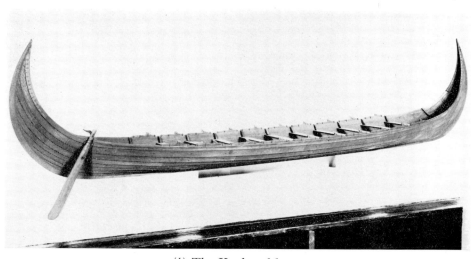

(*b*) The Kvalsund boat.

PLATE VII

The bronze stag and iron ring from the top of the standard.

(*about ⅝ actual size*)

PLATE VIII

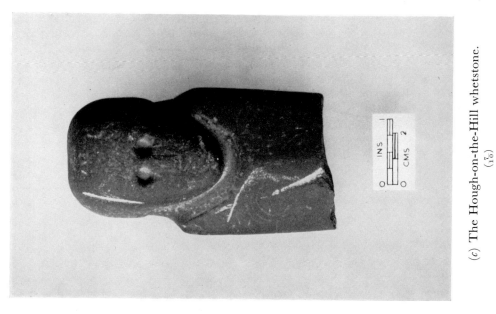

(c) The Hough-on-the-Hill whetstone.
($\frac{7}{10}$)

(a, b) The Sutton Hoo ceremonial whetstone.
(a, $\frac{2}{9}$ b, $\frac{2}{3}$)

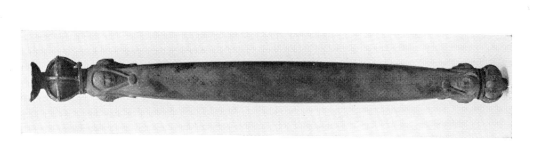

PLATE IX

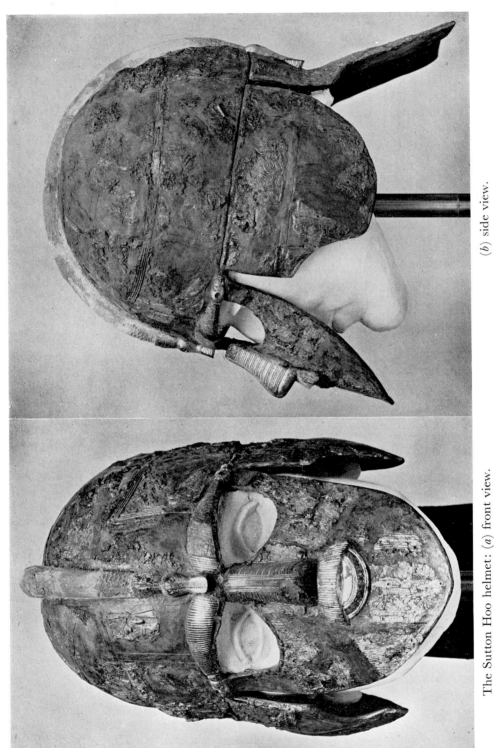

The Sutton Hoo helmet: (a) front view.

(b) side view.

PLATE X

The Sutton Hoo shield: front view.
$(\frac{1}{7})$

PLATE XI

The Sutton Hoo shield: back view.

PLATE XII

(a) The Coptic bowl.
(about ⅓)

(b, c) The gourd-cups.
(about ⅔)

(d) The pottery bottle.
(⅘)

PLATE XIII

(*a*) The large hanging-bowl.
$(\frac{5}{12})$

(*b*) Enamelled bronze
fish on internal
escutcheon.
$(\frac{4}{5})$

(*d*) Bronze animal mask
from beneath an
escutcheon.   (*about* $\frac{1}{4}$)

(*c*) The silver
patch with bird's
head decoration.
$(\frac{4}{5})$

PLATE XIV

(*a*) for suspension.

(*d*) from inside the bowl.

Escutcheons from the large hanging-bowl, decorated with red and green enamel and millefiori glass.

(*slightly less than actual size*)

(*c*) from below the bowl.

(*b*) intermediate.

PLATE XV

(*a*) The harp.

(*b*) A square-headed brooch of Leeds'
'Kenninghall' (Bi) type from Ipswich.
(*about* $\frac{2}{3}$)

PLATE XVI

The great
silver dish:
(*a*) top view.
(*about* ⅛)

(*b*) side view.

(*c, d*) the control
stamps of the
Emperor
Anastasius.
(²⁄₁)

PLATE XVII

(*a, b*) Two of the nest of silver bowls.
(*about* $\frac{2}{7}$)

(*c*) The fluted silver bowl.
($\frac{1}{4}$)

PLATE XVIII

(a) The silver cup.
(⅔)

(b) The bowl of the ladle.
(⅔)

(c) The silver spoons inscribed SAVLOS and PAVLOS.
(⅖)

(d) a side view of one of the spoons.

PLATE XIX

The great gold buckle.
($\frac{1}{1}$)

PLATE XX

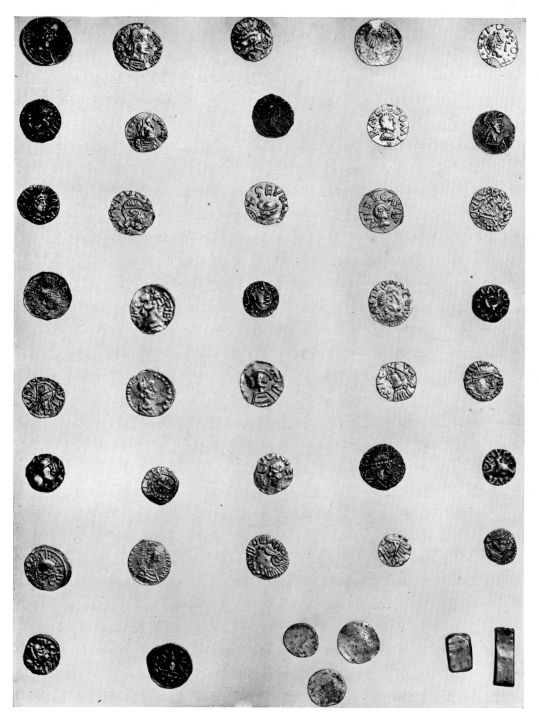

The Merovingian gold coins and billets found with the purse.

$(\frac{1}{1})$

PLATE XXI

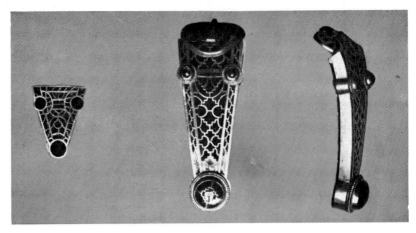

(a)   (b)

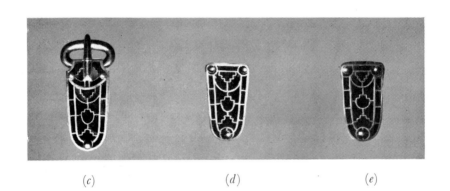

(c)   (d)   (e)

(f)   (g)

Gold and jewelled buckles and mounts.

$(a, b, \frac{3}{5}$ $c\text{-}g, about \frac{7}{10})$

PLATE XXII

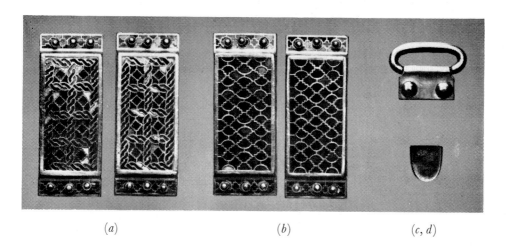

(a) (b) (c, d)

(e) (f)

$(a\text{-}f)$ Gold and jewelled buckles and mounts.

$(a, b, \frac{5}{6} \qquad c, d, \frac{2}{3} \qquad e, f, \frac{5}{6})$

(g) (h)

(g, h) Panels (reconstructed) from the Sutton Hoo helmet.

(slightly enlarged)

PLATE XXIII

(a) The Sutton Hoo sword.

(⅓)

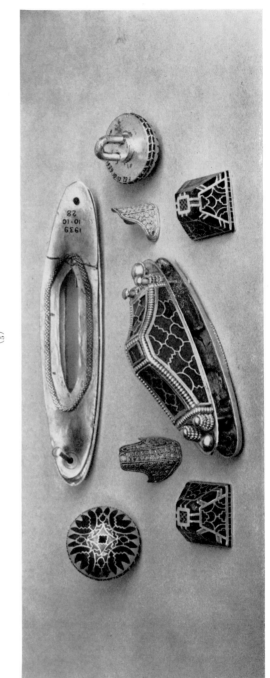

(b) Details of the sword-hilt and scabbard-mounts.

PLATE XXIV

PLATE XXV *opposite:* One of the jewelled clasps.——→
(*slightly enlarged*)

which also makes use of the lidded-cloison technique. The curved ends of the clasps are in the form of interlocked boars and in the spaces between heads and legs there are filigree fillings. The boars themselves are of garnet with the shoulders in mosaic glass. The gold hinge-pins have animal-head terminals with applied filigree; the eye-sockets, though now blank, were originally picked out in garnet.

The smaller strap-mounts are jewelled only in garnet but all have features of interest. Of these, the four rectangular mounts have great significance for they hold in the details of their workmanship much of the evidence which enables the origin of this jewellery to be assessed. Two of the mounts show a two-strand twist arranged as the cable-framework of eight small squares, each containing stepped cloisons. Between the strands of the cables, each loop shows a tiny central gold nodule, a feature of importance to be discussed below. The other pair of rectangular mounts have a geometric pattern of stepped cloisons, elaborations of the mushroom-pattern.

Another mount is T-shaped, being composed of a rectangular top with a hinged pendent stem. The dominant shape of its cloisons is the simple mushroom, which is also seen either in simple or somewhat elaborated form both in the smaller mounts and in the three jewelled buckle-plates. The latter, apart from the addition of loops and tongues, are very similar to the mounts. Two of the smaller buckles have plain gold loops but the third, which has its plate bent into a slight curve, has its loop set with garnets and bears jewelled bosses capping its attachment-rivets.

These harness-mountings by no means comprised all the jewelled pieces for the sword and its appendages were also richly decorated. The sword lay in its scabbard and, as was discovered in the laboratory, blade and sheath were so joined together by rust that they could not be separated. The scabbard itself appears to have been of wood covering an inner leather sheath, the wood itself being further reinforced in places with a fabric binding. As now preserved, the overall length from pommel to scabbard-tip is some 33 inches, the blade being about 28 inches. At a little more than 4 inches below the hilt, the scabbard bears two jewelled bosses. Each is hemispherical and bears a loop on the flat back for attachment to the scabbard. The cross-bar of the hilt is of gold with filigree-work on its upper surface; the grip is fitted with two shaped gold mounts which are filigree-decorated and the pommel, also of gold, is embellished with garnets set in stepped and quatrefoil cloisons. Two tiny gold pyramids set with garnets and mosaic glass seem to have been attached to the sword-knot. A rather similar pyramid of garnet-decorated gold, but not in true cloisons, was found in the seventh-century grave at Broomfield in Essex from which came the iron 'lamp'. In this grave also there lay a sword in a wooden tape-bound sheath, but from this sword the hilt-fittings had disappeared; it seems likely that this pyramid was also from a sword-knot. The two filigree strips, included above in the count of metal fittings on the harness, were found lying on the scabbard and may just possibly belong to the sword-complex and not that of the harness. Of these the larger looped strip bears four garnet studs.

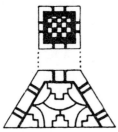

FIG. 23. Design of ornament on pyramids from sword-knot ($\frac{5}{3}$)

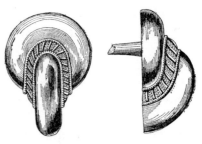

FIG. 24. Gilded bronze "ring" from the pommel of a ring-sword ($\frac{5}{4}$)

And lastly there must be mentioned the detached 'ring' from the pommel of a 'ring-sword'. This had not been seen during the excavation of the chamber, but fell from a crusted sand-lump in the laboratory. Of gilded bronze, it appears to have been removed from its parent sword—not the one described above—and deposited in the grave as a separate piece. Ring-swords are recorded in literature—*Beowulf*, for example, mentions them—but they seem not to have been common. The earliest specimens belong to pagan Anglo-Saxon times and are found in Kent where several have been recorded; the hilt of a fine example in silver-gilt was illustrated by J. Y. Akerman in his *Pagan Saxondom* (1855, Pl. 24). In these earliest examples, there is rigidly affixed to one side of the pommel a ring with which is linked another movable ring. It has in the past been suggested that these rings were functional and carried the 'peace-strings'. But of this there is considerable doubt and as the ring soon became fixed and then solid, it is generally held not to have had utilitarian value but to be a mark of high rank. In the later examples found in Scandinavia this solid knob as it became is enormously swollen and, long before the finding of the Sutton Hoo burial, it had been suggested that the Swedish examples from Uppland had developed from the earlier English type. This Sutton Hoo specimen though by no means of the exaggerated type, has lost all appearance of a loose ring and is present merely as a solid 'disc' incorporated in the 'knob' which carries it. Its closest parallel however as Mr. Bruce-Mitford has seen, is another detached 'ring' which had been used to decorate a drinking horn found at Valsgärde in Sweden.

Cloisonné jewellery of the pagan Anglo-Saxon period has long been known from the graves of East Kent where its finest examples are undoubtedly the garnet- and shell-decorated disc-brooches. The earliest disc-brooches were roundels of bronze or silver cast with animal-ornament carried out in the so-called 'chip-carved' style. Into shaped hollows in these castings were set three or four evenly-spaced garnets of wedge- or T-shape. But as the jeweller's craft progressed, more ambitious creations resulted. The finest are those composite brooches made of two metal plates bound together with strips of gold. The internal space between the plates is filled with a chalky composition and the whole face of this composite disc is then embellished with jewels and filigree-work. A close analysis of the development of this art-style and its chronology was given by Thurlow Leeds in his *Early Anglo-Saxon Art and Archaeology* (1936) and many examples of these brooches have been illustrated and may be conveniently studied in Mr. R. F. Jessup's *Anglo-Saxon Jewellery* (1950). The finest example of this Kentish series is acknowledged to be the Kingston brooch, a circular disc-brooch some 3.3 inches in diameter. It carries five concentric zones of cloisonné-work in red garnet and blue glass—or lapis-lazuli—alternating with panels of fine beaded filigree interlace-patterns. The centre has a boss of white shell[1] surrounding an inner ring of cloisonné-work and there are also four subsidiary roundels in cloisonné and shell. The cloisons are square, triangular, stepped or semi-circular—these with an inner stepped core—in outline. Other brooches of this school, though in design basically a series of concentric zones, yet show star- or cross-shaped geometric patterns in garnet, blue glass and shell cloisonné, with backgrounds of filigree in various small pattern-units. Though many other jewelled objects such as buckle-plates and pins have been found, it is the Kentish disc-brooches which display most clearly the characteristic designs and methods of treatment of this cloisonné-work.

This method of decorating brooches by the application of garnet-set cloisons was certainly of Frankish origin and was derived from Frankish

---

[1] The white substance used to form these bosses is commonly called 'shell or meerschaum', but it has also been suggested that some of them at least are of ivory.

centres on the Middle Rhine. The earliest examples found in Kent appear to have been imports from the continental workshops in the first half of the sixth century. Thurlow Leeds on the evidence available in 1936 had inferred that they first appeared in the first decade of that century. Since then exhaustive surveys of the continental material have been made; these, summarised recently by Professor C. F. C. Hawkes (1956), suggest that this date must be placed some twenty years later. It is however certain that within a few years of their appearance a local Kentish 'school' arose, by which this type of jewellery was fabricated. Though simple at first, the products of this school became more diversified as the craftsmen gained experience and the lines of development diverged from those of the continental workshops. Towards the end of the century the Kentish lapidaries and goldsmiths began to produce not only simpler forms for poorer folk, but the great cloisonné- and filigree-decorated brooches which mark the apogee of Kentish art. It has also been noted that as the seventh century progressed, there was some falling-off in the quality of workmanship. The cloison-shapes themselves and the 'finish' of the work both show evidence of slipshod craftsmanship, symptoms of that 'boredom' which tends to be manifest when once the highest standards have been evolved and lesser men continue to copy their predecessors' work.

From time to time finds of garnet-decorated jewellery have been made in other parts of England though not in considerable numbers and it has generally been agreed that most of these, though certainly not all, were probably strays from the Kentish workshops. The concentration of brooches and the evidence of other archaeological finds have combined to point to Faversham as the most likely centre for the production of this jewellery. Faversham was a *villa regalis,* a district centre of which there were ten in Kent. It has further been suggested that after the founding of the Kentish kingdom, Faversham may have been the most important seat of the kingly power until in A.D. 597, Ethelbert the king was converted to Christianity by Augustine, who was aided by the persuasions of Ethelbert's Frankish wife, herself a Christian. After that there would naturally be a tendency for a transfer of power to be made to Canterbury which became the bishop's see and after that of the Primate of England.

The preliminary survey of the Sutton Hoo jewellery was made, before it was sent away to safety, by Sir Thomas Kendrick, who speedily recognised many of the more outstanding features of its designs. It was he who saw the importance of the mushroom-cell as an innovation derived directly, as he said, from the Rhineland where it originated, a unit of design which was not used by the Kentish jewellers. It does indeed occur on a single brooch found at Faversham, but he also saw in the brooch a twist-pattern with the same tiny gold nodule in its loop which is present in the cable-border of the rectangular mounts at Sutton Hoo. These and the Faversham brooch were the only examples of this odd constructional method known to him and, in view of their dissimilarity to the normal Kentish work, Sir Thomas concluded that this anomalous Faversham brooch was most probably

FIG. 25. Interlace motives in cloisonné-work where the beaded cloison is used: *a*, Sutton Hoo rectangular strap-mount; *b*, Faversham, Kent, composite disc-brooch. (Enlarged)

a product of the workshop of the 'Sutton Hoo jeweller' introduced into Kent, rather than a local Kentish artifact.

More recent research by Mr. Bruce-Mitford seems to confirm this for he has at last found a third example in the fragment of yet another pyramidal sword-knot from the western mound at Uppsala, Sweden, one of the three royal barrows there covering cremated remains of three early Swedish kings. As he has pointed out, though the pyramids are not uncommon in either England or northern and central Europe, yet the true cloisonné-decorated examples are limited to Sutton Hoo and this Swedish site.

As will have been realised from the foregoing descriptions, the mushroom-cell is certainly the most characteristic feature of the Sutton Hoo cloisonné-work. In its double-stepped form it has been known for many years on a jewel-encrusted piece from Forest Gate, Essex, on the outskirts of London. This piece is apparently the head of an ornamental pin; it is roughly a double pyramid of gold with the apices truncated and the faces set with garnet-filled cloisons in elaborate step-patterns, which include double-stepped mushrooms. Present also are what appear to be lidded-cloisons of Sutton Hoo type, so that this pinhead may also be attributed to the 'Sutton Hoo jeweller'.

It has also been known in its simple form in a gold and garnet pendent cross found more than a century ago at Wilton in Norfolk and now in the British Museum. This cross has three fan-shaped arms and a fourth rectangular arm bearing a barrel-shaped suspensory loop. The arms are attached to a border surrounding a central medallion which consists of a gold coin of Heraclius I (610-40). The arms and border are encrusted with cloison-set garnets, the arms showing the mushroom-cells and the border the alternating long and short panels seen also at Sutton Hoo, notably on the purse-frame. In 1937, before the Sutton Hoo discovery, the presence of these mushroom-cells in the Wilton cross had led Sir Thomas Kendrick to compare it with a garnet-encrusted brooch set on the 'celebrated Egbert shrine' of tenth-century date, at Trier on the river Moselle in western Germany. This Trier piece also exhibits rectangular border cells of alternating lengths and other minor features, not then clearly paralleled, which show resemblances to other pieces at Sutton Hoo. At the time, Sir Thomas suggested that this 'exotic' Wilton cross—as it then seemed—must be equated with the Trier brooch and was therefore of sixth-century Merovingian manufacture, the coin having been inserted at a later date into a central space not originally made to hold it. As the coin does not fit very well, this last may well be true.

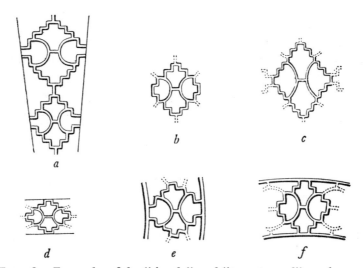

FIG. 26. Examples of the "simple" and "two-stepped" mushroom-cell designs: a, b, c, Sutton Hoo; d, Tongres; e, Wilton cross; f, Egbert shrine, Trier. (All slightly enlarged)

The finding of the Sutton Hoo jewel-hoard has of course reopened the whole question. The Wilton cross, it is now agreed, is a product of the 'Sutton Hoo workshop' and the brooch on the Egbert shrine is another, an English-made piece which later found a continental home as an embellishment on the shrine. Still more examples of the mushroom-cell have been found by Mr. Bruce-Mitford. These are on two Swedish sword-pommels. One bears the characteristic simple cell; the other, which also has the quatrefoil-cell of the Sutton Hoo sword-pommel, has the mushroom-cell in a slightly modified form. In fine, the evidence points to this mushroom-cell being, in Sir Thomas Kendrick's own words, 'the hall-mark of an Anglian cloisonné style'.

Since the above pronouncement was made, the story has perhaps become more complicated, for the writer has himself recognised the possible significance of yet another example of the mushroom-cell, this time in an unusual setting. This was indeed mentioned in passing by Sir Thomas in

FIG. 27.   The Sutton Brooch, showing true and bungled mushroom-cells (× 2)

1940, but he did not then follow up its implications. More than a century ago—about 1835 in fact—the front of a characteristic Kentish disc-brooch was discovered by a ploughman in the parish of Sutton in Suffolk. Having first removed the jewelled settings which he threw away, he sold the golden remnants. This plate with its cell-work passed into the Fitch collection and has been preserved in the Castle Museum at Norwich.[1] Its Kentish style is undoubted for it bears four concentric zones round a bead-edged central setting and the second zone from the outer edge is also marked

[1] The Sutton brooch was transferred in October 1962 to the Ipswich Museum as part of an interchange of Norfolk and Suffolk material between the two museums.

87

by four evenly-spaced subsidiary circular settings (see Fig. 27). The outermost and third zones bear normal Kentish filigree-work while the second and fourth bear cloisons. Its innermost zone has cloisons of a type specifically described by Thurlow Leeds as 'a series of stepped diagonal bars, of which the uppermost angle of one is linked to the lowermost of the next by a plain diagonal bar'. He regards this, in fact, as 'a hall-mark of the greater part of these splendid brooches', leaving us in no doubt that this feature and the filigree-work combine to make certain its Kentish origin. Yet the second zone, divided into four panels by the subsidiary circlets, bears in each one, two or three mushroom-cells alternating in direction, each one set in the 'base' of the space formed by a pair of diagonal stepped bars.

Coming from the same parish as the ship-burial, this Sutton brooch—not infrequently referred to as the Woodbridge brooch—seems to have great significance. A close examination suggests that the mushrooms may have been almost accidentally produced by placing a slightly-curving strip across the small space between the ends of the two stepped diagonals, in one the 'head' being reversed.[1] If so, it may be that in this brooch and not in the Rhineland workshops lies the original inspiration of the 'Sutton Hoo master-jeweller'. Seizing upon this apparently insignificant feature, he built up the designs centring on single- and double-stepped mushrooms and so evolved a whole new style of cloisonné-work which was to mark his output and which, as we shall see in Chapter IX, was to find its way across the North Sea and the Scandinavian peninsula to be buried in great men's graves near the Baltic shore.

If this derivation can be confirmed, it will carry important chronological implications. In view of its developed style the Sutton brooch must have been made, on Thurlow Leeds' dating, not earlier than the end of the sixth century and very possibly in the seventh; the starting-date of Sutton Hoo mushroom-cells is therefore well into the seventh century. And with them must go the Wilton cross, the Trier brooch, the Forest Gate pin and the Swedish sword-pommels. The Wilton cross, universally agreed to be a Christian piece, may then perhaps be equated with the early days of Bishop Felix and the whole episode of East Anglian mushroom-celled cloisonné-work may fall into a single lifetime, roughly the second quarter of the seventh century. That this has important bearings on the question of the Swedish connexion is evident and the whole subject is discussed in Chapter IX. But it also carries other chronological implications at which we must now glance.

[1] It should be noted that the figure of this brooch in vol. I of the *Victoria County History* is incorrect.

In his preliminary survey of the grave-goods in 1940, Sir Thomas Kendrick paid special attention to the large hanging-bowl with the moulded fish. This bowl, it will be remembered, has the enamel of its escutcheons further embellished with millefiori glass, similar glass being also used to fill cloisons in some of the jewellery. The use of millefiori was a survival in the British Isles from the Roman world and it was certainly in production in Ireland in the fifth, sixth and seventh centuries. At the same time, the inclusion of millefiori in the cloisonné-work of the harness-mountings, which was undoubtedly made in East Anglia by a Teutonic goldsmith, has re-opened the whole question of the manufacture of the hanging-bowls. Sir Thomas pointed out the relationship of these Sutton Hoo escutcheons to others in England, stressing particularly their relationship to others from Scunthorpe, Lincolnshire. He also saw that these, together with others which though less closely related, yet had many decorative and technical details in common, formed a group the members of which had been found mainly in the eastern part of England. This, together with the important link provided by the use of millefiori, led him to suggest that somewhere in East Anglia or in its neighbouring areas must lie the place of origin of these bowls.

Sir Thomas also discussed what he called the 'hair-spring coil' motif seen in the decoration of the Sutton Hoo escutcheons; he pointed out its similarity to that seen in many Irish examples, but reached the conclusion that it could not have been directly introduced from Ireland. Irish monks certainly came to England in the seventh century to preach the gospel to the Angles but too late, Sir Thomas thought, for their coming to have influenced the design of the Sutton Hoo bowl. He therefore expressed the view that the use of the 'hair-spring coil' must have resulted rather from a parallel development than from a direct borrowing. And his final words relating to the millefiori are to the point: 'The vitality of this surviving glass-industry in the British background to Saxon England seems to me to be a most significant new fact. We certainly cannot pretend to disbelieve in the existence of such an industry now that we know it was of sufficient prominence to invite the respectful attention of one of the best goldsmiths who ever made Saxon cloisonné jewellery.'

There are however real difficulties in believing that the fine champlevé enamel-work of hanging-bowl escutcheons was produced in Eastern England for, apart from them, no other enamel-work of similar quality is known from the area. All that we have in fact are a few Anglian brooches, certainly of local manufacture, which in addition to their normal cast ornament have a crude smear of enamel. So long ago as 1923, Sir Cyril

Fox suggested that a simple industry producing them had survived in a small sub-Roman community on the eastern edge of the Fenland, for it was in the pagan cemeteries of this region that most of these enamelled brooches had been found.

More recently a most interesting suggestion has been put forward by Mdlle. Françoise Henry, a French scholar whose primary studies for many years have been of early Western enamels. She has long held the view that hanging-bowls were of Irish- not British-Celtic origin, but the apparent lack of them in Ireland has stood in the way of her views being generally accepted. In a recent (1956) short survey, she has brought forward new evidence from Ireland, both for the presence of the bowls and of the manufacture of millefiori. She then draws attention to the Irish Fursey's settlement at Burgh Castle in north-east Suffolk (see p. 93) which took place about 635-6; it was, she suggests, the Irish brethren of Fursey's monastery who either brought the Sutton Hoo bowl from Ireland or perhaps made it there in the decade following their advent, the former alternative being the more probable. The 'Sutton Hoo jeweller' she infers, must either have seen this bowl or acquired it in some way and studied it carefully. And then he learnt the secret of making millefiori, or actually got supplies of the glass, from the Burgh Castle monks to incorporate it in some of his best pieces. She concludes with the words that this 'completely unusual element in Saxon cloisonné is certainly due to contact with the Irish enamellers'.[1]

Now it is clear that if Fursey's party brought the bowl from Ireland about 635, the origin of the hair-spring coils must be in Ireland and the relationship is explained. And if the Anglian jeweller, as earlier paragraphs have suggested, was at that time in active production of fine work, he still had upwards of twenty years in which to learn the secret of millefiori and produce his masterpieces such as the purse and the clasps before they were buried, as we shall see, in 655. These pieces then would seem to mark the second and more successful part of the life of a great unknown artist whose work has added lustre to the English name.

[1] Some confirmation for this may be found in a furnace-pit perhaps for glass-making, which was revealed in the 1958 excavations at Burgh Castle.

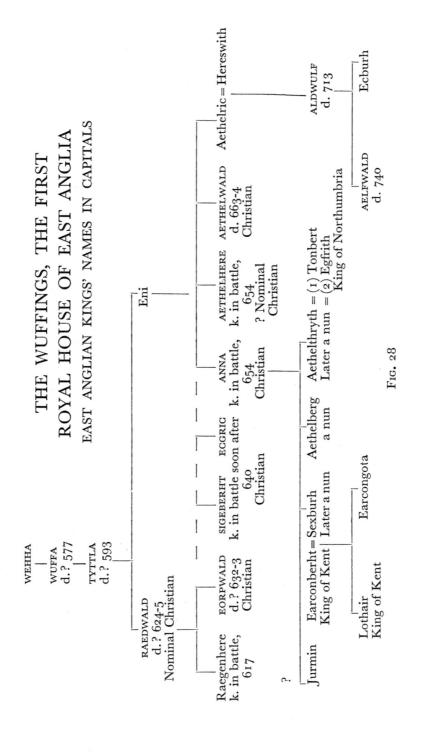

THE WUFFINGS, THE FIRST
ROYAL HOUSE OF EAST ANGLIA

EAST ANGLIAN KINGS' NAMES IN CAPITALS

FIG. 28

VI

THE KING–BURIAL:

WHICH KING?

SOME UNCERTAINTY shrouds the first establishment of the East Anglian dynasty, the Wuffings as they are known from one of their founders, Wuffa, in their new kingdom. And though the names of the successive kings during the seventh century are well-enough known, the relationships of some of them have long been obscure or confused by earlier writers, many of whom had followed the errant summary of the Norman chronicler known as Florence of Worcester. A recent study by Sir Frank Stenton (1959) however, has now disentangled many of these obscurities and his conclusions are embodied in the accompanying table. Though most of these men were in themselves not of great importance in the Anglo-Saxon world, yet a knowledge of these relationships and such of their history as can be rescued from obscurity is essential when the identity of the subject of the ship-burial has to be discussed.

From the pages of Bede's *Ecclesiastical History*, eked out by occasional entries in the *Anglo-Saxon Chronicle*, comes also the outline of the story of East Anglia's conversion to Christianity which also has great relevance, though the detail is not always clear. In particular the dates are often uncertain and there are frequent slight discrepancies in these as given in the different records. The story begins with the nominal conversion of king Raedwald in the early years of the seventh century. Raedwald, so Bede tells us, had been 'admitted to the sacrament of the Christian faith in Kent, but in vain; for, on his return home, he was seduced by his wife and certain perverse teachers and turned back from the sincerity of the faith; . . . in the same temple he had an altar to sacrifice to Christ and another small one to offer victims to devils; which temple, Aldwulf, king of that same province, who lived in our time, testifies had stood until his time and that he had seen it as a boy'. Aldwulf was the grandson of Raedwald's brother Eni and, as he died in 713, he can hardly have been born much before 650 and possibly not until after that date. What is more, Raedwald's temple would seem rather to have been a heathen fane with a subsidiary Christian altar rather than a Christian church with a heathen altar. If so, its survival until after the middle of the century points strongly to some survival of the old religion, though Bede has nothing to say on this. But as Bede was about forty years old when Aldwulf died, it is clear enough that his record of the temple's survival is contemporary and may be trusted.

Raedwald died before 626—probably in 624—and was succeeded by his son Eorpwald who had certainly been reared as a heathen. Soon after his succession he was persuaded by Edwin, king of Northumbria, 'with his whole province, to receive the faith and sacraments of Christ'. Edwin himself was not converted by Paulinus until Easter Day, 627, and the *Chronicle* tells us in an entry for 632 that 'In this year Eorpwald was baptized'. But the conversion of the province cannot have been more than nominal for within a very short time Eorpwald was killed 'by one Richbert, a pagan; and from that time the province was under error for three years, till the crown came into the possession of Sigeberht, brother to the same Eorpwald, a most Christian and learned man'. Sigeberht it appears had been banished to France because of the enmity of Raedwald and there he became a Christian. Though called Eorpwald's brother, his parentage is very obscure and he was perhaps a brother only of the half-blood. Nor are we told specifically who governed East Anglia in the three years between Eorpwald's death and the coming of Sigeberht, though perhaps the rule of the pagan Richbert is implied. The very date of Eorpwald's death is uncertain, but by 635 Sigeberht was king in East Anglia. Early in his reign Felix who had been sent to East Anglia to preach the gospel, was established probably at Dunwich as bishop of the province. About this time too an Irish monk Fursey left his own land to preach the gospel to the English. He came into East Anglia and was settled by Sigeberht at Burgh Castle in Suffolk, where he built a monastery within the walls of the old Roman fort of the Saxon Shore.

Sigeberht himself had founded a monastery at Bury St. Edmunds— as it was later to be known—and, wishing himself to undertake the religious life, made over the kingship to his kinsman (*cognatus*) Ecgric, who previously had been governor of part of the province. Of Ecgric's parentage nothing is known and, though he may just possibly have been the eldest son of Eni, this is most unlikely as Bede was careful to describe in terms of relationship to Anna, all those of Eni's children and grandchildren who are named in his narrative. However this may be, Sigeberht was not left long in enjoyment of his religious seclusion. Soon after 640, though the exact year is not known, the warlike Penda, pagan king of the Mercian Angles, attacked East Anglia. The East Anglian leaders, in the hope that his presence would fortify their men's morale, begged Sigeberht to join them and when he demurred, they took him forcibly. In the battle which followed Penda triumphed and both Sigeberht and Ecgric were slain.

The crown now reverted to the younger branch of the Wuffings, the sons of Eni, Raedwald's younger brother. Anna the king, as Bede tells us many times, 'was a good man, and happy in a good and pious offspring'. He was undoubtedly a good and active Christian. He founded a monastery at Blythburgh where he was later buried according to a positive statement in the *Liber Eliensis* or Ely Chronicle. He and his nobles embellished Fursey's monastery at Burgh Castle with stately buildings and donations. His eldest daughter married Erconberht king of Kent and, after she was widowed, entered the religious life and finally became the second abbess of Ely in succession to her sister Aethelthryth the founder and first abbess. Another daughter of Anna's became abbess of Brie in France. During Anna's reign, Penda of the Mercians extended his power over the Midlands and then over both Wessex and East Anglia. In the last few years of his reign therefore, Anna was in some sense subordinate to Penda. Conflict between them flared up and in 653 or 654—as different manuscripts of the *Chronicle* have it—Anna was killed and, as has been said, was buried at Blythburgh where his tomb was venerated for centuries.

To the throne then came his brother Aethelhere, of whose religious beliefs we know little. It would seem reasonably certain that he was at least a nominal Christian but perhaps no more. For he was acceptable to Penda his 'overlord' and within a few months of his accession, he is found to be in more active alliance. Penda had resolved on the subjection of Northumbria and marched north with a large army, a contingent of which was under the command of Aethelhere. They were met near Leeds by the Northumbrian king Oswy and the Mercian army was destroyed. Penda was slain and so was Aethelhere 'with all his soldiers' as Bede relates. He goes on to say: 'The battle was fought near the river Winwaed which then, with the great rains, had not only filled its channel, but overflowed its banks, so that many more were drowned in the flight than destroyed by the sword'. The traditional date for this battle was in 655, but there is good reason to believe that it was fought on November 14, 654.

Aethelwald, a younger son of Eni, succeeded his brother Aethelhere. Of him we know little, but that he was a Christian is certain for Swithhelm, king of the East Saxons, was baptised by his bishop Cedd at Rendlesham, Aethelwald's royal seat, where Aethelwald stood godfather for him. Aethelwald was dead by 664 and his successor was his nephew Aldwulf the son of Aethelric, another of Eni's sons. Aldwulf reigned until 713, as has been told above; after him came his son Aelfwald who died in 740. There were later kings of East Anglia, but their origin and relationships are obscure and it is probable that Aelfwald was the last of the Wuffing line.

When the great ship-burial was first found and the grave-furniture brought to light, it was at once realised that here was a grave in the heathen tradition and at that one of outstanding richness. Such an exceptional wealth of equipment it was thought would only have been given to a member of the royal house if not, indeed, to a reigning king. With this the name of Raedwald was quickly linked, Raedwald the last of the true pagans and in his day Bretwalda of Britain. But as the coins found in the purse were studied, this identification was first made doubtful and then shown to be not tenable, so that the discussion was re-opened.

Professor Birger Nerman, influenced by the ship-burial and the obvious similarities of some of the grave-goods to Swedish counterparts, expressed his conviction that the grave was actually that of a Swedish prince. This solution proved not to be generally acceptable as, though some Swedish influence was clearly apparent, it was certain that most of the grave-goods were definitely Anglian. There were also distinct evidences of Christian influence and the 'christening spoons' were held to be good evidence of the subject having at least been baptised. And finally his countryman Sune Lindqvist pointed out that though the ship-burial in some ways reflected Swedish pagan practice, it differed significantly from that practice in many ways. He saw it in fact as 'a typically Christian arrangement, but only conceivable during a period of transition from paganism which was of very short duration in all parts of England.' And with this opinion English archaeologists have since found themselves in substantial agreement.

The problem of the coin-dating is not an easy one. Forty of them were present in the purse, of which three had been rubbed smooth, perhaps for re-striking. The remaining thirty-seven were all Merovingian Frankish issues of the type known as *tremisses*, which the Franks had copied from the coinage of the Byzantine Empire and which increasingly diverged in style and treatment from the original models. None of these coins carries the year of issue so that the numismatists' dating has to be based to some extent on style and treatment. Furthermore, the issue of Merovingian coinage was not limited to one mint and these thirty-seven coins come from mints in all parts of what is now France as well as from towns east of the French border. At this time of course, there was no Anglo-Saxon coinage, the first gold thrymsas (*tremisses*) not appearing until the last quarter of the seventh century and the succeeding silver sceattas at about the end of the century.

The first hasty survey of the coins, made by Mr. Derek Allen of the British Museum, was published late in 1939. Briefly summarised, his conclusions were that it was impossible for the burial to have taken place before A.D. 600, most unlikely that it could have happened before 640-50 and may have been nearer 670. As Raedwald was certainly dead before 626 and probably in 624, this made it difficult but perhaps not impossible to identify him as the subject of the burial. But after the war, opportunity came for more careful study of these coins by Mr. John Allan, Keeper of Coins in the British Museum. In 1946 he announced that the hoard contained a coin of King Dagobert I (628-38) which immediately showed it to be impossible that the burial was Raedwald's cenotaph. Mr. Allan was also able to detect other features in the design of some of the coins which must have appeared after 630. Finally he summed up: 'We are certainly on the safe side if we say that the hoard was put together after 650, but I have little doubt the date is nearer A.D. 670.' Since then the increase in our knowledge has enabled Mr. P. H. Grierson (1952) to close the gap a little more and he has said that the earliest date for the burial lies between A.D. 650 and 660. This comparatively close dating is reliable and makes it quite certain that the burial does not commemorate Raedwald.

Now the personal accoutrements in the ship-burial are those of a man and point clearly to its subject being a male member of the royal house. But the presence of the standard and the ceremonial whetstone seems to make it certain that this was a king's memorial, for it is difficult to believe that the symbols of power and office should be given to one who did not himself hold them in life. If this is so, there remain three possible candidates for the final choice, three of the sons of Eni. First there is Anna who died in 653-4, Aethelhere in 654 and Aethelwald in 663-4. The next king to die was Aldwulf in 713 and all that we know of Anglo-Saxon burial customs makes it quite certain that the ship-burial could not have been as late as 713. As Sune Lindqvist said, it must belong to the short transition period between the first conversion and the full establishment of Christianity as the accepted religion and this must have been well before 713. In 653 died Bishop Felix, who had been bishop of East Anglia for seventeen years. His successors, all of whom are known to us by name, followed him regularly and it is impossible that such an open expression of paganism could or would have been thought necessary in the eighth century. In fine, the attribution must be made to one or another of Eni's three kingly sons. Of the three, Professor Lindqvist named Aethelwald, but this choice was made because he apparently misunderstood Mr. John Allan's pronouncement and thought that the burial could not have preceded A.D. 670. In this however he was mistaken and in this attribution he has not been followed. Aethelwald though certainly a Christian was clearly no outstanding figure, much less so than his elder brothers and was hardly the man to merit a pagan 'hero's funeral'. The choice, it seems, is really limited to Anna or Aethelhere and here the difficulties are heavy.

Anna himself, Bede's 'good man' and good Christian, seems at first glance hardly to have merited a pagan cenotaph. As he was buried at Blythburgh, however, the absence of his body can be accounted for and, as he died in battle facing the Mercian enemy, it has been thought that the pagan party at the court may well have raised to him this memorial. Mr. Bruce-Mitford himself, after having tentatively suggested the name of Aethelhere, is now inclined to choose Anna as the cenotaph's subject.

On the other hand the evidence in favour of Aethelhere has force. He died within a year of Anna, so that the dating evidence provided by the grave-goods does not help in making a choice between them. Aethelhere died in battle and that in Northumbria, where in the floods many of his followers were lost. This, it has been considered, may well explain why his body was lost. And though doubtless he had been baptised in his youth, there is no evidence that he was a convinced Christian. His alliance with Penda indeed may well point to his having had pagan sympathies. It is true that his reign was short and lacked the achievements of that of his brother Anna, but by surviving pagan elements in the province, Anna's activities may well have been disliked and disparaged. To these arguments, the present writer would add another, apparently not before advanced, which seems to strengthen the case for the identification with Aethelhere.

Bede of course is primarily concerned in his history with the story of the church and its establishment in England. When once that has happened in a province with the support of its king, he does not detail all the surviving pagan elements in nominally Christian communities; but he does from time to time make clear that paganism did survive well into the middle of the seventh century. For example, we are told that Earconberht of Kent, husband of Anna's daughter, succeeded his father in 640. He reigned until his death in 664 and during that reign was the first English king to order the destruction of pagan idols in his kingdom. Now Ethelbert's conversion, the first of an English king, happened in 597 so that upwards of fifty years were to pass before his descendant felt strong enough to suppress overt paganism. And yet the falling away after the death of Ethelbert in 616 lasted only a few months for Eadbald, who at first refused to follow his father's religion and drove the bishop away, had returned to his Christian practice and recalled the bishop within a year after he had left. Bede in fact has made it clear that when the evangelising missionaries first entered a new province they did so by royal permission and their first task was to attempt the conversion of the king himself and of the members of his family and court. When this was done the royal support enabled them to continue their work, and the example set by the kingly leader doubtless influenced many of that king's subjects. But if the king or his successor reverted to the old faith, the bishop's position became difficult or impossible to maintain, certain evidence that in both the court-nobility and the commonalty there was still a strong pagan sympathy.

Now as has been told above (p. 92) Raedwald's temple, with its pagan and Christian altars described by Aldwulf, must have survived until about 650 or even later; it may even be suggested that it was there until 654 at least. Felix became bishop of East Anglia in about 636 and did not die until 653. Anna the pious Christian reigned from about 640 until 654. And yet the temple and its pagan altar survived, sure evidence of a strong pagan party which, in the eighteen years since the coming of Felix, had not been suppressed. But if this party, in spite of the pressure of a king such as Anna and a bishop such as Felix, could maintain its influence well enough to preserve its temple, there must have been strong leadership in the court itself, a leadership probably given by a member of the royal family. Aethelwald the Christian could hardly be that man. His younger brother Aethelric, the father of Aldwulf, was probably a pagan as his Christian wife had left him, but his name is not even mentioned by Bede and his influence must have been small. It would seem therefore that it was Aethelhere, Anna's own successor who was the leader of the pagan party. From the *Ely Chronicle* we also learn that Anna had a son Jurmin, who like his father was buried at Blythburgh—though some chroniclers have called him Anna's nephew—but he did not succeed his father. At Anna's death the crown fell to the mature Aethelhere and it is clear enough that he had strong support. And immediately the royal power came to him he entered into active alliance with the pagan Penda, to lose his life in the autumn of the same year on the banks of the Winwaed river. With his death the story of East Anglian paganism ends. What scanty evidence remains to us does suggest that, after Aethelhere's death, East Anglia was a Christian land increasingly under the influence of Penda's Christian successors.

The weight of evidence therefore points to Aethelhere as the last royal leader of strength who maintained pagan practice in East Anglia. To him therefore would seem to be due the last great manifestation of pagan funeral-ritual. And this burial, which could hardly have taken place before the beginning of 655—Aethelhere's death being on November 14, 654—

was probably the last ship-burial to take place at Sutton Hoo. To make this probable attribution also raises the question of how far it is possible to identify the persons in the other barrow-burials. The evidence is slight but may at least be surveyed and the possibilities assessed.

Ship-burial at this early date is known to have been practised only in Suffolk and in the Uppland province of Sweden and there is good evidence to suggest that the fashion was brought to England from that province. The full significance of this Swedish connexion is discussed in Chapter IX and need not be further enlarged on here. But the excavation of many Swedish graves at Vendel and Valsgärde, where pagan boat-burials continued to be made to the end of the Viking period, has shown that this practice was the custom only of a few leading families whose successive members were interred in this way in a family cemetery. It has also established, as Sune Lindqvist pointed out, that certain features of these Swedish burials, such as the interment of horses, harness and other animals and birds, did not take place in Barrow No. 1 at Sutton Hoo. The similarity in the selection and precise arrangement of the grave-goods is not close and the presence of the boat itself is really the linking factor. This dissimilarity had indeed been one of the factors in identifying the subject of the cenotaph and has been considered to confirm the view that this was a belated pagan revival in an early Christian setting, at a time when men had become unfamiliar with the true pagan ritual. It has further led to the suggestion that the obvious anachronisms in the Beowulf story, in which ship-burial was attributed to the early sixth century in conjunction with cremation and, in that of Scyld Scefing to an even earlier date, are due to the memory of this last Sutton Hoo burial having survived until *Beowulf* in its present form was composed. For the poet was certainly a Christian addressing a Christian audience and he appears to have described what he believed was an early pagan practice.

In other parts of Scandinavia ship-burial is not known until a later day. In Denmark it was always rare. But in Westfold, the district around the Oslo Fjord, the royal house who were known as the Ynglings and who later became kings of all Norway, claimed descent from the old Swedish royal house as is told in Snorre Sturlason's 'Ynglinga Saga', the first in his *Heimskringla*, the sagas of the Norse kings. To this family are attributed those great burials at Gokstad, Oseberg and perhaps Borre and Tune. Later the practice spread with the Vikings 'west over the sea' and Viking boat-burials have been found in different parts of the British Isles as well as in many parts of Norway.

In Sweden this practice does not seem to have begun before the end of the sixth century. Its earliest date in England therefore would seem to be not before A.D. 600. And the three certain English boat-burials seem to confirm this dating. Apart from the great ship-burial, we have the smaller Sutton Hoo burial in Barrow No. 2 and the Snape boat-burial. The Caister variants certainly do not antedate the middle third of the seventh century and for Ashby Dell there is no evidence at all. Even for the Snape and smaller Sutton Hoo interments no very close dating can be achieved; but after a careful study of the Snape burial, Mr. Bruce-Mitford has given it an approximate date of A.D. 635-50. This is based largely on the details of workmanship shown by a gold ring found in that burial. This ring, which holds in its bezel an onyx intaglio of Roman workmanship, is decorated with filigree-work of rather unusual type which apparently could hardly have been made before 625. As the ring had certainly been worn for a time before it was buried, 635 is fixed as the probable earliest date for the interment. Of the other grave-goods, which were not spectacular, the only ones of any chronological significance were a glass 'claw-beaker' and a fragment of another vessel of dark blue glass. The former cannot be closely dated, but Dr. Harden has placed its date of manufacture as well into the sixth century. More important is the dark blue fragment, for this seems to belong to the 'squat jar' series, which is divided into sub-groups by their decoration; here we are concerned only with those having a body decorated with 'trails' forming a lattice-pattern. Two were found in the seventh-century grave at Broomfield, which has already been mentioned and fragments of another were in the boat-burial in Barrow No. 2, at Sutton Hoo (Fig. 5). All the vessels in this sub-group are of dark blue glass; they are placed by Dr. Harden as 'certainly seventh-century pieces'. He also points out that dark blue glass in Anglo-Saxon graves is normally late and probably belonged to the seventh century. All types of squat jar, he believes, were made in England, probably in a glasshouse at Faversham in Kent.

Now this independent dating of the glass agrees well with that derived from the other evidence and places the Sutton Hoo No. 2 boat-burial in the seventh century, though doubtless well before the great ship-burial. If we are to accept this barrow-group as that of the royal house only, on the analogy of family cemeteries of boat-burials of great folk in Sweden, it should be possible to arrive at some approximation to their number. Counting the male members of the Wuffing family in England to the last possible date for barrow burial, we have Wehha, Wuffa, Tyttla, Raedwald Eni, Raegenhere, Eorpwald, Anna, Aethelhere, Aethelwald and Aethelric, a total of eleven which is the same as the barrow number. Sigeberht and Ecgric almost certainly were not true Wuffings, at least in the legitimate line, and so are omitted. Of those named, Aethelwald can hardly be buried here, Anna was certainly not and in view of the postulated gap before the great cenotaph, it seems rather unlikely that he too was memorialised here. Eorpwald, certainly a Christian, though only for a short time in a predominantly pagan community, may well lie here. Raedwald, his son Raegenhere and his brother Eni are most probably buried under one or another of these mounds together with their predecessors. There are then two mounds only which are perhaps not accounted for and these may well cover sons of the house whose names are not mentioned in Bede's history. Until more of the mounds are excavated, little further identification is possible for on the evidence of a single boat-burial—that in No. 2— the comparative richness of different burials cannot be assessed. As however this No. 2 burial was apparently rather poorly furnished and its date in the seventh century is fixed by the glass jar, it would perhaps seem more probable that this grave was that of either Eni or his nephew Raegenhere, neither of whom was ever king. One further suggestion may be offered. If Barrows Nos. 7 and 10 are shown at some future date to have covered ship-burials, they also may be expected to be of seventh-century date and Raedwald himself may yet be found to lie in one of them.

There is indeed further support for the barrow-group's being that of the Wuffings. It has already been mentioned that Rendlesham, a few miles higher up the Deben valley, was a seat of this kingly house. In this immediate area of Suffolk, the 'Sandlings' as it is known, many finds of exceptional richness have been made, some of which have been mentioned earlier. The custom of burying king and chief under a barrow, which is very rare elsewhere in East Anglia, seems to occur in this area. Thus apart from the Sutton Hoo group itself, there is such a burial already described at Snape where the seventh-century boat-burial lay under one of a small group of barrows. Of these one only now survives; it has not been scientifically excavated. The others were apparently destroyed many years ago during road-making activities and no record of their contents survives. Further north at Bloodmoor Hill, on the borders of Gisleham and Pakefield near Lowestoft, another barrow was opened as long ago as 1758. Some record remains of the burial and the objects themselves are preserved in the Ashmolean Museum. Here lay the skeleton of a man with two pendants attached to a necklace of rough garnets. One of the pendants was an onyx intaglio of Roman workmanship which may be compared with that preserved in the Snape ring. But the more important of the two was the pendant made of a gold coin set in a hoop. In the past this coin has generally been attributed to Avitus who was declared emperor in Gaul in A.D. 455, but who resigned to become a bishop. However a recent examination of this coin by Dr. J. P. C. Kent has enabled him to state that this is a Late Visigothic copy of a coin of Justinian I (527-65), which makes the grave not earlier than the latter part of the sixth century and quite possibly anything up to fifty years later.

Now at Snape the boat-burial was made on the site of an earlier cremation cemetery, some of the urns lying undisturbed—until the excavation—under the sides of the mound. Others, cut into by the digging of the trench for the boat, appear to have been incorporated in the body of the mound, while those surrounding the barrow lay closer to the surface than is usual; this seemed to result from the topsoil having been removed to build the mound. At Sutton Hoo, however, no such cemetery is known. The humbler members of the Rendlesham community were buried it seems in a cemetery at Rendlesham itself, from which no evidence whatever of a possible royal interment has come to light. There can be little doubt that the 'Sutton Mounts' are the last resting-places of the ancient Wuffings. For more than a thousand years they have lain there, not far from their Rendlesham home, but overlooking the estuary by which they had entered their kingdom.

VII

NORTH SEA CROSSINGS

FOR UPWARDS of 250 years, North German pirates and settlers were crossing the North Sea from the Continent to Britain. By what route did they come? To this question, no satisfactory answer has been given in the past. It has, indeed, been generally assumed that Angles crossed from Schleswig to the Humber and the Wash, Saxons, Frisians and Jutes to the Thames estuary and the Channel shore, as well as to the Wash. The problem, in fact, has hardly been seen as a problem. They were seamen, they had sea-going vessels and so they crossed. But such an assumption avoids real difficulties, for to understand the various phases of the Anglo-Saxon settlement, and particularly the East Anglian settlement-pattern, it is necessary to have a clear picture of how the settlers got there. Their Continental homes have already been discussed, and we are here concerned only with the seafaring problems which confronted them. We have reviewed at some length the ships used in these North Sea crossings and found that the normal vessel was a rowing galley of some 60-80 feet long, somewhat cranky and ill-suited to survive a North Sea gale. We must now try to estimate the composition of the boats' companies and, for this purpose, the Nydam ship with its thirty oars, will be used as the standard type.

It is easy to see that, in the earlier days of piracy, such a boat could have carried a crew of from sixty to eighty men, so that reliefs were available for the oars. But when, in the true Migration Period, family parties began to cross, as is certain from Bede's account, as well as from the graves and their contents, the problem changed. The captain of the galley would generally be the leading man of a village- or family-group. The thirty oarsmen would be his kinsmen and dependents, some adolescent and some older men. With them would be perhaps as many girls and women, together with a number of small children. The ship would certainly be very full and if, in addition to food and water, some bulky personal possessions were also brought, it would probably be uncomfortably so. The later Viking vessels of approximately the same length normally carried from three to five times as many men as there were oars, but these later vessels were proportionately much broader and had higher freeboard—i.e. higher sides above the waterline—so that eighty persons would be a very full company for the Nydam ship. And with a mixed party, though many of the women could take an oar for a time in an emergency, the general practice would doubtless be not to overwork the oarsmen.

Severely limiting, too, was the absence of clock, chart or compass. All navigation, in a sea notorious for its mists, strong winds, shoals and swift tides, would have to be by dead reckoning. And what could an Anglian farmer-fisher from the Baltic coast of Schleswig know of the topography of the former Roman province of Britain? Certainly after a century or more of piracy or trading, most North German seamen of the North Sea coasts would have some knowledge, either by experience or by hearsay, of Britain's general position and configuration. But this would have been learned while stalking and raiding, or by serving aboard, Roman merchantmen trading between the Rhine or the north Gaulish ports such as Boulogne, and the south-east coasts of Britain. It would seem, therefore, that to make a desired landfall, they would first wish to reach those Continental coasts from which they knew a safe passage to Britain could be made with some certainty.

The leaders, then, of parties from Schleswig, both because of the heavily-laden ships and of the limits of their topographical knowledge, would incline to make first, or be forced to make first, a coasting voyage to the Low Countries. From there they could cross the Narrow Seas by a comparatively short passage. And, indeed, on a clear summer's day, the English cliffs are to be seen from Cap Gris Nez, so that even the most cautious shipman could be assured of a fair landfall. We may also go further and say that, except by the accident of weather or ignorance, no direct passage from North Schleswig to England was ever made at this time. It was, normally speaking, an impossible voyage to make without a steady north-east wind and a lifting square-sail, which they had not got, and could only have succeeded by good fortune and under exceptionally favourable conditions. Of this the truth may easily be demonstrated.

To grasp the difficulty of the North Sea crossing, either direct or by the coastwise route, it is necessary to choose a specific date in the year and, working with the sun and tide data for that and following days, make a theoretical crossing. Here it is enough to summarise such a coastwise voyage, as well as the almost impossible direct crossing. But in an appendix, the details of the coasting voyage to England, from Esbjerg on the south-west coast of Jutland, are given and some attempt is made to show how specific difficulties would be overcome. For this purpose, it has been assumed that the crew could row a vessel of Nydam type at a steady speed of 5 knots for periods up to six hours or more. But this is fairly certainly an over-estimate for these migrating family-parties, and as is explained in more detail in the appendix, the true rate should be about 3 knots, and that only for a comparatively limited period.

The direct passage may first be considered. As conveniently high tides occur on or about April 24 at Esbjerg, this date for the departure has been chosen for, if the season is good, the fair weather is likely to persist for several days. Leaving Esbjerg at dawn (high water 03.30 hours and sunrise about 04.10 hours)[1] and rowing at 5 knots on a course of about west-south-west for Spurn Head at the mouth of the Humber, the tides will modify the estimated position by several miles from time to time. But if there is no wind and the steered course never varies, the end of the journey will be some 13 miles south-south-east of the objective and the ship will come ashore between Saltfleet and Mablethorpe on the Lincolnshire coast at about 20.30 hours on April 26 (sunset at 19.14) as darkness falls. This means that 30 men will row at a steady 5 knots for sixty-five hours, while the leader steers a perfect compass course without a compass and all the time there is no wind.

To attempt a somewhat more realistic estimate than this impossibly swift and accurate crossing, another journey between these points was plotted. But this time the rowing speed was reduced to 3 knots and it was further assumed that the vessel lay to a sea-anchor from sunset to sunrise. In the absence of wind, therefore, it was tide-drifted only during the night. With these altered conditions, a ship which left Esbjerg at dawn on April 24 would reach Sutton-on-Sea in Lincolnshire about midday on May 2, a passage of 8½ days. And again this presupposes that a true course was steered whenever the crew was rowing and that no wind blew. These conditions are clearly impossible; and even an open-sea passage of 8½ days would not be undertaken with a heavily-laden ship, when a comparatively easy coasting voyage was possible. Had such crossings been attempted, they would almost inevitably have ended in disaster.

The coasting voyage down the West Schleswig coast and westward along the East and West Frisian island-fringe to Texel, lasted from April 24 to midday on May 3. This passage was again based on a rowing speed of 5 knots and a daily passage; no allowances were made for bad weather, mishap, sickness or ignorance of local waters. From Texel, two courses were open. One was to put to sea on a course due west and make the Wash.

---

[1] All local times are reduced to Greenwich Mean Time (G.M.T.), and the twenty-four-hour clock is used. All distances by sea are given in nautical miles, i.e. minutes of latitude, or about 1⅐ English Statute Miles (E.S.M.).

Holding this course, again at 5 knots, the ship landed on Sheringham beach in twenty-four hours, a landfall a few miles south of the estimated position. The other alternative was to continue coastwise southward from Texel to Flushing or Dunkirk, and cross the Narrow Seas more rapidly. From Flushing, it was calculated, a passage to Harwich, with the same ideal conditions, would have taken 16½ hours, so that by this route, a ship which left Esbjerg on April 24 at 08.00 hours reached Harwich on May 7 at 20.30 hours, some fourteen days. By extending the coastal voyage for another day down the Belgian coast, the open-sea crossing would be considerably reduced; made from the neighbourhood of Calais on a day of good visibility, land would never be out of sight.

It is certain, therefore, that with an average rowing speed of 3 knots, together with all the delays due to weather, to human frailty and to the condition of the ship, most passages from Schleswig to East Anglia must have taken some two months. In bad seasons, it may well have been six months. And many more must have failed altogether. Some of these parties may have been lost by shipwreck and drowning. Others, by forced choice due to sickness, lack of fortitude or by the loss of their ship, may have settled on any part of the continental coast as far west as Calais, if only the local inhabitants were not too hostile. Evidence for scattered settlements of this kind has been found, for cremation urns of early fifth-century type, deriving from the homeland to the north, are well known both in Belgium and South Holland. It is clear, also, that such lengthy voyages would lead to some intercourse between the travellers and the local people, for food from time to time would have to be obtained. Odd trinkets might well be acquired at the same time and the occurrence of an odd Saxon or Rhenish brooch in a purely Anglian village-cemetery in England may mean no more than such a trivial commercial contact.

So far we have dealt only with the parties who put to sea from the West Schleswig coast. But the centres of Anglian population seem rather to have lain in the eastern half of Schleswig and many, if not most, Anglian ships were doubtless kept in the fjords and bays of the tideless Baltic coast, to which they were better suited. It is less easy to decide how these ships made their journeys. Probably enough, many of the parties may have embarked at some staithe in the Schlei Fjord or the Als Sound and made the journey round the Jutish coast. Other parties perhaps crossed to the west coast by land, an average journey of some 40 miles and there met their ships which had been taken round Jutland by a skeleton crew. This preliminary voyage would have been along the shore of the Little Belt and the Cattegat, through the Liim Fjord—in those days open, though today in part silted up—and south along the west coast of Jutland to the North Frisian island-fringe. By this route the comparatively hazardous passage round the Skaw would be avoided and, indeed, some distance saved, a matter of some importance when rowing was the motive power. Nevertheless, this preliminary passage would add nearly another month to the overall time of the voyage to England.

Saxons from the Elbe estuary and the East Frisian shore would have followed the same coastwise route, but for them the journey would be somewhat shorter. And, indeed, their landings in south and south-east England point strongly to their having coasted as far as Cap Gris Nez, though some may have crossed to the Wash and so penetrated to the Midlands by the major rivers, as Leeds' studies have shown. During these voyages there must, under these conditions, have been much contact between Angles and Saxons on passage. Under the hazards of travel, slight differences of pronunciation of a more or less common tongue, the wearing of different brooches, and other minor cultural variations, must all have been forgotten; mutual aid and fraternisation would lead to different groups joining forces to establish a footing on the English shore. This point needs no labouring and the occurrence, particularly of Saxon-type urns and brooches in the predominantly Anglian eastern counties, need cause no surprise. More odd, indeed, would have been their entire absence. Traces of Anglian culture found from time to time in predominantly Saxon territory may be similarly explained.

One other uncertain factor must be mentioned. These hypothetical voyages have been assessed in relation to the present-day coastline. Now it is certain that, during the Migration Period and, apparently, for some centuries before it began, conditions on the Frisian shore had been deteriorating due to the encroachment of the sea. Archaeological investigations have shown that, in the areas close to the coast, homesteads were wont to be built on artificial mounds—*terpen* as they are called—which lifted the houses above the water-table of the surrounding marshland. Indeed, it is well-recognised that this slow submergence of the land of an expanding people set up population-pressures which were one of the causes of such large-scale migration. Tentative reconstructions have been made of the coastline as it then was. It is fairly clear that many of the East and West Frisian islands were larger than they are today and the mainland behind the island-fringe was less indented by great estuaries. Conversely, the Belgian coast, or at least the dry mainland, lay rather inshore of its present-day line. But though the topographical detail of today differs in many ways from that of 1,500 years ago, it is unlikely that there is any essential difference in the basic conditions. The shore would still be low-lying with impeding banks and tidal channels between the islands and mainland. Sunrise and sunset, times of high and low water and the tidal streams would not be significantly different.

The passages therefore have been worked out for a route outside the islands, so that a local variation in inshore channels does not invalidate the calculations. It is probable enough that, when going ashore for the night, the leader would take advantage of the shelter of a channel-entrance. Saxon leaders who knew the coast well would doubtless use inshore channels for daytime passages, when a stiff onshore breeze was blowing. But it is unlikely that an Angle from East Schleswig would know them with sufficient intimacy, particularly as his seafaring in the tideless Baltic was but poor preparation for the tide-rips and rushing streams of the Frisian coast.

APPENDIX

To make clear the duration of a voyage from Schleswig to England, a detailed itinerary is given below. This has been calculated, as I have said above, on the assumption that the crew could row a vessel of Nydam type at a steady speed of 5 knots for periods up to 6 hours or more. But, as this seemed certainly to be an over-estimate, I have discussed the matter at some length with the coxswain and some senior members of the Caister lifeboat crew, as well as with a former coxswain who, in his younger days had worked in the beach yawls as well as in pulling lifeboats. The agreed opinion was that an average speed of 3 knots was the best that could be achieved, unless there were frequent reliefs. The further opinion was that, unless the voyage were urgent, the whole company would tend to rest for a day after a fairly long pull, more especially if the weather was not very good. This means that the following itinerary is impossibly fast and should, for normal crossings, be at least trebled. Many crossings would have taken much longer and a bad season would have meant considerable delay in reaching the final destination.

I have chosen Esbjerg on the south-west coast of Jutland as the most northerly point from which Anglian departures were made. Many, however, must have left the mainland coast at points behind the fringe of North Frisian islands, thus reducing the crossing-time by some days. The times of high water at the named places are taken from the tables of tidal constants given in various nautical almanacs, my own being *Reed's Nautical Almanac*

(Sunderland, published annually). The direction and speed of tidal currents have been calculated from the series of charts in *Brown's Tidal Streams for the Whole of the British Coasts, Ireland and North Sea* (Thirteenth Edition, Glasgow, 1952). An adequate explanation of the modern theory of tide-formation, and the co-tidal lines centring on the various amphidromic points in the North Sea, may be found in Doodson and Warburg's *Admiralty Manual of Tides* (London, 1941). Admiralty Chart No. 301, *British Islands and Adjacent Waters*, showing co-tidal and co-range lines, may also be consulted. This chart makes quite clear that, during a passage from the Schleswig-Holstein coasts to northern East Anglia or the Humber, two such systems are traversed, the coastal points of their meeting lying between Texel and Terschelling on the north coast of Holland and near Cromer in Norfolk. Therefore, during a crossing from Schleswig to the Wash, following the coastwise route, the voyage would begin in system No. 2—numbered southward from the Norwegian coast—pass into No. 3 off the Dutch coast and return to No. 2 on the north Norfolk coast. Because of this, the crew would experience great changes in the range of tidal rise and fall, perplexing to a Baltic seaman. There are also considerable differences in the rates of tidal streams. Thus, on the east coast of Norfolk, during spring tides, the southbound flood-stream may run as fast as 4 knots for some hours. Against this a Nydam-type ship could make no headway. How far these difficulties and the determination of individual parties to press on, or stay near the first landfall, influenced the choice of settlement-site will never be known. But it is clear that in some such way, much of the cultural admixture which is apparent in the distribution of urn-types and trinkets, may be explained. Together with the suggestions already made above, this gives three distinct ways in which admixture took place.

It is only when one works out the details of crossings by various routes that the real difficulties become apparent. Using the relevant data from almanac and tide-chart, I have chosen to begin on a date late in April, when the spring tides are high and the weather is often suited to such a voyage. The 'unit of travel' is a single daily passage at a rowing speed of 5 knots with no allowances made for bad weather, sickness, damage to ship or error due to lack of knowledge of the coast. But the absence of clock, compass and chart must again be stressed. A further complication has also to be noted. Standard time in Denmark and Germany—based of course on the sun's passage—is one hour ahead of Greenwich and, in Holland, 20 minutes. On the West Schleswig coast, sunrise and sunset are roughly 36 minutes earlier than at Greenwich. All times shown below, therefore, are reduced to G.M.T. Allowances have also been made for the different speeds of tidal streams at springs and neaps. Distances are given in nautical miles with English Statute Miles (E.S.M.) sometimes shown in brackets. The narrative is cast in the form of a log and, for convenience in presentation, two ships are supposed to have sailed in company.

April 24. Left Esbjerg at about 08.00 hours as the tide turned to flood south along the Schleswig coast. It reached a speed of 2 knots and then slackened, turning again to ebb NNW at about 14.00 hours. The east coast of Sylt was reached, a distance of 38 miles (44 E.S.M.).

April 25. Left Sylt at about 08.00 near low water. 6 hours' rowing brought the ship to the north coast of Pellworm.

April 26. Left Pellworm at about 09.00 near low water. 6 hours' rowing on the flood tide made Büsum on the NE side of the Elbe estuary entrance.

In the approaches to the Elbe, conditions changed. The bay of the estuary had to be crossed. A theoretical passage, similar to those already made, would be to Wangeroog, the most easterly of the East Frisian islands. From Büsum, this would be reached by setting a direct course to the Scharhorn and then across the Weser-Jade entrance to Wangeroog. To do this Büsum would have to be left 1-2 hours before high water. The last of the flood would at first make progress slow, but would soon ease and then a favourable ebb would enable the ship to reach Wangeroog about high water or a little later. But on April 27, sunrise at Büsum was not until about 04.00 hours and sunset at about 18.50. Therefore, as the morning high water was at 03.19 hours, it would have meant putting to sea 2 hours or more before sunrise. On the afternoon tide, leaving Büsum at about 14.00 hours would have meant that the Scharhorn would not have been reached until near sunset, with another 20 miles across the Weser-Jade entrance to traverse mainly in darkness, which was impossible. Therefore—

April 27. Left Büsum at about 07.00 hours at half ebb and, passing down the channel towards the Scharhorn, entered the main Elbe channel at low water, whence the flood-tide took the ship to Cuxhaven by high water at 13.00 hours.

April 28. Left Cuxhaven at high water at about 04.00, which was also the time of sunrise. Off Scharhorn at about 06.15 and changed course for Wangeroog, where arrived about low water, a little before 10.00.

April 29. Left Wangeroog (east end) soon after dawn at high water (sunrise, 04.04) and steered W outside the island, to reach the W end of Norderney at about low water, 11.30 hours, passing inside the island in slack water and on the first of the flood.

April 30. Left Norderney at about 05.00 (high water) and steered N outside Juist on the ebb. There was scarcely time to make Schiermonnikoog before the tide turned, so went ashore at Rottum.

Between Rottum and Texel the tides are difficult, due to the contact of two rotary tidal-wave systems. Furthermore, at low water *inside* the West Frisian islands, the ebb-stream outside still runs W for a time, and correspondingly, east after high water. Accordingly—

May 1. Left Rottum at about 06.00 hours when the tide-stream slackened. Steered W to Schiermonnikoog and then to Ameland. Owing to the earlier times of high water towards the W went ashore on Ameland at about low water (10.00 hours).

May 2. Left Ameland at about 06.30 hours (sunrise 04.20) when the tide was slack and, though progress at first was slow, it soon improved with an increasing westbound stream along the Vlieland coast and so across to the west side of Texel. The tide just enabled the ship to reach the S end of the island before it began to run W at about 13.00 hours.

Two possible courses were now open. The first was to push out to sea and cross directly to the north Norfolk coast and the Wash. The other was to coast still further south to Flushing, or even to Dunkirk, and then cross the Narrow Seas to Harwich. Of these, Ship No. 1 took the open-sea route and Ship No. 2 coasted.

SHIP No. 1

May 4. Left Texel at about 10.30 hours steering due W, when the tide was running roughly W. Rowing for 12 hours at 5 knots, the estimated position was about 53° N 30° E. But the tide, moving in turn W, NW, N, NE, E, SE and S for various periods and at different speeds, had carried the ship roughly in a semicircle in relation to its estimated course, leaving it on that course but some 3 miles to the E of its supposed position, which was about half way across. Continuing to row for another 12 hours at 5 knots, the estimated position was a few miles N of Cromer. This time the tide was rather more helpful. The ship was carried in turn NW, N and S, leaving it 3½ miles SW of its estimated position, i.e., on Sheringham beach.

From Esbjerg to Sheringham, therefore, by this route had taken 12 days, including an open-sea crossing of 24 hours rowing steadily at 5 knots and steering an accurate course, in practice an impossible feat.

SHIP No. 2

May 4. Left Texel at about 05.00, when the northbound stream slackened a little after high water. Steering S with a southbound stream, reached Ymuiden in slack water at about 10.00 hours.

May 5. Left Ymuiden at slack water at about 05.00 and with some hours of favourable tide, reached the Hook of Holland at about 11.00 hours.

May 6. Left the Hook in slack water at about 06.00 and steered outside the islands with a favourable tide towards Walcheren, reaching its SW point at about 12.00, just after the tide had turned. The eastbound flood then carried the ship into Flushing Bay.

May 7. Left Flushing at sunrise (04.00) and steered towards Harwich (roughly W by N ½N). At first the tide set W and NW but later turned to SW. At the end of 6 hours rowing, the ship had advanced 30 miles direct and had been set some 7 miles to the SW of its estimated position. During most of the next 6 hours' rowing, the tide was setting NE, so that the ship's actual position was roughly some 5 miles NE of estimate. For the next two hours, the tide was nearly slack, first setting NE and then SW, so that the divergences from true course cancelled each other. Finally, in two to three hours, on the SW-running flood-tide, the ship reached Harwich at about 20.30. Sunset that day was at about 19.30, so that dusk was rapidly falling as the shore was approached.

Ship No. 2, therefore, had spent 14 days voyaging from Esbjerg to Harwich including an open-sea crossing of over 16 hours.

These imaginary passages, worked out with chart and almanac, at an impossibly fast rowing speed and with the assumption of a knowledge of destination, good landing-places and tide-conditions, have shown the theoretically possible minimum time in which the passages could be made. It will be noted that the rowing speed has only just enabled certain more arduous crossings, such as the Elbe estuary, the Weser-Jade estuary and the Narrow Seas, to be made in fairly good time. At the more realistic speed of 3 knots, with all allowances made for bad weather, mishap, sickness, ignorance of local waters and the needs of travel, the minimum allowance of two months or more is fully justified. And, apart from those families which stayed on the continental shore, there must have been many deaths during the various voyages. Doubtless the dead were buried with due ceremony where possible, and so the exotic cremation urns would stay to mark the temporary halt of a migrant group.

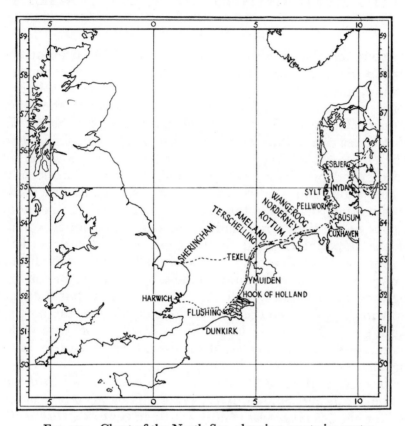

FIG. 29.   Chart of the North Sea, showing coastwise routes

VIII

THE BEGINNINGS OF EAST ANGLIA

THE STORY of the English settlement and the transformation of Roman Britain into Anglo-Saxon England begins in the third century, more than 100 years before the last Roman soldier left the land. For it we must turn to the Imperial records where the salient facts are enshrined. There is a Roman official document, the *Notitia dignitatum et administrationum tam civilium quam militarium in partibus orientis et occidentis*, the *Notitia Dignitatum* or *Notitia* in common usage, which is still available in four medieval copies. These are preserved in various European libraries, one of which is our own Bodleian at Oxford. It is, as its title states, a list of civil and military officials in the Roman Empire and also includes a note of the troops under their command. In modern parlance it would be the Chief of the Imperial General Staff's copy of the 'battle order' of his forces. It was compiled about the middle of the first half of the fifth century —say, between 420 and 430—and includes a list of the British garrisons, including those of Hadrian's Wall. As it seems certain that these garrisons had been withdrawn before the date of the compilation, the part referring to Britain is generally taken to be the list as it was before that withdrawal, doubtless retained for reference as, at the time, there was every intention of replacing the troops as soon as possible.

Our interest in the *Notitia* centres on a list of coastal forts which lay between the Wash and Southampton Water. They are *Branodunum* (Brancaster in Norfolk), *Gariannonum* (Burgh Castle in Suffolk), *Othona* (Bradwell in Essex), *Regulbium*, *Rutupiae*, *Dubris*, *Lemanis* (respectively Reculver, Richborough, Dover and Lympne, all in Kent), *Anderida* (Pevensey in Sussex) and *Portus Adurni* (Portchester in Hampshire). Apart from the Second Legion, or a part of it, which was stationed at Richborough, the headquarters of the defence scheme, the units were all of auxiliary troops, either cavalry or infantry, and all were under the command of the Count of the Saxon Shore. The walls, or a part of them, of most of these forts are still standing and the identifications, with the possible exception of *Othona* and *Portus Adurni*, are certain. The slight uncertainty about Bradwell and Portchester arises from there having been two others not far away which are not mentioned in the list. A few miles north of Bradwell, at Walton on the outskirts of Felixstowe in Suffolk, stood Walton Castle. It was finally destroyed by the sea in the eighteenth century, but we still know something of it from contemporary descriptions and prints, and its details seem to be those of this type of fort. The remains of another, at Carisbrooke in the Isle of Wight, have been recognised under the later castle which stands there. It may, of course, be that the two which are unnamed in the list had not been garrisoned for some time before the withdrawal and so were omitted.

Though the general organisation of these forts and their use in the fourth century are known to us from the *Notitia*, the exact date of their construction and original purpose are still obscure, in spite of partial excavation of some of them. From the style of the commander, this section of our coast is commonly known as 'the Saxon Shore', but it is not yet certain that the name was used here in the third century. At that time the northern coast of France was certainly styled 'the Saxon Shore' and it is also certain that, in the second half of the third century, Saxon pirates began to raid Roman merchant ships crossing the Narrow Seas. In their defence the Roman fleet in the Channel, which was based on Boulogne, was strengthened under the command of the admiral, Carausius, who had considerable success in dealing with the pirates. But Carausius fell under the displeasure of Rome, as he was thought to have used his position to enrich himself. When recalled, he refused to obey and established himself as Emperor of Britain in A.D. 287. For a time the authorities in Rome were too preoccupied with other troubles to deal with the rebel. He was provisionally recognised by the imperial power and given also dominion over the opposite shore of Gaul. He survived until 293, when the newly-appointed Caesar, the future emperor Constantius Chlorus, retook the Gaulish coastal strip and prepared to cross the Channel. Carausius was then slain by his lieutenant, Allectus, in 293. But in 296 Constantius landed in Britain, slew Allectus and re-established the imperial authority. It would seem that, after this settlement, the fleet was broken up into detachments, one of which was based in each of the estuaries protected by a fort, the latest of which were probably built at this time, though some had certainly been standing for perhaps half a century and Reculver at least from the beginning of the third century. By this means and by placing the general command in the hands of a land-based officer, it was hoped to prevent that excess of power, such as Carausius had found himself to possess, falling into the hands of one man. For more than a century after this reorganisation the defence scheme worked fairly well, the ships dealing with pirates at sea and the land-based forces protecting the naval dockyards and their stores and repelling overland raids.

At this time the Roman Empire was beset with troubles. A century or more earlier the Migration Period had begun, the period of the wanderings of the Germanic peoples who were now pressing on the frontiers of the Empire. Later, the frontiers of Rhine and Danube were to crumble; Frank and Burgundian, Lombard and Goth were to spread to the Mediterranean and Atlantic and sweep the old Western Empire out of political existence. But at the beginning of the fourth century the frontier, though threatened in many places, still held. Troops and more troops were needed to hold it and could no longer be recruited within the imperial bounds, so that more and more men were enlisted from the Germanic tribes. In addition to this, whole tribal groups from time to time were admitted and settled along the frontiers to stiffen the resistance to their own kinsfolk, who were pressing in behind. The Barbarian, though at times he slew and looted, yet respected the imperial name; the collapse when it came seems rather to have been due to inherent weaknesses in the imperial organisation than of set intent to destroy it on the part of the invaders. Their need was primarily for food and the land on which to grow it; the organisation was not sufficiently elastic to allow the newcomers to be incorporated in the economic system.

At this time the province of Britain was under threat from west, north and east. From the west came pirates and settlers from Ireland, from the north Pictish raiders from beyond Hadrian's Wall and from the east came the Saxon pirates. In the first half of the century they were held, but later they became stronger and allied themselves to gather a formidable force. Aided by the semi-barbarous troops who guarded the Wall, they broke through into the province, and in the black year of 367 Pictish raiders were looting the villas of Kent. In this strife both the Duke of Britain and the Count of the Saxon Shore were slain. In 369 Count Theodosius, father of the emperor of that name, crossed the Channel and restored order. He re-established Hadrian's Wall, disbanded the traitorous auxiliaries who had failed to hold it and established a series of signal-towers along the coast to supplement the work of the navy and the Saxon Shore garrisons. About this time too, we know from the historian Ammianus Marcellinus that Alamanni under their king were brought from the Middle Rhine and established as *fœderati* somewhere in Britain. Where this was we do not know, but it was doubtless somewhere near the southern half of the North Sea coast and very possibly in East Anglia. This happened nearly a century before that settlement of *fœderati* in Thanet under their leaders Hengist and Horsa, a story known to every schoolboy, which historians in the past have so generally accepted as the true *Adventus Saxonum*. But archaeologists are now beginning to amass new evidence to show that, though the Hengist story may well be true, yet substantial settlement had already taken place long before the middle of the fifth century.

This evidence has been largely drawn from a closer study of early Anglo-Saxon pottery. Dr. Myres has shown that from certain cemeteries in Yorkshire, Lincolnshire and East Anglia, there have come cremation urns of early Anglian type, called by him Anglo-Frisian, which if found in their original continental home would be dated as early as A.D. 400 and occasionally even earlier. Apart from these early true Anglo-Saxon pots, an entirely new type of pottery has also been recognised. This is a late Roman provincial ware or wares, made on the wheel but having decoration of bosses, impressed dimples and incised lines in true Germanic style. Not all archaeologists are yet convinced of the validity of this 'Romano-Saxon' pottery, as they deem it to be copied primarily from Roman silver vessels. This indeed is probably the source of the designs, but the derivation seems originally to have taken place in the Rhineland and the units of design were to appear again at a slightly later date on the true early Anglo-Saxon hand-made pots. Furthermore, the shapes of the Romano-Saxon pots are few; the most common, which are greatly in excess of the others, seem to be those of the hand-made cremation urns but made to a smaller size. Even more significant is the distribution of this ware. It is found on the East Anglian coast from Caister-on-Sea near Yarmouth to Colchester and occasionally on other riverine sites as far inland as the Fens. A few pots with similar decoration, but of rather different fabric, are known from the north Kentish shore and, more recently, odd vessels which are rather similar have come from Roman sites near the western edge of the Lincolnshire Fens. Dr. Myres in 1956 and again in 1958 expressed the view that it might well have been made primarily to accord with the tastes of such settled *fœderati* as Freomar's Alamanni. But the evidence now available leads to a rather different conclusion.

From 1951 to 1954 the writer's excavations in the Roman town at Caister-on-Sea produced the fragments of more than sixty of these Romano-Saxon pots, more than all the others known. When Dr. Myres wrote, Burgh Castle, the Saxon Shore fort across the estuary from Caister, had not been excavated and the few fragments of this ware from that site were chance finds only. Since then the writer in three seasons' excavations inside the fort has produced fragments of ten such vessels only. Clearly the concentration of this hybrid pottery lies rather in the civilian seaport town and not in the related military establishment. If then we are to see in this pottery a product of the provincial kilns designed to suit Germanic settlers or visiting customers, it is primarily among the civilian population that they are to be sought. And to find them is perhaps not a difficult task.

Now the towns of the Middle Rhine such as Cologne, which is marked by its name as a Roman *colonia*, were the great manufacturing centres north of the Alps. From here came so many of the manufactured goods traded to the ports of south and east Britain in exchange for British corn and wool. The same pressures which drove so many of the coastal tribesmen to piracy would send many more to employment as seamen in the merchant ships and as labourers in the ports. Such a cosmopolitan seaport as Caister then was, doubtless heard German dialects in its streets as often as the provincial Latin which was its 'official' tongue. This Romano-Saxon pottery was certainly in use at Caister at least from the beginning of the fourth century so that, by the early years of the fifth, when the collapse of the fiscal system brought an end to most of the trade and therefore to piracy, the population of Caister and the other eastern ports such as Colchester and perhaps London and Richborough, had doubtless a considerable mixed Germanic element composed of Saxons, Frisians and perhaps some Franks and Swabians. Intermarriage and local movement would spread these Germanic elements, though they would doubtless tend to be more strongly concentrated near the estuaries, where also lived the half-Germanic children of the garrisons.

The growth of place-name studies based on sound philological foundations is doing much to clarify our Dark-Age studies. The wild guesses of a former day are now being replaced by the disciplined work of the Place-name Society, whose first county volume was published in 1925. These volumes and a few others by modern scholars of repute are clarifying many obscurities in the story of the English settlement, though it has not always been possible to substantiate the conclusions drawn from this evidence by parallel conclusions from archaeological sources. Workers on East Anglian material have remarked on the almost complete absence of Celtic roots in the East Anglian place-nomenclature, many even of the rivers having Germanic names. This has led to the suggestion that the old Celtic speech of the Icenian tribesmen had virtually disappeared. When after the breakdown of the Imperial administration, the Latin-speaking officials and the more wealthy administrative and business classes tended to leave the province, many of the humbler folk of mixed origin who were still resident may well have spoken a somewhat modified Low German dialect.

But before this took place, the Germanic element in the area was certainly strengthened by the advent of new settlers. The old cantonal capital was *Venta Icenorum* at Caistor by Norwich. Here outside, but close to its massive town wall, has been found and excavated a great Anglo-Saxon cemetery. The results of the excavation have not yet been fully published, but a short summary of them will suffice. The earliest types of Anglian pottery to be found in England are from this cemetery and, together with other evidence, suggest that a settlement of Angles outside the walls of the town had begun before the end of the fourth century. These were certainly not somewhat romanised seamen employed by the Rhineland merchants and shippers. Their earliest cremation urns point to their being mainly an Anglian community of men and women straight from the homeland in Schleswig though, even at this time, there were some urns of pure Saxon type. It seems impossible that this settlement could have been made at a time when the imperial control was still effective, unless by official consent. Here it would seem was a considerable tribal settlement of the *fœderati*-type, designed and permitted as an assistance in guarding the cantonal town, its provincial governors and its provincial treasury against the dangers of the time. A few other very early cemeteries may be as early in their beginnings and their disposition suggests that the primary settlements to which they were attached were, in part at least, placed by arrangement with the provincial governors as a protection against raiders from the north (see Fig. 31).

The story of Hengist and Horsa may perhaps tend to confirm this. Part of the story is given by Gildas and more by Bede. The *Anglo-Saxon Chronicle* in its entry for A.D. 449, though the account is based on Bede's story, also mentions the British (sub-Roman) ruler Vortigern who engaged Hengist and Horsa and their war-band as mercenary troops; the ninth-century Nennius in his *Historia Brittonum* has given a more circumstantial story of the event. Nennius is a dubious authority, but he seems to have thrown together into one book a mass of evidence drawn from various sources and has not altered the various narratives in order to make a consistent story. Though the reliability of his different sources is uncertain, this crude editorship has left us some information of value which, when it can be tested, may be used with caution. Vortigern, it seems, was a sub-Roman 'king', one of those who for a time filled the gap left by the departure of the senior administrative officials and under whose governance the Roman way of life continued in a somewhat enfeebled and dwindling form during much of the fifth century.

Harassed in particular by Pictish raids from the North, Vortigern engaged this band of mercenaries and, as Bede states, 'assigned them to reside in the eastern part of the island. . . . They engaged with the enemy,

who were come from the north to give battle, and obtained the victory.'
After this victory they sent across the North Sea for more men; it is
apparently at this time that they appeared in Thanet, soon to revolt and
begin the war with Vortigern which led to the conquest of Kent. But it is
unlikely that their first home 'in the eastern part of the island' was in Kent,
as this was by no means the best position from which they could screen the
country from Pictish raiders. East Anglia or possibly Lincolnshire would
seem to be much more likely places for their initial settlement. And though
this story was no more than a tradition, for even Bede did not finish his
history until about 280 years after the reputed date of Hengist's landing,
there are internal features in the story which tend to confirm its substantial
truth. But that his was the first warrior-band or the only warrior-band to
be employed by this date can no longer be maintained with confidence.

Nevertheless the first coming of Hengist and Horsa, which can be
dated as about A.D. 445, seems to mark the beginning of substantial independent immigrant settlement. It was now that the family parties whose
fortunes we have followed in Chapter VII began to appear. The brothers
Hengist and Horsa are generally called Jutes and no doubt the core of their
war-band was Jutish also. But the glimpse of the 'Finnesburh' story we
are given in *Beowulf* and the slight further evidence in the so-called *Finnesburh Fragment* seem to show that Hengist was employed by a Frisian king as
commander of his troops somewhere on the Frisian shore. In a war with his
own people, called 'Danes' in the story, he seems at one point to have
broken faith with his Frisian lord and was doubtless driven from Frisia.
With him when he came to Britain there would also be many Frisians
and Franks, adventurers from the Lower Rhine who followed a famous
leader. This seems to explain why the Kentish people, named after their
leading group, were later known as Jutes and why in fact so many Frankish
features are found in that county.

But in East Anglia proper, the first settlers were certainly men of true
Anglian stock from Schleswig. In these pages it is impossible to describe
the range of objects found in the settlers' graves from which these attributions are largely made. In the earlier stages when cremation was the
normal Anglo-Saxon practice, the pottery cremation urns which hold the
calcined bones are themselves the best evidence, for so many of the trinkets,
if indeed they are present, have themselves 'passed the fire' and so do not
often survive in a form suited to close study. But from a comparatively early
period of the settlement there began that 'flight from cremation', as Thurlow
Leeds termed it. Some of the Saxons indeed seem to have inhumed their
dead from the earliest period of their settlement, though in their North

German homeland cremation had been their usual custom. But when once inhumation begins to be common, the buried grave-goods and particularly the brooches and other trinkets of the womenfolk, are found to be the material most suited to classification and study; from time to time among them are found brooches which were certainly brought from the continent, where they can be dated with fair accuracy. Of this a single instance may be given.

From the Saxon homeland between Weser and Elbe came the few 'equal-armed brooches' which have been found in England. They have been dated by Professor F. Roeder and range from about A.D. 450 to 500. Two have appeared on the very borders of our area, beyond which Saxon features predominate. Of these one comes from the great cemetery at Little Wilbraham in south-east Cambridgeshire and the other from Haslingfield, a few miles outside Cambridge town. Both of these are dated as about 500; they were in good condition when buried and so had probably not been worn for a long time before burial. Mr. Lethbridge has drawn attention to the dangers of dating a grave by what may be buried 'heirlooms' of an earlier day and has shown that this may happen. At Holywell Row in north-west Suffolk, he uncovered the grave of a ten-year-old girl; her brooches and girdle-hangers were old and patched and her string of beads was much too large for her. They were, he suggests, old cast-off trinkets perhaps once belonging to her grandmother. We have also seen something of the kind in the Sutton Hoo ship-burial. But in general the groupings of the various objects found in these graves show that most people were buried with the objects they had themselves used in their lifetime and so they may be safely used for dating purposes.

There is also to be considered the question of what proportion of the sub-Roman population survived to amalgamate with the newcomers. There is scope here for differences of opinion and it has even been suggested that the sub-Roman wife of an Anglo-Saxon might be buried wearing characteristic Germanic beads and brooches. Trinkets, we are told, are no evidence of racial identity. This is quite true for single examples. But if large numbers of such intermarriages had taken place at this early time, there would have been far more survival of late Roman objects than in fact took place. Even the presence of decorative motifs derived from Roman art found on Anglo-Saxon trinkets does not prove intermarriage. This recurrence of Roman patterns is well-evidenced but is by no means confined to Britain. For example, the equal-armed brooches already mentioned, which have been found in large numbers in north Hanover, all show ornamentation of classical inspiration hardly removed from its Roman prototypes. The presence of ornament derived from Roman models therefore is no evidence that it was evolved in Britain, even if the object which carries it was made there.

During the early pagan period frequent intermarriage between the two peoples seems rather unlikely. In the earlier days when soldiers, unaccompanied by their womenfolk, were stationed in Britain, such matings were common enough. But when once true family migration began and Anglo-Saxon village communities were established, intermarriage would be much rarer. The presence of Romano-British objects and pottery-fragments in pagan Saxon graves, where they are often found, is hardly good evidence for village continuity. The twentieth-century graves in the parish cemetery at Caister-on-Sea commonly have Romano-British potsherds in their filling, sometimes together with such objects as bone pins; this arises from its position, which is close to the old Roman town-site. Such remains, if no more definite evidence is forthcoming, mean no more than an identity of site. When Christianity was introduced towards the middle of the seventh century, the cultural differences of two centuries earlier would probably have largely disappeared and blending of the two stocks was doubtless in process; before the consolidation of the kingdom in the mid-sixth century, when settlements were probably independent units, its incidence would be much less frequent.

These considerations are strengthened by evidence from another source. In a recent summary of some place-name evidence from Norfolk and Suffolk, Dr. O. K. Schram[1] has stressed the homogeneity of the early English nomenclature in the two counties. The earliest names are generally considered to be those in -*ing*, derived from an earlier -*ingas* denoting tribal occupation, and in -*ingham*, from an earlier -*ingaham*, often the headquarters of that tribe. The distribution of these names is shown in the accompanying map (Fig. 30). The personal names enshrined in these 'give the impression of extreme antiquity'. Many are to be found only in East Anglia and others have parallels only on the continent. He then stresses the very considerable number of names in -*ham* which indicate 'the main strength of the early Anglian settlements'. It is also to be noted that the same personal names and, in fact, exactly the same village names occur frequently both in Norfolk and Suffolk and on the Cambridge border, a similarity which, Dr. Schram says, 'may be regarded as constituting a clear proof that the two counties making up the Kingdom of East Anglia formed a distinct linguistic as well as an ethnic unit from the earliest centuries of the Anglo-Saxon period'.

[1] Dr. Schram is at present engaged in preparing the 'Norfolk' volume for the Place-name Society. This summary was prepared for a visit of the British Association to Norwich in 1961.

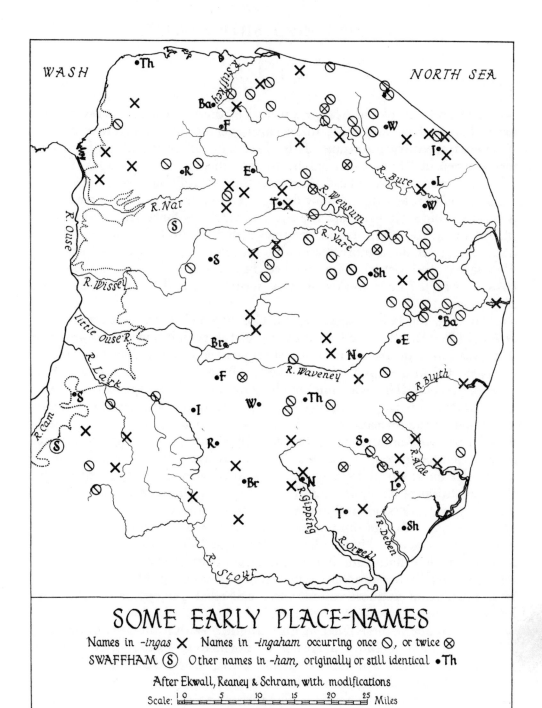

WASH

NORTH SEA

SOME EARLY PLACE-NAMES

Names in *-ingas* ✕ Names in *-ingaham* occurring once ⊘, or twice ⊗

SWAFFHAM Ⓢ Other names in *-ham*, originally or still identical •Th

After Ekwall, Reaney & Schram, with modifications

Scale: 1 0   5   10   15   20   25 Miles

Fig. 30

APPENDIX

The problem of the relative survival of the sub-Roman peasantry has never been solved and to it there can never be an authoritative answer. Nineteenth-century historians of the Freeman school visualised an almost clean sweep of Romano-Britons by the conquering Anglo-Saxons, at least in the eastern half of England. The most they would allow were a few slave-women and perhaps an odd male drudge. To this assumption there was later a considerable resistance and the survival-rate was for a time undoubtedly placed much too high, as has been suggested in the Introduction. Here, I have tried to make a more reasonable estimate. The figures are obviously speculative and are therefore placed in an appendix, but at least the basis on which I have worked may be scrutinised and my results amended if necessary.

In 1929 the late Professor R. G. Collingwood in his *Town and Country in Roman Britain* attempted an estimate of the population of the province. This was based on the information summarised in the *Ordnance Survey Map of Roman Britain* (Second edition, 1928). His original result was, in round figures, 500,000. This was quickly challenged by H. J. Randall and, after controversy, the total suggested by Sir Mortimer Wheeler was nearer 1,500,000. Some revision of the first figure was clearly necessary and in his major work on Roman Britain, first published in 1936, Collingwood placed it as a round figure of 1,000,000. This is probably not very far from the truth and on it my following estimates are based. Now this represented the population at its highest figure; it included military garrisons, imperial officials and traders, as well as town workers, miners and those engaged in agriculture and all the country trades. Between A.D. 350 and 450 there must have been a sharp fall, particularly in the latter part of this period. Soldiers and officials had left, trade had dwindled and the country was reverting to a simpler subsistence economy which meant smaller numbers. By 450, the total population at most cannot have exceeded 750,000 and may have been much less.

How many of these lived in East Anglia? Within the area of our map (Fig. 31) which includes a corner of north-west Essex, strictly outside East Anglia, there are three walled towns, Caistor-by-Norwich (*Venta Icenorum*), Caister-on-Sea and Chesterford, Cambridge lying just outside the western margin. To make a comparison with the rest of the Roman province I have used the schedules included in the explanatory text to the *Ordnance Survey Map of Roman Britain* (Third Edition, 1956). Though there has been some addition to our knowledge since their publication, they provide an adequate basis for these calculations.

The first group of walled towns includes London, the four *coloniae* and the cantonal capitals. The size of the *colonia* at York (as distinct from the legionary fortress) is not known, but its area has been included here as 50 acres, almost certainly an under-estimate. The approximate total area inside the walls of these major towns is some 2,080 acres. That of Caistor-by-Norwich, the only East Anglian town in this first group, is 35 acres. East Anglia's major town population therefore is one-sixtieth of the total. In these towns at the peak of their prosperity the average density was perhaps some 50 persons to the acre. By A.D. 450 this must have fallen greatly and many may have been almost empty. But to be generous I have placed it at 25 to the acre, which gives a total for all of 52,000 and therefore for *Venta Icenorum* of 875. And deducting 52,000 from 750,000, we have a total of 698,000 for the small towns and the countryside.

The schedules list many types of sites including minor walled towns, major and minor settlements without stone walls, country buildings including villas and those of uncertain status, and potteries. Excluding all military establishments, mines and temples, we have a total of 919 sites, of which 71 are in our area, a fraction of almost 1 in 13. Dividing 698,000 by 13, we get 53,692 as East Anglia's proportion. On this basis therefore, East Anglia in the first half of the fifth century had a population of 54,567, which may in round figures be called 55,000. Of these an appreciable proportion would be wholly or partly of Germanic blood, descended from soldiers enlisted in the Rhineland, *fœderati* and civilian settlers in the ports. During the next century, the time of the major immigration, many of these sub-Romans would disappear, either by violent death or by their moving away from an area where their normal mode of life had become impossible. This loss cannot be at all closely estimated but should mean that by A.D. 550, the mixed population would perhaps include the 'equivalent' of between 25,000 and 50,000 sub-Romans, very many of whom would be sub-German by descent.

Our unit of calculation for Anglo-Saxon parties was a ship with a company of 80 persons. Ten ships a year would mean 800 immigrants; if this were repeated annually for a century, roughly the length of the major immigration period, we get a total of 80,000. It is almost certain, of course, that a large proportion of the immigrants had arrived by the end of the fifth century, so that the rate after that would have dwindled rapidly. If so, the number of Anglo-Saxons would tend to be higher proportionately, as their rate of increase would, after they were established, tend to rise rather more rapidly than that of the dispossessed and socially depressed sub-Romans. Even if this Anglo-Saxon number is too high, it is clear that, by the time of the Danish settlement in the ninth century, the population of East Anglia, by then well blended, could not possibly have been more than one half of sub-Roman blood and much more probably had less than one quarter. Before the conversion to Christianity, intermarriage between pagan settler and Christian sub-Roman would be much less common than after, so that in the pagan graves the proportion of persons of sub-Roman stock may well be far less than 10 per cent.

IX

THE SETTLEMENT OF THE SANDLINGS

B Y THE early years of the sixth century there had been a considerable Anglian settlement in the new East Anglian home. Archaeological surveys of the province, published in the past by Sir Cyril Fox, Mr. R. Rainbird Clarke and the writer, have all shown that, since about 2000 B.C., the prehistoric and Roman agricultural communities had tended to be concentrated on the lighter drier soils overlying the chalk in the western half of the province. To quote the writer's own words: 'All these distribution maps point to one conclusion. From the beginning of the Bronze Age, at least until the early days of the Anglo-Saxon settlement, the primary concentration of population in Norfolk and northern Suffolk lay in the west, along the line of the Icknield Way and westward to the fen-edge. A secondary concentration around the site of Norwich is to be noted throughout the period. Elsewhere a "scatter" of finds shows a relatively sparse occupation . . . These conclusions follow broadly those of Fox (1933, 1943) and Clarke (1938, 1940*a*). . . . ' Since then Mr. Clarke's *East Anglia* has appeared and his maps again stress this basic conclusion.

With the causes of this grouping of population we are not here concerned, but its incidence explains why, in the early stages of the English settlement, a somewhat similar pattern should be found. The primary need of the settlers was for cultivable land and in these long-occupied areas lay cleared land readily available. Later, as the communities grew, new land to meet the needs of the additional population was cleared towards the east. The earliest settlements show a simple grouping (see Fig. 31). First there are several in the Norwich region on the rivers Yare, Wensum and Tas, originally placed there as has been said to guard the cantonal capital. A few more, north of the Roman east-west road which runs across north Norfolk, would seem to be a barrier against inland raids from the lonely northern coast. On the west the settlement-sites were approached from the East Fenland rivers and are clustered near to the Icknield Way and its companion Roman road, now known as 'Peddar's Way', from the Nar valley in the north to Little Wilbraham in Cambridgeshire.

But by this early settlement the Sandlings of East Suffolk were almost

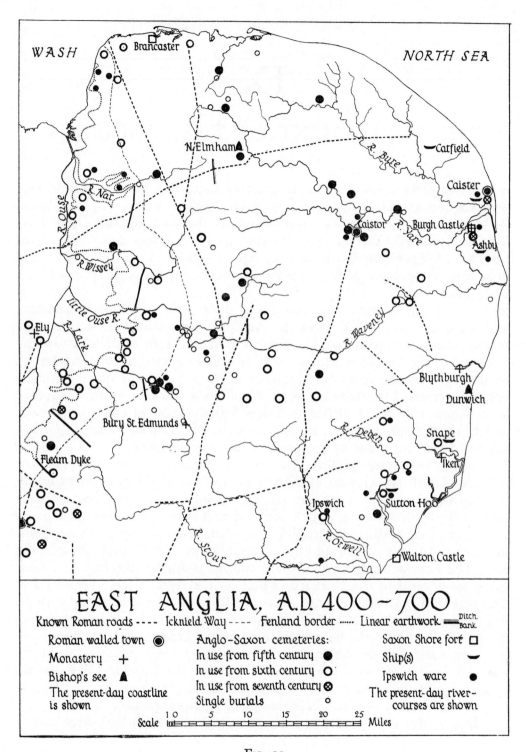

WASH

NORTH SEA

Brancaster

N. Elmham

R. Nar

Catfield

R. Bure

Ouse

Caister

R. Wissey

Caistor

R. Yare

Burgh Castle

Ashby

Little Ouse R.

Ely

R. Lark

R. Waveney

Blythburgh

Bury St. Edmunds

Dunwich

Snape

R. Deben

Iken

Fleam Dyke

Ipswich

Sutton Hoo

R. Stour

R. Orwell

Walton Castle

EAST ANGLIA, A.D. 400~700

Known Roman roads ----	Icknield Way ----	Fenland border ······	Linear earthwork ▬ Ditch Bank

Roman walled town ◉

Anglo-Saxon cemeteries:

Saxon Shore fort ▫

Monastery ✛

In use from fifth century ●

Ship(s) ◗

Bishop's see ▲

In use from sixth century ○

Ipswich ware ●

The present-day coastline is shown

In use from seventh century ⊗

The present-day river-courses are shown

Single burials ○

Scale |⊢⊢⊢⊢⊢⊢⊢⊢⊢⊢⊢⊢⊢⊢⊢⊢⊢⊢⊢⊢⊢⊢| Miles
1 0   5   10   15   20   25

Fig. 31

unaffected. Outside the true Sandlings there is a cemetery at Eye approached from the Waveney by the Roman road and another at Waldringfield close to the Deben estuary; these are the only certain fifth-century cemeteries in this wide area. Other cremation cemeteries at Ipswich and Snape may perhaps have begun late in this century, but so early a date cannot be given to them with certainty. Between this coastal strip and the valleys of the West Suffolk rivers where there was certainly a considerable concentration of population, lay the dense forest which covered the heavy boulder-clay country of Mid-Suffolk. That this was a real barrier to easy communication, and which tended to segregate east from west, is shown by the absence of main roads. The separation culminated in the nineteenth century when local administration by county councils began; Suffolk, because of this poor communication, was divided into two parts and each part was given its own County Council, which survive to the present day.

The cemeteries shown as beginning in the sixth century may sometimes contain slightly earlier elements, but these cannot be dated with certainty. In west Norfolk, Suffolk to the west of the Icknield Way and that strip of Cambridge lying between the Icknield Way and the fen, their distribution points to the arrival of later settlers by the East Fenland rivers and perhaps some colonisation from the first settlements. Only in north central Suffolk do we see a group which seems to indicate expansion into the forest area from the Lark valley. Apart from the Waldringfield community, there is no evidence of desire to be near the coast. The settlers it seems were all farmers by choice and, when once they had chosen their land, their seafaring came to an end.

At about the beginning of the sixth century or a little later, there began a new invasion which was to give a new orientation to East Anglian life. In the early years of the present century, a large cemetery on the west side of Ipswich was excavated and the finds published in 1907 by Miss Nina Layard. The main part of the cemetery held inhumation burials only, but a small area on the south had also a number of cremations. Further to the west were remains of more urns, but it has not been possible to prove that this was a continuous burial area. The contents of these inhumation graves, most of which were of the sixth century, differed significantly from those of most East Anglian graves of the same period. The characteristic Anglian cruciform brooches and wrist-clasps were wanting; the poorer quality 'small-long' brooches were equally absent. On the other hand, there were two early-type Kentish cast disc-brooches with wedge-shaped garnet insets. Other finds include no less than five glass vessels, three squat jars of different sub-types and two palm cups. Most important of all were a number of the so-called large square-headed brooches of a type which certainly originated in Denmark towards the end of the fifth century, at the time when the characteristic northern animal-ornament was in its earliest stages of development. This brooch-type, named by Thurlow Leeds the 'Kenninghall brooch' after a fine example found a century ago at Kenninghall in Norfolk, is also known from several East Anglian cemeteries of the sixth century; they come from the Norwich area, north-west Norfolk and the Lark valley, so that they are well distributed over the whole area though not in large numbers.

Now these newcomers were not Jutes from Jutland. As in the preceding century, the emigration of Angles and Jutes from North Schleswig and Jutland progressively emptied so much of the peninsula of its inhabitants, fresh invasions from the east brought in new tribes to take their place. They came originally from Halland and Scania, the western provinces of South Sweden; they had already occupied the islands in the entrance to the Baltic and were now colonising the Jutish peninsula. They came first into the most northerly part, between the Skaggerrak and Liim Fjord and spread slowly southward, but when Bede wrote they had not yet occupied South Schleswig, which explains his mention of *Angulus desertus*. These newcomers were the ancestors of the people later known to us as the Danes and the changes brought about by their advent are reflected in the archaeology of Jutland, for the old custom of cremation gave place to inhumation and new styles of ornament became dominant.

With them to Jutland came too the earlier types of those gold pendants known as bracteates. Of these there were various types; some originated in Sweden and some in Denmark, but even the Swedish types reached their fullest development further west. At a slightly later date than the first appearance at Ipswich, another variant of the square-headed brooch appeared in Kent. The origins of this type seem also to lie in Denmark. And in Kent there have also been found several of these northern bracteates. Thurlow Leeds surveyed the English specimens in 1946 and was able to enumerate twenty, of which seventeen were from Kent. That these, with one possible exception, came from Denmark is certain and so they provide further evidence of Anglo-Danish intercommunication in the early sixth century.

It must again be stressed that at this time there were no sailing ships and that all these voyages were made in rowing galleys of a developed Nydam type. These sixth-century 'Danes' who first ventured as far as England and who certainly were not North Sea seafarers in the earlier centuries, must have coasted the mainland shore as far south as Belgium. They crossed the Narrow Seas to the Kentish shore and then rowed northward across the wide Thames estuary and, in the sparsely-populated heathlands of south-east Suffolk, in many ways so like their Jutish homeland, they made their new home. The occasional occurrence of a bracteate near the coast of Hanover or Frisia need not then surprise us, though Thurlow Leeds, who habitually thought in terms of direct voyages by open-sea passage from Jutland to England, was not quite sure that the bracteates had not first come to Frisia and then been brought further from there. And though settled in England, these people did not at once lose contact with their old northern home, for archaeological evidence makes continued intercourse a certainty.

Though the Danish origin of both bracteates and square-headed brooches had earlier been realised, the settlement in the Sandlings by a party of 'Danish' migrants was first propounded by Mr. Rainbird Clarke in 1960. To call them Danes at this date, in view of the later settlements on the East Coast by Danish Vikings in the ninth and tenth centuries, would, he thought, be confusing and so he proposed that they be known as the 'Ipswich People' from their cemetery at that place. As, however, the name 'Ipswich' was already in use for both a brooch-type and a later pottery industry, as will be seen in Chapter X, both Mr. Clarke and others have realised that this name was somewhat ill-chosen; they will here be referred to as the 'Sandlings Folk'.

Now in earlier chapters we have seen that the Sandlings was the district where the East Anglian royal house was seated and in which a new style of cloisonné jewellery flourished. The Sutton brooch, the Faversham brooch of East Anglian type, the Kentish glass and other evidences, all point to connexions between north Kent and east Suffolk throughout the sixth century and after. At the beginning of the seventh, as has been told above in Bede's own words, Raedwald, the reigning king of East Anglia, was baptised during a visit to Kent and, later in the century, Anna's daughter married the Kentish king. Clearly enough these facts are evidence of a continuing contact between the two kingdoms, a contact made easy by the use of coastwise shipping. For Kent was the first, or last, port of call on the voyage to and from the Baltic.

We have also seen that the Sutton Hoo grave-goods show evidence of Scandinavian connexion; but this was with a different province, that of Uppland on the Baltic shore of Sweden, far from Danish Jutland. But before trying to establish a connexion between them, we must first consider again the royal house of East Anglia. Counting back from Raedwald, who probably became king about A.D. 593, we see that his grandfather Wuffa, from whom the dynasty was named, must have been king about 550. If he was preceded by his father Wehha, as one account tells us, Wehha must have been established in England between 520 and 530. Is it then possible to see in Wehha or Wuffa one or other of the leaders of the Sandlings Folk? An answer to this question, posed rather differently, has already been given by Professor Lindqvist and for the basic evidence we must turn again to the poem *Beowulf*.

Its hero, the man Beowulf, was a prince of the Geats, as they were known in Anglo-Saxon speech, or Gautar in the Scandinavian form. The Geats lived in that part of south-west Sweden lying between the west coast and Lake Wener and in the valley of the Gotha river. In his youth Beowulf visited the Danish king at his great hall of Heorot, believed to have stood at Leire in the Danish isle of Sjaelland, where he slew the monster Grendel. Later he accompanied his uncle, Hygelac, king of the Geats, in a raid on the Frisian shore, probably at a place not far from the mouth of the Rhine. Hygelac was slain and in due course Beowulf himself became king, to be killed in old age after slaying a dragon which preyed on his people. Of Beowulf himself we have no true historical evidence, but Hygelac was a real man whose attack on the Frisians was recorded by Gregory of Tours, historian of the Franks. His original raid it seems was successful, but Theodoric, king of the Franks, who was the Frisian king's overlord, sent an army to the rescue and Hygelac was defeated and slain by these Franks. Professor Chambers, in his analysis of the evidence, gives the date of this raid as 'after A.D. 516 and probably after 520, although perhaps before 522 and certainly before 531'.

Now Beowulf's companion at his death was a young kinsman, named in the poem as 'Wiglaf, son of Weohstan, a valued shield-warrior, prince of the Scylfings, kinsman of Aelf here'. With the date of Hygelac historically fixed, Wiglaf would therefore be a man in the prime of life towards the middle of the century; his family the Scylfings were the royal house of Sweden seated at Uppsala in Uppland. Though related both to Swedish and Geatish royalty, this young princeling seems to have thrown in his lot with the latter. In the poem we are also told of the fall of Hygelac's son in battle with the Swedes and it was after his death that Beowulf came to the throne. To turn to historical fact, it was at about this time that the Geats were finally conquered by the Swedes and incorporated in the Swedish kingdom. Wiglaf could then have been exiled for his share in such a conflict, to seek his fortune elsewhere. And to be brief, Sune Lindqvist has suggested the identity of Wiglaf the Scylfing with Wuffa of East

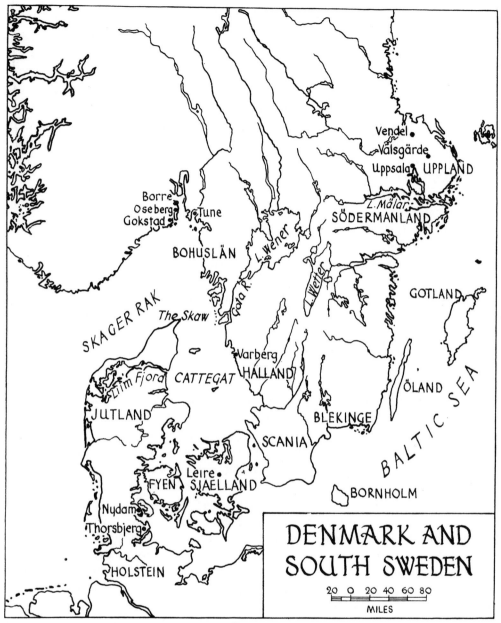

Vendel
Välsgärde
Uppsala UPPLAND

L. Mälar
SÖDERMANLAND

Borre
Oseberg
Tune
Gokstad

BOHUSLÄN

L. Wener

Göta R.

L. Wetter

GOTLAND

SKAGER RAK

The Skaw

Varberg
HALLAND

ÖLAND

CATTEGAT

Lim Fjord

BALTIC SEA

JUTLAND

BLEKINGE

SCANIA

Leire
FYEN SJAELLAND

BORNHOLM

Nydam
Thorsbjerg

HOLSTEIN

DENMARK AND
SOUTH SWEDEN

20 0 20 40 60 80
MILES

FIG. 32

Anglia, Wiglaf's father, Weohstan, being none other than Wehha, father of Wuffa.

As we have seen in the survey, the evidence given by the grave-goods of the Sutton Hoo ship-burial points strongly to a connexion with the Uppland province. First we have the burials in boats, itself sufficiently unusual as it was practised nowhere else in the North at that time. But ship-burial, as we have also seen, was a custom developed after the Wiglaf-Wuffa period, as it seems not to have begun until about A.D. 600. This alone points to continued contacts between the Sandlings and Scandinavia at least until the end of the sixth century. During that century, though inhumation had become the Danish burial-practice and was to appear in Suffolk at the Ipswich cemetery, the Swedes of Uppland still cremated their dead.

At Old Uppsala, the Scylfing royal seat, there are three burial mounds known as 'the King Barrows'. These have been excavated in the past and though the records are not those of the best modern standards, enough is known for attributions to have been made. They have been assigned to three early kings named Aun, Egil and Aðils. The first was dead by A.D. 500, Egil about 510 and Aðils between 570 and 580. Aðils' father, Ottarr Vendelcrow, was buried below another mound at Vendel about 525-30. All these burials were of cremated remains. Now three of these kings are mentioned in *Beowulf*, Egil appearing in Anglian form as Ongen-theow, Ottarr as Ohtere and Aðils as Eadgils, which confirms the dating already suggested by Hygelac's raid and death. And in similar fashion the two Sutton Hoo barrows which did not cover boat-graves also held cre-mated remains, though the barrow-construction was simpler than that of the Swedish ones, doubtless due to the absence of good building-stone.

Mr. Bruce-Mitford has compared the finds from these Swedish barrows, all sadly damaged by fire and very fragmentary, with those from Sutton Hoo. He has pointed out that from one came a fragment of stamped bronze sheeting showing a warrior which is so similar in detail to one on the Sutton Hoo helmet that it may well have been struck from the same stamp. So many indeed are the similarities between the Sutton Hoo helmet and those of the Uppland graves, both in decorative styles and structural method that its fabrication by an Uppland helmet-smith seems to be established.

The Sutton Hoo shield also, as we have seen, appears to be a Swedish piece which incidentally provides important dating evidence. The many repairs carried out in gilded gesso are deemed to have been made at the time of the burial. The shield, it is thought, was an ancient one brought from Sweden in the past and which had hung for many years on a wall in the royal hall. It was in fact one of those heirlooms which are frequently mentioned in early Northern story. Neither helmet nor shield, in spite of the general similarities, has been precisely paralleled by any found in the Uppland boat-graves. But the earliest of these are perhaps half a century or more later in date than the arrival in England of the Sutton Hoo specimens. The Uppland equipment is also that, not of royalty, but of wealthy free-holders, so that some difference in quality may be expected. And as in the sixth century the grave-goods of Swedish royalty seem to have been burned with the body and so were largely destroyed, exact comparison has not been possible. The case for their Swedish origin is further strengthened by the absence of any other from Anglo-Saxon graves with which they may be compared. The Benty Grange helmet, the only certain Anglo-Saxon helmet known, is quite different from that of Sutton Hoo, as we have seen. And though very many shield-bosses and fittings are known in England, both from the graves of simple ceorls and wealthy chiefs, like the man of the Taplow barrow, none is at all similar to that at Sutton Hoo.

The third item in the equipment which shows strong Swedish affinity is the sword. Now an X-ray examination of the blade in the British Museum has shown that this is 'damascened', or 'pattern-welded', to use Mr. Maryon's preferable term. These pattern-welded blades were made in the Rhineland, where the sword-smiths had not lost all the skills of the past. The British Museum tests have also shown that the swords from both the Taplow and the Broomfield burials are similarly decorated and so have a similar Rhenish origin. Though most blades of this period are so rusted that this ornamentation is not visible, yet an X-ray examination reveals the presence of the patterned metal and further work on Anglo-Saxon swords is making clear that pattern-welded blades were not uncommon in England in the pagan period. It is therefore quite possible that a Swedish pommel was fitted to a Rhenish blade in England. At the same time Mr. Bruce-Mitford points out that the mounts on the grip of the sword, though very possibly Swedish or at least paralleled in Sweden, bear filigree-decoration which is certainly of English workmanship. English, too, are the two garnet-decorated domed bosses on the scabbard. The pommel itself may well have been made in Sweden; if so, it doubtless arrived in England as part of a Swedish sword and was later removed and fitted to a finer blade, of which the scabbard was embellished with English jewellery. If the pommel is not of Swedish origin, it was doubtless made in England by a Swedish craftsman.

Other links between the Sandlings and Sweden have been mentioned. There is the sword-pommel with East Anglian mushroom-celled garnet

135

cloisonné-work, found in Södermanland, the province south of Uppland on the far bank of Lake Mälar. There is another with quatrefoil decoration and with other details of the garnet-treatment which led Mr. Bruce-Mitford to say was certainly made by the 'Sutton Hoo jeweller'. This pommel comes from the modern Bohuslän province, the ancient home of the Geats. Yet another is from Blekinge, the province in the extreme south-east corner of Sweden. The 'ring' from the pommel of a ring-sword, most closely paralleled in Sweden, is probably another example of Swedish workmanship. More important even than these are the 'Daniel in the Lion's Den' plaques on the purse, of which the basic design has been shown to agree closely with Scandinavian models. To summarise the evidence simply, this 'man and lions' motif is known to exist in two main forms, one Frankish and the other Scandinavian, and between them are significant differences of posture and other detail. That on the Sutton Hoo purse follows the northern pattern and gives us, translated by an Anglo-Saxon craftsman into the finest jewelled-work of his insular style, a theme seen in Sweden on stamped metal plates used for building up decorated helmets. Though the purse is certainly English, the theme is as surely Swedish and the design may well have been taken from another helmet of the Sutton Hoo type.

Yet another example of this use of a Swedish theme by an English craftsman is the great gold buckle. Its Swedish affinity has already been mentioned, but it is unquestionably an English-made piece by a craftsman who deliberately used the ornamental patterns known to us on objects from Vendel graves. Clearly he had access to and was familiar with Swedish models; from these he took his designs and so transmuted them with his English 'touch' that Swedish archaeologists are, we may suspect with reluctance, driven to disclaim as Swedish-made the beautiful piece which has been called 'without doubt the finest Germanic buckle known'.

And there is further confirmation of the Swedish link from other finds in Suffolk. At the Museum of Bury St. Edmunds are two bronze sword-fittings which were described by Reginald Smith in 1911, long before the Sutton Hoo discovery. He likened the twist- and interlace-decoration of these fittings to parallels in Sweden which were closer to them than any English work. Another small piece, also described by Smith, was a decorated buckle found in the cemetery at Mitchell's Hill, Icklingham, in the Lark valley. The peculiar decorated panels on the buckle-loop are quite unlike normal English work, but can be compared with Swedish prototypes.

To summarise this somewhat briefly-reviewed evidence, there is no doubt that intercourse between Sweden and Suffolk began in the first half of the sixth century and was to some extent maintained until the beginning of the next. In a mid-seventh-century Suffolk grave are found Swedish heirlooms of a century earlier, objects which when made were of the highest quality, suited to the dignity of a royal prince and not seen in the graves of those of lesser rank. Suffolk-made pommels of a later date, found in different parts of Sweden, point to return journeys to the old homeland, as does the appearance of seventh-century boat burial, which can hardly be an independent invention in this sub-Swedish *milieu*. From Kent and other parts of England comes evidence also of continued contact not only with north Denmark, but also with southern Norway. For proof of this we may turn to the conclusions of Haakon Shetelig and H. Falk. In their *Scandinavian Archaeology* (1937) they point out that in the fifth and sixth centuries there was a close connexion between the southern coasts of Norway and those of England and France, a connexion which ceased in the seventh. Shetelig had already inferred this many years before from his study of the development of cruciform brooches.

At the same time the close linkage between Sweden and England is not just one of casual trading contact, for the secondary pieces, such as the gold buckle, show the Swedish traditions transmuted into English forms. And yet in the ship-burial places of high honour were given to the ancient Swedish pieces, which were carefully refurbished for the ceremony. This close interlocking of Swedish and English traditions for at least a century makes impossible the suggestion that it could have been a memorial to a visiting Swede. As we have already seen, the cenotaph must have been in honour of an East Anglian king, Aethelhere being the most probable choice. But the Swedish past is none the less real and the status of this Swedish ancestor was royal. If then Wuffa—and perhaps his father, Wehha—be seen as an adventurous Swedish prince who had gathered around himself a largely Danish war-band, we have just what is needed to explain both the Swedish links shown by the royal burial and the Danish influences visible in the grave-goods of the Sandlings commonalty, which also show evidences of Anglicisation. The continued contacts with the Baltic shores also confirm the retention of seafaring habits by these settlers, habits which we have seen were discarded by the earlier Anglian settlers when once they had found their new homes. All these conclusions may be reached from a study of the archaeological evidences of the Suffolk graves. And when we turn to *Beowulf*, though this is but a 'heroic' story blending fact and fiction, there is in its background of history and its choice of heroic figures just that evidence needed to explain the reason for this early Scandinavian migration and to place in his former royal setting its leading actor who became the eponym of his English descendants.

For further support we may briefly examine the internal evidence in *Beowulf* itself. Professor Whitelock in *The Audience of Beowulf* (1951) has made quite clear that the poem is not merely a pagan theme with Christian additions made at a later date, but one composed by a Christian for a Christian audience, telling a tale of the pagan past. Its hero is a Geat; it lauds his host, the Danish king and his house and, at the end, praises his young cousin and follower, Wiglaf the Scylfing. The method of its telling implies some understanding of the past history of these peoples by the audience. One reference only is made to early Anglo-Saxon history, when Offa, the fourth-century king of the Continental Angles, is praised as a warrior and a statesman.

The critical literature of *Beowulf* is voluminous, and much of it has been devoted to a discussion of the date of composition of the poem; for many years it has generally been thought to belong to the age of Bede, which might just bring it within the middle third of the eighth century. If Professor Whitelock is right in her estimate, it might even be as late as the middle of the century. It was certainly composed in an Anglian dialect, and the isolated reference to the ancestral Offa has led to the suggestion that it was composed for the court of his descendants, the kings of Mercia. But the Mercian court would seem to have little connexion with Danes, Geats and Swedes. And as Dr. Whitelock points out, the references to early Danish history are so slight that the detail must have been familiar to the audience, whereas that of the Geats is rather more carefully explained as though the audience were less familiar with it. This is, of course, not the only possible explanation of this slight difference in treatment, for it might perhaps result from the amount of detail available to the poet in his sources. But the former explanation seems to be the more likely. In summing up, Dr. Whitelock surveys the possible places of origin. She mentions in passing that Aelfwald of East Anglia, to whom Felix had dedicated his *Life of St. Guthlac*, was a possible patron of the poet. Finally, influenced by the name of the first Offa, she suggests that the reign of Offa of Mercia (A.D. 757-96) is not impossibly late and it may have been at his court where the poet dwelt. So would the reference to the famous ancestor and namesake be explained.

But the archaeological evidence available to us, insofar as it may be used, does not favour this last suggestion. If we must seek an audience with a Danish background, we must look to the Sandlings Folk who, so far as we know, were the only ones in England who had it. Their familiarity with Geatish lore would be somewhat less and so this had to be treated in more detail. But the Geatish story was necessary, as it was the fame and kinship of Beowulf the Geat which had drawn Wiglaf the Scylfing to the Geatish court to be involved in its ruin at the hands of his Scylfing kinsmen. He would naturally then take refuge with Beowulf's old friends of the Danish court. There he gathered a following and went adventuring to found a new kingdom in their English home. East Anglia in Aelfwald's reign (713-40) was under the overlordship of the Mercian kings and so the reference to their great ancestor Offa finds its place. The poet as we also know had a somewhat erroneous picture in his mind of a pagan funeral; but it was one which might well have been derived from a description heard in his youth from one who had seen Aethelhere's cenotaph burial. If then *Beowulf* may be seen as an early eighth-century poem composed in East Anglia for the descendants of the Scylfing prince and his Sandling Danes, the theme of the tale and its treatment are more easily explicable than if it is given a Northumbrian or Mercian birthplace.

It is possible that Wiglaf the Scylfing may be no more than a fictional character in a heroic lay of the North. If so, we may believe, his story is but a rationalisation of that of Wuffa as seen by his descendants and their men at a time when, after a glorious past, they had fallen under the sway of a Mercian lord.

X

THE CONSOLIDATION OF THE KINGDOM

THOUGH IT was Wuffa who gave his name to the East Anglian dynasty, one chronicler, Nennius, tells us that Wuffa's father, Wehha, was the first king of East Anglia and we have seen that the first settlement by the Sandlings Folk must have occurred during Wehha's lifetime. There is insufficient evidence for us to be sure of the events of that period, but the dates suggest that Wehha may in fact have been the senior leader of this new party of immigrants and, because of that seniority, was quite probably the actual founder of the settlement. But to found a new settlement in an almost unpopulated coastal area was not to establish a new kingdom which included the whole East Anglian province. This great venture, it is likely enough, was not successfully completed until after Wehha's death and so Wuffa may well have been the first king of all East Anglia. If so, his name would naturally be the one which the landsfolk used when referring to their kingly house.

Our discussion of the settlement and its pattern revealed by the maps (Figs. 30 and 31) has shown that in the first part of the fifth century, the distribution of the earliest settler-villages displays a certain strategic unity planned, it would seem, by the sub-Roman provincial governors at Caistor-by-Norwich. At the beginning of the sixth century that semblance of control had long vanished and the great body of newcomers had established many new settlements which led to important changes in the distribution-pattern. There was a fairly continuous line of villages running southward from the Wash coast of north-west Norfolk to the north-west border of Essex and lying between the margin of the Fens and the Peddar's Way. The older group in the north formed a smaller and more scattered series in the upper valleys of the Bure and Wensum, in the terrain between the north coast of Norfolk and the east-west Roman road. A third group in the Norwich region and others on or near both banks of the Middle and Upper Waveney and its tributaries show how scanty were the settlements in the middle of the province other than those placed in the earlier phase.

Dr. Schram's place-name studies give evidence of a dominant ethnic group, the Schleswig Angles, though there are also distinct traces of

Saxons from the country between the estuaries of the river Weser and Elbe. In addition we may note the occurrence twice of the name Swaffham—as well as Swavesey, west of Cambridge and just outside our map-area—which is evidence of Swabians, or Swaefe, presumably from the west Schleswig coast. But it is difficult to believe that there can have been, during the later fifth century, any central authority after the break-down of the sub-Roman provincial government. When that had gone, the various settlements must have continued as independent villages. The land was tilled, the edges of the forest were cleared and the settlements spread, either by taking in new land or by founding small daughter settlements to meet their growing needs. And yet, long before the end of the sixth century, all East Anglia was under the sway of a king, probably seated at Rendlesham in the extreme south-east of the province. So well had this consolidation been effected that, by the beginning of the seventh century, the power of the reigning king Raedwald was so great that he was Bretwalda of Britain in succession to Ethelbert, whose Kentish kingdom had been closely knit for nearly a century and a half.

To consolidate and organise so large an area with such poor land-communications was a remarkable achievement. And the fact that, until the final disappearance of this royal line, rule seems to have been exercised from the Sandlings and not from Caistor-by-Norwich, where the Roman roads largely centred, shows that an entirely new factor had been introduced. That new factor was seapower; it was by the maintenance and use of their sea-going ships that the Wuffings were able to exercise their power and sustain their ascendancy. This lasted until the scattered settlements of the great Northumbrian province were in turn so firmly drawn together that the English leadership passed into the hands of the king seated at Yeavering and York.

It has sometimes been suggested that the East Anglian kingdom was no more than a re-emergence of the old Icenian province in a new guise. That the territorial bounds were roughly similar is true enough—though the southern part of Suffolk was probably never Icenian territory—but this is due to the geographical unity of the area, which is clearly demarcated on three sides by the Fenland and the sea. But the shift of power from the old cantonal capital to the very borders of the kingdom, in an area which in pre-Roman and Roman times was the least considered and least populated part of the whole territory, makes certain that this organisation was new. New men with new methods, who had no loyalty to and, probably enough, no knowledge of an outworn order long since fallen into decline and now vanished, built a new kingdom from a new centre. This kingdom survived, though later acknowledging some control by the Mercian neighbour, until a Viking Dane and his men late in the ninth century re-oriented the province on a new centre perhaps at Thetford. And this in turn survived for two centuries until the Norman began to exercise his sway from Norwich and laid the foundations of the modern order.

Of the method by which the province was united the chroniclers tell us nothing. But done it was and, in the absence of a direct record, it is legitimate to assess the geographical and archaeological evidence and endeavour to sketch a very tentative outline of the process. The archaeological evidence is perhaps scanty and some of its implications are uncertain, but a vague pattern is discernible and the conclusions to be drawn from it are not without interest.

To discuss the geographical factors graphically, it is necessary to see them through the eyes of an adventurous Swedish prince who had little or no knowledge of English topography other than that gathered during a voyage from the Baltic by the coastwise route. To the west of the new settlement, some twelve miles inland, there was a road running north through the forest from Colchester to Caistor-by-Norwich and, at about the same distance away to the north, a minor road led from this main road to a small settlement of which we today know nothing. Between these roads and the sea there were a few scattered Anglian villages where men farmed the land and possibly did a little estuarine fishing. The royal party had come to the Sandlings by sea from the south and the further exploration of the territory would be carried on towards the north. To follow the fortunes of that explorative party, a measure of speculation may profitably be permitted.

While the father Wehha consolidated his holding in the Sandlings, his son Wuffa with some ships explored northward along the coast. He would enter the estuary of the Alde and find a village at Snape, beyond which his ships could hardly go. The estuary of the Blyth was next inspected, but here there were no settlements nor had been, it would seem, for 1,000 years or more. Then he would come to the great Yare estuary, still largely open to the sea, though with a central island where Yarmouth was later to stand. The valley of the Waveney was open to him, perhaps as far as Bungay, but he would find few human occupants. Returning to the Yare, he could penetrate as far inland as the confluence of the Wensum with that river, where Norwich now stands. In this area he would find a scatter of settlements long established and secure. From the men of these villages he would doubtless be able to gain intelligence of the northern settlements. The latter were less easily approached by water; though they lay in the upper valleys of Wensum and Bure, a passage so far up these streams in Nydam-type longships was not possible, as the upper reaches were too shallow.

After returning down-river to the sea where, on the northern shore of the estuary stood the ruins of Roman Caister, later to be settled by his own people, Wuffa would follow the Norfolk coast northward and westward. From Morston or Wells he may well have visited the valley of the river Stiffkey, though as this would hardly be deep enough to take his ships, a journey by land to the Walsingham settlement may have been made. Then, after making his way back to the sea and cruising westward to Hunstanton, he would pass the Brancaster ruins and perhaps a ruined port at Holme-next-the-Sea. Working southward along the Wash shore he would enter in turn the rivers of the Fenland basin and creep along the upland edge; here in every valley-mouth he would find new settlements. Finally, in the Cambridge area, his progress by water would cease, for the rivers ran too small. Here it was at a later date that his successors seem to have constructed the Fleam Dyke, the final south-western boundary of the new kingdom, which ran from fen to forest near the headwaters of the river Stour. There he may have learned, though it is hardly likely at this early date, that this same river Stour was the boundary-river which ran south-eastward through the forest to enter the sea hard by his new Sandlings settlement. Retracing his route to the estuary of Deben or Stour, having cruised by sea and river some 400 miles, an exploratory trip of many weeks' duration, Wuffa would have visited three sides of the new kingdom, the Stour valley being the only boundary still unknown.

On such a first journey, there could scarcely have been any exercise of force and indeed force may never have been really necessary. Annual visits by a well-armed band with leaders bearing the trappings of royalty, which were backed by some small traffic in the manufactured articles so desired by these outland folk, may well have been enough to establish an association and dependence which bore fruit when later pressures and needs had to be met.

While this and succeeding, perhaps annual, voyages of the kind were being made, Wehha it would seem sent back from time to time an expedition to the homelands bordering the Cattegat. His primary need would be more followers and his leading men were doubtless able to recruit more Danes and Geats and perhaps a few Swedes to swell his English settlements. Passing along the coasts of Kent, the Rhine-mouth and Frisia, these visitors would keep in being those contacts lost by the earlier Anglian settlers when they gave up seafaring. And these continental voyages, continuing throughout the sixth century, would bring in many Rhenish and Kentish goods which before had not been seen in East Anglia.

The above few paragraphs, as has been suggested, are speculative in that they personalise an inferred sequence of events. But every item of the evidence we have points to their substantial truth. The distribution-map of the square-headed brooches of the type used to suggest the origin of the Sandlings Folk is almost a map of our inferred voyage. Beginning at the Ipswich cemetery where there were several, they have been found at Brooke and Catton near Norwich and at Hunstanton in the extreme north-west corner of Norfolk. In the west, one came from Bridgham and three from Kenninghall in the valley of the river Thet and more from both Lakenheath in the Little Ouse valley and Mildenhall on the river Lark. In none of these outlying settlements are they common; they occur as somewhat exotic units among grave-goods which are mainly of Anglian type.[1]

The distribution of Kentish and Frankish objects follows the same pattern. Glass vessels, which are either of Rhenish or Kentish origin, are found in small numbers and all are on the line of the voyage, with a larger concentration in the Ipswich area. Thus from Ipswich come three squat jars, two palm cups and what is probably a claw-beaker of this period. A squat jar occurred in Barrow No. 2 at Sutton Hoo and a claw-beaker was in the Snape boat-burial. From Bungay in the Waveney valley came a pouch bottle and from Caistor-by-Norwich what seems to be a fragment of another claw-beaker. In the western area the only glass vessel seems to be a small bowl from Lackford in the valley of the Lark. This is an early piece and if taken there by the Sandlings Folk it must have been at the beginning of their occupation.

The Coptic bowls imported from the continent are mainly found in the Sandlings area. Apart from that in the Sutton Hoo ship-burial, one came from Badley near Needham Market and another from Sudbury on the river Stour. In Norfolk one was found in the Caistor-by-Norwich cemetery. From the Ipswich cemetery came a fine Frankish brooch and from Melton, near Woodbridge, the plate of a jewelled buckle of Kentish type. There are the 'Swedish-type' mounts and buckle in the Lark valley, garnet-decorated brooches of the earlier Kentish type at Ipswich and Little Wilbraham in Cambridgeshire and two fine plaques from an inhumation burial in a barrow on Allington Hill, Bottisham, not far from Cambridge. These are

[1] These brooches are of course, not all exactly contemporary. Collectively they display the stages in the development of this brooch-form throughout the sixth century. A few later examples have been found in the Anglian territory west and north of the Fens.

of decorated bronze-gilt with bosses of shell and garnet and are doubtless of Kentish origin, made early in the seventh century. Cambridge, of course, was easily accessible from London by the old Roman road, and it is always possible that objects of Kentish origin reached the Cambridge area by that route. But so little from Kent is found there that there cannot at this time have been any regular trade-route by this road and before the middle of the seventh century the communication with the eastern border of the Fens was largely from the north by way of the river valleys. At Lakenheath, too, was found a wheel-made rouletted pottery vessel of Frankish type, to which several parallels are known from Kent; yet another was found in the Broomfield grave in Essex. And finally, the spread of boat-burial itself, a custom of the early seventh century, was along the coast where men of the Sandlings communities still had their sea-going boats.

To sum up our evidence, the communications maintained until the end of the sixth century with the countries round the entrance to the Baltic, which have long been recognised from a mass of archaeological evidence, are confirmed by the interchange between the Sandlings and the south Scandinavian region. The Sandlings Folk who, unlike the other East Anglian settlers, maintained their ships, as the graves show, played an important part in this continental traffic which in the next century fell almost entirely into the hands of the Frisians. Because of their use of the coastwise route they were able to act as a link between the Frisian and Rhenish shores and Kent, as well as Suffolk. By this wise use of shipping they were also, in spite of their peripheral position in East Anglia, to utilise the sea and the larger inland waterways to establish and maintain their dominion. Nowhere does the distribution-pattern give any suggestion that the East Anglian communications were by road. It was ships and the sea which gave the Wuffings their success in kingdom-building, a success which must largely be attributed to Wuffa himself.

In East Anglia, the sea-routes were still the main lines of communication in the seventh century. On the map (Fig. 31) will be seen the distribution of 'Ipswich ware', which has already been mentioned. When in 1947, the second edition of Sir Frank Stenton's *Anglo-Saxon England* appeared, he was able to say in reviewing his evidence that 'the history of English pottery is virtually a blank from the seventh century until the Norman Conquest'. Four years later, Middle Saxon pottery was being found in the settlement at Caister-on-Sea and Late Saxon pottery, now known as Thetford ware from the town of that name where its kilns have been recorded, as well as other types, began to be found there a few years earlier. This Middle Saxon Ipswich ware, so named because kilns for its manufacture have been found in that town, was soon realised to be in use during the seventh century, to last until replaced in the second half of the ninth century by the more satisfactory Thetford ware. As was mentioned in Chapter I (p. 28) a sherd of this ware was found in the filling of the boat-grave in Barrow No. 2 at Sutton Hoo and therefore must date from the early part of the seventh century, this being the earliest dated fragment known.

Now this pottery, though showing Rhenish affiliations in design and manufacture, was made on a slow wheel, a less satisfactory implement than those in use in the Rhineland. It seems that in one of their voyages to the continent, men of the Sandlings Folk learnt something of this, to them, new machine and in their own home they experimented and produced this characteristic ware until it was superseded by the true Rhenish type, made on a fast wheel which first appeared about the time of the Viking invasions. More evidence is needed to confirm these provisional conclusions; but the distribution of this Ipswich ware, unlike that of the Late Saxon wares, is confined to the East Anglian coast, to the head of the Yare estuary and to the Fenland edge. It has been found nowhere else,[1] apart from a few vessels from Castor-by-Peterborough in the Nene valley and Godmanchester in the Ouse valley on the western edge of the Fens and this distribution is clearly that of the coastwise traffic which had been in existence for a hundred years or more. Something of confirmation is found also in the early Christian cross-pendants with cloisonné decoration. Of those from East Anglia, the Wilton cross was found near the fen-edge in the Little Ouse valley and the Ixworth cross came from a tributary-valley of the same river. Another garnet-set pendant, though not a cross, was found at Bacton on the north-east coast of Norfolk. All these are virtually on the same coastwise route and add to the growing evidence of its employment.

During the seventh century, the Mercian threat became severe and, as we have seen, several East Anglian kings were slain in war with their stronger neighbour. It was probably in the early days of this threat, though the dating cannot yet be finally proved, that the 'Devil's Dyke' and then the 'Fleam Dyke' were thrown up across the Icknield Way, to bar intruders from the Midlands by the Cambridge route. The construction of these

---

[1] As this went to press, it was announced (*The Times*, November 9, 1962) that Ipswich ware had been found in the Saxon hall below the Treasury building off Whitehall in London. Since the map (Fig. 31) was drawn, a few more sites have been added to the list, but these do not modify the pattern.

great bank-and-ditch earthworks, lying across the open country between forest and fen, must have involved a great co-operative effort; their presence shows how well the Wuffings had organised their kingdom and secured the allegiance of their people. But the pressure was too great. East Anglia could not withstand the attacks of so powerful a foe and the ultimate control passed to the Mercian king.

The military genius of Penda and the much greater resources of men and supplies at his command were responsible for this subjugation and in the so-called *Tribal Hidage*, probably compiled in the eighth century, we have some evidence of this disparity. The *Hidage* lists the regions of England south of Northumbria and gives the area of their lands in conventional 'hides'. Some of the smaller groups cannot with certainty be identified, but it is clear enough that those which formed the Mercian Kingdom had upwards of 80,000 hides, whereas East Anglia had no more than 30,000. After the death of Aethelhere, we hear no more of war in East Anglia for more than two centuries. The last Wuffing, so far as we know, died in 740 and, after that, there were sub-kings of unknown origin until the foundation of Guthrum's Viking kingdom in 879.

After more than two centuries of rule, the Wuffing adventure in kingship came to its end. Historians have long known the names of the leading actors in its drama, the anecdotes of the chroniclers and the judgements of Bede. But these were never more than the skeleton of a story. Twelve hundred years after that story came to an end, it has fallen to our generation to reveal the burial-hoard of Sutton Hoo and clothe the skeleton of the Wuffings' story with the flesh and blood of its valiant humanity.

BIBLIOGRAPHICAL SUMMARY

To PROVIDE a full scholar's bibliography here is unnecessary. So much of the relevant matter is published in articles in learned journals that it would be fulsome to name them all. However, the main papers dealing with the Sutton Hoo find are first listed and in these full bibliographical references may be found. I have then made a selection of the more important works in English, in which further references occur, and for the boats I have added a few references to publications in other languages where this seemed desirable.

The first account of the excavation is by C. W. Phillips, 'The Excavation of the Sutton Hoo Ship-burial', in *Antiquaries Journal*, 20 (1940) and a description of the ship by him is also given in 'The Sutton Hoo Burial Ship', *Mariner's Mirror*, 26 (1940). Constructive criticism of this by R. C. Anderson appears in Vol. 28 (1942) of the same publication; this volume also contains Guy Maynard's 'The Smaller Boat from Sutton Hoo'. A more general account by Mr. Phillips, 'The Excavation of the Sutton Hoo Ship-burial', is in *Recent Archaeological Excavations in Britain* (edited R. L. S. Bruce-Mitford, London, 1956).

In 1940, the editor of *Antiquity* devoted the March number of Vol. 14 to Sutton Hoo and its treasures. The contents include: 'I. The Excavation', by C. W. Phillips; 'II. The Gold Ornaments', 'III. The Large Hanging-bowl', 'IV. The Archaeology of the Jewellery', all by T. D. Kendrick; 'V. The Silver', by Ernst Kitzinger; 'VI. The Coins: A Summary', by O. G. S. Crawford; 'VII. The Salvaging of the Finds', by W. F. Grimes and 'VIII. Who Was He?' by H. Munro Chadwick. Other preliminary descriptive articles appeared in the *British Museum Quarterly*, 13 (1939) and notes by T. D. Kendrick on a Celtic masked whetstone and the Sutton Hoo gourd-cups appeared in *Antiquaries Journal*, 21 (1941).

Since the war, important papers have been published by R. L. S. Bruce-Mitford. They include *The Sutton Hoo Ship Burial: A Provisional Guide* (London: British Museum, 1947), 'Saxon Rendlesham', *Proceedings of the Suffolk Institute of Archaeology*, 24 (1948) and in the following year (1949) in the same publication, Vol. 25, appeared his 'The Sutton Hoo Ship-burial', a long paper of prime importance. Here also may be mentioned his 'The Snape Boat-grave', in Vol. 26 (1952) of the same *Proceedings*. This paper gives full references to the original descriptions by Davidson, Hele and

Francis. Other papers by Mr. Bruce-Mitford include 'The Sutton Hoo musical instrument' *Archaeological News Letter*, 1 (1949), 'The Problem of the Sutton Hoo Cenotaph'. *Archaeological News Letter*, 2 (1950) which summarises a lecture and 'The Sutton Hoo Ship-burial' which appears as an appendix in R. H. Hodgkin's *A History of the Anglo-Saxons* (Third edition, Oxford, 1952). This book is itself a valuable general history of our period and need not be mentioned again. A collection of Mr. Bruce-Mitford's papers, together with new material, is due to appear shortly under the title of *Sutton Hoo Studies*. Professor Sune Lindqvist's important paper, 'Sutton Hoo and Beowulf', translated from the Swedish, is in *Antiquity*, 22 (1948). H. Maryon's papers, 'The Sutton Hoo Shield' and 'The Sutton Hoo Helmet', appeared in *Antiquity*, 20 (1946) and 21 (1947) respectively.

An attempt by Dr. Gordon Ward to maintain the attribution of the cenotaph to Raedwald appeared as 'The Silver Spoons from Sutton Hoo', in *Antiquity*, 26 (1952). This was answered by Mr. Bruce-Mitford later in the same volume and his paper, 'Sutton Hoo: A Rejoinder' was followed immediately by P. H. Grierson's 'The Dating of the Sutton Hoo Coins'. Other interesting papers are J. W. Walker's 'The battle of Winwaed and the Sutton Hoo ship burial', in *Yorkshire Archaeological Journal*, part 145 (1948) and Sir Frank Stenton's 'The East Anglian Kings of the Seventh Century', in *The Anglo-Saxons* (edited by P. Clemoes, London, 1959). Miss V. I. Evison's 'Early Anglo-Saxon Inlaid Metalwork', in *Antiquaries Journal*, 35 (1955) is also of interest.

A 'Chronological Bibliography' of writings dealing with Sutton Hoo was published by F. P. Magoun in *Speculum*, Vol. xxix (1954) and this J. B. Bessinger supplemented in the same journal for 1958. The standard history of the Anglo-Saxon period is Sir Frank Stenton's *Anglo-Saxon England* (Second edition, Oxford, 1947) and D. M. Wilson has recently published a general survey of Anglo-Saxon archaeology in his *The Anglo-Saxons* (London, 1960), in which he discusses some of the Sutton Hoo problems. A newly-published book, H. R. Ellis Davidson's *The Sword in Anglo-Saxon England*, (Oxford, 1962) discusses 'ring-swords' and illustrates many examples. Pattern-welding is also described and illustrated.

The standard editions of the early chroniclers in Latin or Anglo-Saxon are well-known to students and need not be enumerated. For English renderings, a new translation of the manuscripts collectively known as *The Anglo-Saxon Chronicle* (translated by G. N. Garmonsway) has been published (1953) by J. M. Dent & Sons in the Everyman Library. This Library also contains a translation of Bede's *Ecclesiastical History of the English*

Nation (1910) and Professor R. K. Gordon's *Anglo-Saxon Poetry* (revised edition 1954). The latter, which includes 'Beowulf', is rendered in English prose and is a valuable anthology of the early work. Gildas' *De Excidio . . .* and Nennius' *Historia Brittonum* are included in *Six Old English Chronicles* (edited by J. A. Giles) in Bohn's nineteenth-century 'Antiquarian Library', now not easily obtained. Recent translations of *Beowulf* and Bede's *History* have also been published by Penguin Books Ltd. of Harmondsworth.

The writings of Edward Thurlow Leeds are far too numerous to be listed here. His important books are *The Archaeology of the Anglo-Saxon Settlements* (Oxford, 1913), *Celtic Ornament in the British Isles down to A.D. 700* (Oxford, 1933) in which he deals with the problem of the hanging-bowls, *Early Anglo-Saxon Art and Archaeology* (Oxford, 1936) and *A Corpus of Early Anglo-Saxon Great Square-headed Brooches* (Oxford, 1949). Of his many papers, 'The Distribution of the Anglo-Saxon Saucer Brooch . . .', *Archaeologia*, 63 (1912), 'The Early Saxon Penetration of the Upper Thames area', *Antiquaries Journal*, 13 (1933), 'The Distribution of the Angles and Saxons archaeologically considered', *Archaeologia*, 91 (1945) and 'Denmark and Early England', *Antiquaries Journal*, 26 (1946), are perhaps the most important. A full list of his works was published in his *Festschrift* volume, *Dark-Age Britain* (edited by D. B. Harden, London, 1956). This valuable book comprises many papers; those referred to in the text of this book include 'Romano-Saxon Pottery', by J. N. L. Myres, 'Irish Enamels . . .', by Françoise Henry, 'The Jutes of Kent', by C. F. C. Hawkes, 'The Anglo-Saxon Settlement in Eastern England', by T. C. Lethbridge and 'Glass Vessels . . .', by D. B. Harden.

Reginald Smith's important surveys are to be found in the relevant volumes of the Victoria County Histories in which, county by county, he described the 'Anglo-Saxon Remains'. His also was the British Museum *Guide to Anglo-Saxon and Foreign Teutonic Antiquities* (1923), now alas out of print. His other very numerous papers are scattered through the publications of the Society of Antiquaries of London. Professor G. Baldwin Brown's best work is in the various volumes of his *The Arts in Early England*, the first of which was published in 1903. Those dealing with finds from the graves are volumes 3 and 4, 'Saxon Art and Industry in the Pagan Period' (London, 1915). His *Arts and Crafts of our Teutonic Forefathers* (London, 1910) may also be used with profit. Sir Thomas Kendrick's studies of Anglo-Saxon art are spread through many papers; their substance, with his considered views, are expounded in his *Anglo-Saxon Art to A.D. 900* (London 1938). Of the papers, three must be mentioned here, 'British Hanging-bowls', *Antiquity*, 6 (1932), 'Polychrome Jewellery in Kent', *Antiquity*, 7

(1933) and 'St. Cuthbert's Pectoral Cross and the Wilton and Ixworth Crosses', in *Antiquaries Journal*, 17 (1937). R. F. Jessup's *Anglo-Saxon Jewellery* (London 1950) may also be conveniently mentioned here. Another important book, Nils Åberg's *The Anglo-Saxons in England during the early centuries after the invasion* (Uppsala and Cambridge, 1926), is mainly devoted to an exhaustive survey of all the known examples of cruciform and other brooches and the establishment of a detailed chronology based on their development.

Of cemeteries in our East Anglian area an excellent survey to 1938 may be found in Rainbird Clarke's 'Norfolk in the Dark Ages, A.D. 400-800', in *Norfolk Archaeology*, 27 (1938 and 1939), which also includes 'The Anglo-Saxon Pottery of Norfolk', by J. N. L. Myres. There is no detailed survey of Suffolk material later than that of Reginald Smith in the *Victoria County History* (Vol. I, London 1911), but Mr. Clarke's recent *East Anglia* (1960) summarises the remains from the two counties in Chapter VIII. For that part of Cambridgeshire included in our area, T. C. Lethbridge's survey of 'Anglo-Saxon Cambridgeshire' in the *Victoria County History* (Vol. I, London, 1938) is the most up-to-date. But mention must be made of a famous pioneer work, Sir Cyril Fox's *The Archaeology of the Cambridge Region* (Cambridge, 1923), still an essential source book on which all later work has been based. The Ipswich cemetery was described by N. F. Layard in 'An Anglo-Saxon Cemetery in Ipswich', *Archaeologia*, 60 (1907). Mr. Lethbridge has published reports on his excavations in several cemeteries near the Cambridgeshire-Suffolk border in both the *Proceedings* and the *Quarto Publications* of the Cambridge Antiquarian Society. Some East Anglian remains may be found pictured in colour in J. Y. Akerman's *Remains of Pagan Saxondom* (London, 1855) and the finds from the Little Wilbraham cemetery are described and illustrated in colour in the Hon. R. C. Neville's *Saxon Obsequies* . . . (London, 1852). *The Mildenhall Treasure* (Second edition, London: British Museum, 1955) is a beautifully-illustrated handbook to this important hoard, written by J. W. Brailsford. The Broomfield grave, first described by Sir Hercules Read in the *Proceedings of the Society of Antiquaries* (second series) 15 (1894) is further discussed and illustrated by Reginald Smith in the *Victoria History of the County of Essex* (Vol. I, Westminster, 1903), where the Forest Gate jewel is also illustrated in colour. The Benty Grange finds were first described by Thomas Bateman in *Ten Years Digging* . . . (London and Derby, 1861). The Hough-on-the-Hill whetstone appears in 'Archaeological Notes for 1956' by D. F. Petch in the *Lincolnshire Architectural and Archaeological Society's Reports and Papers*, 7 (1957).

Dr. J. N. L. Myres' descriptions of Anglo-Saxon pagan pottery are in many scattered papers of which 'Some English Parallels to the Anglo-Saxon Pottery of Holland and Belgium in the Migration Period', *L'Antiquité Classique*, 17 (1948) has special reference to a theme developed in this book. His initial paper on Romano-Saxon pottery has already been mentioned, but this should now be supplemented by the shorter 'Anglo-Saxon Pottery of the Pagan Period', in *Medieval Archaeology*, 3 (1959). In the same volume is J. G. Hurst's supplement to his earlier paper written jointly with S. E. West, 'An Account of Middle Saxon Ipswich Ware' in the *Proceedings of the Cambridge Antiquarian Society*, 50 (1957). For some of his more general historical conclusions, Dr. Myres' 'The Adventus Saxonum' in *Aspects of Archaeology* (edited by W. F. Grimes, London, 1951) should be consulted.

There is no up-to-date account of the Saxon Shore. A very readable book by Jessie Mothersole, *The Saxon Shore* (London, 1924) may still be read with profit, but since its publication our knowledge has greatly increased and many of its conclusions need to be amended. A recently-published book by Donald A. White, *Litus Saxonicum: The British Saxon Shore in Scholarship and History* (Madison, Wisconsin, U.S.A., 1961) is of great interest and has a valuable bibliography, but some of its conclusions are not in accordance with the most recent excavation-evidence. For the general history of the late Romano-British period, R. G. Collingwood and J. N. L. Myres in *Roman Britain and the English Settlements* (Second edition, Oxford, 1937) is still the best, though now slightly outdated.

The published accounts of the early ships are not all easily available as many of them are in German and Scandinavian publications; of some of the English boats there is only the scantiest information. The Waltham-stow boat No. 1 is briefly described by W. Robinson in his *History and Antiquities of Hackney in the County of Middlesex* (London, 1842). Walthamstow No. 2 is mentioned by T. V. Holmes in his 'Geological Notes on the New Reservoirs . . .', in *The Essex Naturalist*, 12 (1902) and by A. R. Hatley in *Footnotes to Local History* (Walthamstow, 1932). The finds from this boat-burial are briefly recorded by Dr. R. E. M. (now Sir Mortimer) Wheeler in his *London and the Vikings* (London Museum Catalogue, 1927). The few available details of the Yarmouth ship are given by the writer and J. N. Hutchinson in 'Part III. The Archaeological Evidence', in *The Making of the Broads*, by J. M. Lambert *et al.* (London, 1960). The description of the Ashby ship appeared in the *Yarmouth Mercury*, January 8, 1927 and all the available data have been incorporated in this book. The Snape boat and those from Sutton Hoo have already been mentioned.

The Bruges boat found in 1899 and described by E. Jonckheere in *L'origine de la côte de Flandre et le Bateau de Bruges* (Bruges, 1903), appears to be later than the Migration Period and so is not described in the survey in Chapter III. Its few preserved remains in the Gruuthuuse Museum were in 1962 in poor condition and little further evidence could be gained from them. Of the Utrecht boat there is a thirty-page account by Hr. Van der Wijk in the *Jaarboekje van 'Oud-Utrecht'* (1932). The later Viking ships, including the Kvalsund and other earlier boats, receive a general description by A. W. Brøgger and H. Shetelig in *The Viking Ships* (London, 1954), a revised English version of their first edition (1951) in Norwegian, the English version being fuller and more satisfactory. An excellent short account in English of the Westfold ships is given by Thorleif Sjøvold in *The Oseberg Find and the other Viking Ship Finds*, a handbook published by the Oslo University Museum (1957). Full details of the Hjortspring boat are available in Danish in *Hjortspringfundet* (Copenhagen, 1937) by G. Rosenberg, K. Jessen and F. Johannessen and of the Halsnøy boat in Norwegian by H. Shetelig in *Bergens Museums Aarbog* (Bergen, 1903). An early account of the Nydam ship, an English version of the finder's original book in Danish, is Conrad Engelhardt's *Denmark in the Early Iron Age* (London, 1866). A full modern description is in German as 'Das Nydamschiff' in *Acta Archaeologica*, I (Copenhagen, 1930) by H. Shetelig. A more satisfactory reconstruction of the steering-mechanism of the Nydam ship is given by J. W. van Nouhuys in 'Some Doubtful Points with regard to the Nydam Ship', in *Mariner's Mirror*, 22 (1936); Shetelig's reconstruction is also criticised by Carl V. Sølver in 'The Rebaek Rudder', in *Mariner's Mirror*, 32 (1946). Engelhardt's other finds from the Danish mosses were described in Danish in *Thorsbjerg Mosefunde* (1863), *Kragehul Mosefunde* (1867) and *Vimose Fundet* (1869), but a short description by H. Jankuhn of the *Nydam und Thorsberg Moorfunde der Eisenzeit* was published by the Schleswig-Holsteinisches Museum (1950) in German. Finally the Galtabäck ship is described in Swedish by N. Niklasson and Fr. Johannessen in *Galtabäcksbåten och dess Restaurering* (Goteborg, 1933) and further by P. Humbla and L. von Post in *Galtabäcksbåten och tidigt båtbyggen in Norden* (Goteborg, 1937). Its lines are reproduced by Mr. Phillips in *Antiquaries Journal*, 20 (1940).

The Romano-British population was discussed by R. G. Collingwood in 'Town and Country in Roman Britain', *Antiquity*, 3 (1929); H. J. Randall replied with 'Population and Agriculture in Roman Britain', in *Antiquity*, 4 (1930), followed in the same number by Sir Mortimer Wheeler with 'Mr. Collingwood and Mr. Randall'. Dr. O. K. Schram's place-name evidence appeared in 'Place-names' in *Norwich and its Region* (Norwich,

1961), the local handbook of the British Association for the Advancement of Science. For the extinct beaver and aurochs, convenient references may be found in J. E. Harting's *British Animals Extinct within Historic Times* (London, 1880), Sir E. Ray Lankester's *Extinct Animals* (London, 1906) and Colin Matheson's *Changes in the Fauna of Wales within Historic Times* (Cardiff: National Museum of Wales, 1932).

The continental literature dealing with the Migration Period is of enormous volume, but a few books and papers may be suggested to outline the continental background. H. M. Chadwick's *The Origin of the English Nation* (Cambridge, 1907), though some of its conclusions must now be modified, is an excellent starting point; H. Shetelig and H. Falk have made a valuable survey in their *Scandinavian Archaeology* (Oxford, 1937). The Vendel graves, so important to Sutton Hoo students, were first described in Swedish (1912) by H. Stolpe and T. J. Arne, but a later edition in French, *La Nécropole de Vendel* (Stockholm, 1927) makes their work more easily accessible to English readers. Two short but valuable surveys by leading German scholars, 'The Continental Home of the English', by H. Jankuhn and 'The Continental Background', by F. Tischler, appeared in *Antiquity*, 26 (1952) and *Medieval Archaeology*, 3 (1959) respectively.

Finally, for the discussions of *Beowulf*, reference should first be made to Professor R. W. Chambers' *Beowulf: An Introduction to the Study of the Poem with a Discussion of the Stories of Offa and Finn* (Second revised edition, Cambridge, 1932). This book has an exhaustive bibliography complete to the time of publication and it need only be supplemented by reference to Professor F. Klaeber's *Beowulf with the Fight at Finnsburg* (Third revised edition, Boston, U.S.A., 1936), Professor D. Whitelock's *The Audience of Beowulf* (Oxford, 1951) and Mrs. N. K. Chadwick's 'The Monsters and Beowulf' in *The Anglo-Saxons* (edited by P. Clemoes, London, 1959), in which she suggests the possibility of an East Anglian origin for the poem for other reasons than those advanced above. For the 'Ynglingasaga', a convenient edition in English of Snorre Sturlason's *Heimskringla* is in two volumes in the Everyman Library.

Mention may also be made of a paper by Rosemary J. Cramp, 'Beowulf and Archaeology', in *Medieval Archaeology*, Vol. i (1957) and Professor C. L. Wrenn's 'Sutton Hoo and Beowulf', in *Mélanges de Linguistique et de Philologie* (Paris, 1959) which also gives the *Beowulf* poem an East Anglian origin.

INDEX

N.B. In the Bibliographical Summary authors' names only are indexed, *not* the titles of books and papers.

ÅBERG, NILS, 151
Admiralty Manual of Tides (1941), 109
Adventus Saxonum, 15, 116
AÐILS, king of the Swedes, 134
AELFHERE, 132
AELFWALD, king of East Anglia, 95, 138, 139, Fig. 28
AELLE, king of the South Saxons, 66
AETHELHERE, king of East Anglia, 94, 96, 97, 98, 100, 137, 139, 147, Fig. 28
AETHELRIC of East Anglia, 94, 98, 100, Fig. 28
AETHELTHRYTH of East Anglia, 94, Fig. 28
AETHELWALD, king of East Anglia, 94, 96, 97, 98, 100, Fig. 28
AKERMAN, J. Y., 14, 82, 151
Alamanni, 116, 117
Alde, river, 142, Fig. 2
ALDWULF, king of East Anglia, 92, 93, 94, 96, 98, Fig. 28
Ale, 75, 76
Alexandria, Egypt, 72
ALFRED, king, 13
ALLAN, JOHN, 96
ALLECTUS, 115
ALLEN, DEREK, 95
Allington Hill, *see* Bottisham
Als Sound, Schleswig, 106
Ameland, Holland, 111, Fig. 29
AMMIANUS MARCELLINUS, 116
ANASTASIUS I, 74
ANDERSON, R. C., 48, 55, 148
Andreas, 51-2
Angles (*see also* Anglo-Saxons), 13, 14, 15, 89, 103, 104, 108, 119, 120, 130, 140, 142, 143, Fig. 1
— contact with Saxons, 15, 106, 107
— East, 15, 122
— intermixture with Saxons, 107, 109, 119, 141
— Mercian, 15, 93, 94, 97, 139, 142
— Middle, 15
— Northumbrian, 15
Anglian continental homeland, 15, 48, 119, Fig. 1
Anglo-Saxon Chronicle, 17, 92, 93, 94, 119
Anglo-Saxon England (1947), 145
Anglo-Saxon Jewellery (1950), 83
Anglo-Saxon Poetry (1954), 20
Anglo-Saxons (*see also* Angles, Early English, Jutes, Saxons), 13, 18, 66, 72, 73, 82, 121, 124, 125
— continental homes, 14, 15, Fig. 1
— migration, 15, 49, 64, 65, 103-13, 120, 122, 125
— pirates and raiders, 13, 73, 75, 103, 115, 116, 118
— seafaring, 19, 48-9, 52, 103-13, 129, 137
— settlement-pattern, 16, 19, 64, 103, 107, 109, 113, 118, 127, 140-1, Fig. 1
Angon-heads, 41, 71, Pl. IIa
Angulus, 15
— desertus, 130
Animal-ornament, 41, 70, 71, 72, 73, 77, 79, 80, 81, 83
ANNA, king of East Anglia, 93, 94, 96, 97, 98, 100-1, 131, Fig. 28
Antiquaries of London, Society of, 19
Antiquity, 20, 32
Aquavit, 75
ARNE, T. J., 154
Ashby Dell boat, *see* Ships and Boats
Ashmolean Museum, Oxford, *see* Museums
Atlantic Ocean, 116
Audience of Beowulf, The (1951), 138
AUGUSTINE, 84

Aun, king of the Swedes, 134
Aurochs (*Bos primigenius*), 73-4
Axe, iron bearded, 26-7
— — francisca, 26, 40, 77
— stone, 30

Bacton (Norfolk) pendant, 146
Badley, Suffolk, 144
Bag(s), beaver-skin, 73
— leather, *see* Leather
Baker, F. T., 20
Baldrick, *see* Harness
Baltic Sea, 104, 106, 108, 109, 130, 131,
     137, 141, 145, Figs. 1, 32
Bamburgh, Northumberland, 68
Barrows, Sutton, *see* Sutton Mounts
Barrow-robbers, 25, 26, 29, 30-1
Bateman, Thomas, 77, 151
Bead(s) Anglo-Saxon, 121
— Bronze Age faience, 28
Beaver (*Castor fiber*), 73
— -skin bag, 73
Bede, 14, 15, 16, 20, 51, 66, 67, 80, 92, 93,
     94, 97, 98, 101, 103, 119, 120, 130,
     131, 138, 147, 149, 150
Beeleigh, Essex, gold-hunt, 31
Belgium, 106, 107, 131
Belt, Sword-, *see* Harness
Belton Fen, Suffolk, 62
Benty Grange, Monyash, Derbyshire, 77
Beowulf, 132, 134, 138
— burials described, 46, 99
— byrnies mentioned, 77
— date of composition, 99, 138-9
— Finnesburh story, 120
— place of composition, 137-9
— ring-swords mentioned, 82
— ships described, 52
Beowulf, king of the Geats, 132, 139
Bessinger, J. B., 149
Blekinge, Sweden, 136, Fig. 32
Bloodmoor Hill, Suffolk, 101
Blyth, river, 142, Fig. 2
Blythburgh, Suffolk, 94, 97, 98, Fig. 31
Boats, *see* Ships
Bodleian Library, Oxford, 114
Body absent from ship-burial, 43
Bohuslän, Sweden, 136, Fig. 32

Bone comb(s), 26, 77
— gaming-piece, 27
— panel, 80
— pins, 122
Bones, domestic animal, 19, 27
— human, *see* Burials
Borre, Norway, 99, Figs. 1, 32
Bottisham, Cambs, 144
Boulogne, France, 104, 115
Bowl(s), bronze, 25, 38, 41
— bronze Coptic, 72, 144, Pl. XIIIa
— — hanging-, 40, 72-3, 76, 89, 90,
     Pl. XIVa
— fluted silver, 38, 40, 74-5, Pl. XVIIIc
— nest of silver, 41, 42, 74, Pl. XVIIIa, b
Bracteates, 130, 131
Bradwell, Essex, Saxon Shore fort, 114, 115
Brailsford, J. W., 151
Brancaster, Norfolk, Saxon Shore fort,
     114, 143, Fig. 31
Bretwalda, 66, 68, 95, 141
Bridgham, Norfolk, 144
Britain, 13, 15, 19, 66, 75, 76, 103, 104,
     115, 116, 118, 120, 121, 122, Fig. 1
British Association for the Advancement
     of Science, 122
British Isles, 89
— Museum, *see* Museums
— — (Natural History), *see* Museums
British Museum *Provisional Guide*, 18
Britons, 13, 15
— Romano-, 75
— sub-Roman, 17, 75, 90, 121, 126
— — intermarriage with Germanic
     settlers, 118, 121, 122, 125, 126
— — provincial governors, 119, 140, 141
— — survival of, 121, 122, 124-6
Brøgger, Dr. A. W., 65, 153
Bronze bowls, *see* Bowls
— bucket-mountings, 75
— buckle, *see* Buckles
— cauldrons, *see* Cauldrons
— condition of, 37
— Coptic bowl, *see* Bowls
— decoration on whetstone, 40, 69, Pl.
     IXa, b
— disc-brooches, *see* Brooches

Bronze disc, decorated, 27
— fish in hanging-bowl, 72, Pl. XIVb
— fragments, 25, 26, 27
— hanging-bowl, *see* Bowls
— helmet-fittings, *see* Helmet
— plaque, gilt, 144-5
— 'ring' from ring-sword, 82-3, Fig. 24
— shield-mounts, *see* Shield
— stag on standard, 40, 66, Pl. VIII
— stamped sheeting, 70, 134, 136, Pl. XXIIIg, h
— stud, 27
— sword-fittings, 136
Brooch(es), Anglian enamelled, 89
— cruciform, 129, 137
— equal-armed, 121
— Faversham, 85, 131
— Frankish, 144
— Germanic, 121
— Ipswich-type, 131
— Kentish disc-, 83, 84, 87, 129, 144
— Kingston, 83
— Rhenish, 106
— Saxon, 106, 107
— small-long, 129
— square-headed, large, 130, 144, Pl. XVIb
— Sutton, 87, 131, Fig. 27
— Trier, 86
Brooke, Norfolk, 144
Broomfield, Essex, *see* Burials
BROWN, B. J. W., 19, 25, 27, 29, 30, 31, 32, 33, 44, 56
BROWN, G. BALDWIN, 14, 150
Brown's Tidal Streams for the Whole of the British Coasts, Ireland and North Sea, 109
BRUCE-MITFORD, R. L. S., 17, 18, 19, 25, 58, 73, 79, 80, 83, 85, 86, 97, 100, 134, 135, 148, 149
Bucket(s), wooden, 40, 43, 76
Buckle(s), bronze, 27, 38
— gold, 78, 79, 136, 137, Pl. XX
— gold and jewelled, 42, 78, Pls. XXII, XXIII
— Kentish, 144
— Swedish-type, 136, 144

Bungay, Suffolk, 142, 144, Fig. 2
Bure, river, 140, 143, Fig. 2
Burgh Castle, Suffolk, 62, Fig. 31
— — excavations at, 90
— — glass-making at, 90
— — monastery, 90, 93, 94
— — Romano-Saxon pottery, 117
— — Saxon Shore fort, 93, 114, 117
Burgundians, 116
Burial-chamber in Sutton Hoo ship No. 1, 31, 32, 36, 44, 66, Figs. 7, 8
— — absence of body, 43
— — clay-pan over, 36-7, Fig. 7
— — collapse of roof, 33, 34, 36, 37, 42
— — construction, 31, 33, 34, 36
— — grave-goods, 18, 31, 32, 33, 34, 36, 37, 38, 40-3, 66-90, 95, 99, 131, 134, Figs. 9, 10, Pls. I, II
— — methods of excavation, 32, 33-4, 37, 38, 40, 41
— — recording of grave-goods, 37-8
— — sandy filling, 33, 34, 37
— — symbols of power at west end, 40, 43, 68, Fig. 9
Burials (*see also* Burial-chamber *and* Ship-burials), Fig. 31
— Anglo-Saxon pagan, 21, 72 (and *passim*)
— animal, 27, 99
— Anglo-Saxon mistaken for Roman, 14
— barrow (*see also* Sutton Mounts), 77, 101-2, 134
— Benty Grange, 77
— Bloodmoor Hill, 101-2
— Broomfield, Frankish pot, 145
— — glass jar, 100
— — iron lamp, 76, 82
— — pyramid, 81-2
— — sword, 135
— cemeteries, 14, 48, 102, 117, 118, 121, 129, 130, 144
— cenotaph, 43, 99, 101, 137, 139
— cremation, 14, 25, 26, 27, 29, 72, 102, 117, 120, 129, 130, 134
— grave-goods, 14, 17, 72, 103, 121, 122, 129, 137, 144 (and *passim*)
— — Sutton Hoo Barrow No. 3, 26-7

Burials, grave-goods, Sutton Hoo Barrow
    No. 4, 25
— inhumation, 120-1, 129, 130, 134
— Kentish, 14
— Swedish, 70
— Taplow, 73, 74, 135
Bury St. Edmunds, Suffolk, 93, Figs. 2, 31
— Museum, *see* Museums
Busüm, Germany, 110, Fig. 29
Byrnie(s), 40, 77
Byzantine Empire, 74, 95

Cable twist with central gold nodule, 81,
    85, Fig. 25
Caenby, Lincs, 79
Caister-on-Sea, Norfolk, Fig. 31
— Anglo-Saxon boats, *see* Ships and Boats
— Ipswich ware, 145
— Lifeboat crew, 108
— Roman walled town, 117, 118, 122,
    124, 143
— Romano-Saxon pottery, 117, 118
— Roman remains in modern graves, 122
Caistor-by Norwich (*Venta Icenorum*), 119,
    124, 125, 140, 141, 142, 144, Fig. 31
Calais, France, 106
Cambridge, 121, 124, 141, 143, 145, 146
Cambridgeshire, 77, 122, 129 (and *passim*)
Canterbury, Kent, 84
Cap Griz Nez, France, 104, 107
CARAUSIUS, 115
Carisbrooke, I.o.W., Saxon Shore fort, 115
Castor, Northants, 146
Catfield boat, *see* Ships and Boats
Cattegat, 106, 143, Figs. 1, 32
Catton, Norfolk, 144
Cauldrons, 43, 76, Pl. Ia
CEAWLIN, king of the West Saxons, 66
CEDD, Bishop, 94
Celtic Britain, 73, 76, 118
Cenotaph-burial, *see* Burials
CHADWICK, H. M., 15, 148, 154
— Mrs. N. K., 154
Chain-mail, *see* Byrnies
Chainwork and bars of iron, 43, 76
CHAMBERS, Professor R. W., 132, 154
Champlevé-work, 79, 89

Channel, English, 103, 115, 116
Chart, *British Islands and Adjacent Waters*, 109
Chesterford, Essex, 124
Christianity, conversion to, 84, 92, 93, 96,
    97, 98, 122, 126
Christian church, 93
CLARKE, R. RAINBIRD, 20, 127, 131, 151
Clasps, gold and jewelled, 42, 78, 80, 90,
    Pl. XXV
Classis Britannica, see Roman fleet
Clay-pan in graves, 26, 36-7
Clench-nails, *see* Ships and Boats
Cloisonné-work, Anglian style, 87, 88, 131
— described, 79
— development and decline, 83, 84
— Frankish, 83
— Kentish, 83, 84, 88
— lidded, 79, 80, 81, 85
— mushroom-celled, 80, 81, 84, 85, 86,
    87, 88, 135-6, Figs. 26, 27
— pendants, 146
— quatrefoil-celled, 81, 86, 136
— rectangular-celled, 80, 85, 86
— stepped-celled, 80, 81, 85, 88
Coastal change, 107-8
Coins, Anglo-Saxon thrymsas and sceattas,
    95
— AVITUS, 101
— DAGOBERT I, 96
— HERACLIUS I, 85
— JUSTINIAN I, 101-2
— Merovingian gold *tremisses*, 42, 95,
    Pl. XXI
Colchester, Essex, 117, 118, 142
COLLINGWOOD, Professor R. G., 124, 152,
    153
Cologne, Germany, 118
Comb(s), Bone, 26, 77
CONSTANTIUS CHLORUS, 115
Coptic bowl, *see* Bowls
Corslet, *see* Byrnies
Count of the Saxon Shore, 114, 116
CRAMP, ROSEMARY J., 154
CRAWFORD, O. G. S., 32, 38, 148
Cremation burials, *see* Burials
— urns, *see* Pottery
Cromer, Norfolk, 109, 111, Fig. 2

Cross, pendent, 85-6, 88, 146
Cups, glass, 130, 144
— Gourd-, 37, 38, Pl. XIIIb, c
— horn, 76
— leather, silver-mounted, 77
— silver, 40, 75, 76, Pl. XIXa
— wooden, 76
CUTHBERT, Saint, 51
Cuxhaven, Germany, 110, Fig. 29
CYNEWULF school of poetry, 52

DAGOBERT I, coin, 96
Danes, 13, 120, 126, 130, 131, 137, 138,
     139, 142, 143, Fig. 1
'Daniel in the Lion's Den' motif, 80, 136,
     Frontispiece
Danube frontier, 116
Dark Age studies, 13, 14, 29, 118
DAVIDSON, H. R. ELLIS, 149
— SEPTIMUS, 58, 59, 148
Deben, river, 21, 30, 101, 129, 143, Figs.
     2, 3
Decorative styles, Anglo-Saxon, 78-9, 80
— Frankish, 83, 136
— Hiberno-Saxon, 80
— Irish, 89, 90
— Kentish, 79, 83-4
— of Roman derivation, 121
De Excidio et Conquesto Britanniae, 17
DEE, Dr. JOHN, 31
DEFOE, DANIEL, 13
Denmark, 15, 52, 63, 109, 130, 131, 137,
     Figs. 1, 32
DENT AND SONS, J. M., 20
Devil's Dyke, 146
Dish, Great silver, 38, 40, 43, 74, 75,
     Pl. XVIIa, b
— assay marks, 74, Pl. XVIIc, d
DOODSON, A. T., 109
DOUGLAS, The Rev. JAMES, 14
Dover, Kent, Saxon Shore fort, 114
Drinking-horns, 42-3, 73-4, 83, Pl. IIb
Dunkirk, France, 106, 111, Fig. 29
Dunwich, Suffolk, 93, Fig. 31

EADBALD, king of Kent, 97
EADGILS, *see* ADILS

Early Anglo-Saxon Art and Archaeology (1936),
     83
Earthworks, Bank-and-ditch, 146-7, Fig.
     31
East Anglia (1960), 20, 127
East Anglia, 15, 17, 66, 72, 89, 93, 94, 95,
     96, 98, 101, 103, 106, 109, 116,
     117, 118, 120, 122, 124, 125, 126,
     127, 131, 138, 139, 140, 141, 144,
     145, 146, 147 (and *passim*), Figs. 2,
     30, 31
— cremation urns from, 117
East Anglian royal house, *see* Wuffing
     dynasty
Ecclesiastical History of the English Nation,
     14, 20, 51, 92, 101
ECGRIC, king of East Anglia, 93, 94, 100,
     Fig. 28
EDWIN, king of Northumbria, 66, 67, 68,
     93
Egbert shrine, Trier, 86
EGIL, king of the Swedes, 134
Eider, river, 15
Elbe, river, 15, 107, 110, 112, 121, 141,
     Fig. 1
Ely, Cambs, 94, Figs. 2, 31
Ely Chronicle, 94, 98
Ems, river, 15, Fig. 1
Enamel-work, 72, 76, 79, 89-90
ENGELHARDT, CONRAD, 153
English Channel, *see* Channel
English, Early, art, 18
— craftsmanship, 18
— history, 18, 138
— language, 14
English people, ancestry of, 13
ENI of East Anglia, 92, 93, 94, 96, 100,
     101, Fig. 28
EORPWALD, king of East Anglia, 93, 100,
     101, Fig. 28
ERCONBERHT, king of Kent, 94, 97, Fig. 28
Esbjerg, Denmark, 104, 105, 106, 108,
     110, 112, Fig. 29
Escutcheons, bucket-, 76
— hanging-bowl, 72, 73, 76, 89, Pl. XV
— silver bowl, 74
Essex, England, 124, 140

ETHELBERT, king of Kent, 66, 84, 97, 141
ETHELFRITH, king of Northumbria, 68
ETHELWALD, hermit of Farne, 51
EVISON, VERA I., 149
Eye, Suffolk, 129, Fig. 2

FALK, H., 137, 154
Faversham, Kent, a *villa regalis*, 84
— brooch, 85, 131
— glasshouse, 100
FELIX, Bishop, 88, 93, 96, 98
Felixstowe, Suffolk, 115, Fig. 2
Fenland, The English, 16, 17, 90, 117,
    127, 129, 140, 141, 143, 145, 146,
    Fig. 2
Ferrules, iron, 41, 71, 77
Filigree-work, 78, 79, 80, 81, 82, 83, 84,
    88, 100, 135
Finnesburh Fragment, The, 120
Fitch Collection, Norwich, 87
Flambeau, *see* 'Lamp-stand'
Fleam Dyke, 143, 146, Fig. 31
Fleet, Roman, *see* Roman
FLORENCE OF WORCESTER, 92
Flushing, Holland, 106, 111, 112, Fig. 29
Fœderati, employment of, 116, 119, 120
Forest Gate (Essex), jewelled pin, 85, 88
Fox, Sir CYRIL, 89-90, 127, 151
France (Gaul), 93, 95, 104, 115, 137
FRANCIS, F., 148
Franks, 13, 15, 77, 95, 116, 118, 120, 132,
    Fig. 1
FREOMAR, king of the Alamanni, 116, 117
Frisia, 107, 120, 131, 132, 143, 145
— East, 15, 107
— — islands, 105, 107, 110, Fig. 29
— North, islands, 107, 108, 110, Fig. 29
— West, islands, 105, 107, 111, Fig. 29
Frisians, 13, 15, 103, 118, 120, 145, Fig. 1
FURSEY, Saint, 90, 93, 94

Galtabäck ship, *see* Ships and Boats
Gaming-piece, 27, 40
GARMONSWAY, G. N., 149
Garnet cloisonné-work, 79, 135-6
— decorated brooch at Trier, 86
— — buckles, 81, Pls. XXII, XXIII

— — crosses, 85, 146
— — Kentish brooches, 83, 84, 129, 144
— — — plaques, 144-5
— — pendant, 146
— — pinhead, 85
— — strap-mounts, 78, 81, Pls. XXII,
    XXIII
— helmet-decoration, 70
— necklace, 101
— purse-decoration, 80, 81, Frontispiece
— shield-decoration, 71
— studs, 82
— sword-decoration, 42, 81, 135, Pl.
    XXIV
Geats (Gautar), 132, 136, 138, 139, 143,
    Fig. 1
German tribes, North, 15, 103, 118
Germany, 74, 86, 109
Gesso, gilt, 41, 70, 71, 134
GILDAS, 17, 119, 150
Gilded bronze, 27, 69, 70, 71, 82, 144
— gesso, 41, 70, 71, 134
— silver, 42, 73, 75
— wooden object, 41
GIRALDUS CAMBRENSIS, 73
Gisleham, Suffolk, 101
Glass bowl, 144
— blue, cloisonné-set, 83
— claw-beakers, 100, 144
— dark blue at Snape, 100
— of Frankish origin, 144
— of Kentish origin, 100, 131, 144
— in lapidary-work, 79, 89
— millefiori, or mosaic, 72, 80, 81, 89,
    90, Fig. 23, Frontispiece, Pls.
    XV, XXV
— palm cups, 130, 144
— pouch bottle, 144
— squat jars, 27, 100, 101, 130, 144, Fig. 5
Godmanchester, Hunts, 146
Gokstad, Norway, 99, Figs. 1, 32
— ship, *see* Ships and Boats
Gold, 17, 32, 37, 42, 46, 77
— bracteates, 130, 131
— brooch-disc, 87
— buckle, 78, 81, 136, 137, Pl. XX
— clasps, 42, 78, 80, Pl. XXV

Gold coin of Heraclius I, 85
— coin, copy of Justinian I, 101-2
— coins, Merovingian, 42, 95, Pl. XXI
— commission to seek, 31
— filigree-work, 78, 80, 81, 82 (*see also* Filigree-work)
— foil, 41, 71, 79
— helmet-embellishment, 70
— ingots, 42
— lidded cloisons, 79, 80, 81
— mounts, 78, Pls. XXII, XXIII
— nodule in cable-twist, 81, 85, Fig. 25
— pendent cross, 85, 146
— pinhead, 85
— purse-frame, 42, 78, 80, Frontispiece
— pyramids from sword-knots, 81, 82, 85, Pl. XXIVb
— ring from Snape, 100, 101
— sought at Beeleigh, 31
— sword-fittings, 81, Pl. XXIV
— Treasure Trove, 46
Goose-feather pillow, 77
Gordon, Professor R. K., 20, 150
Gotha, river, Sweden, 132, Figs. 1, 32
Goths, 116
Gotland, Sweden, 71, Figs. 1, 32
Gourd-cups, 37, 38, 75, Pl. XIIIb, c
Grave-goods, *see* Burials, Ship-burials *or* Burial-chamber
Great Yarmouth, Norfolk, *see* Yarmouth
Green, Barbara, 20
Greenwich Mean Time used, 105, 109
Gregory of Tours, 132
Grendel, 132
Grierson, P. H., 96, 149
Grimes, Professor W. F., 32, 38, 41, 148, 152
Guthfrith of Lindisfarne, 51
Guthrum, 147

Hadrian's Wall, 114, 116
'Hair-spring coil' motif, 89-90
Halland, Sweden, 130, Fig. 32
Halsnøy boat, *see* Ships and Boats
Hanging-bowls, 40, 72-3, 76, 89, 90, Pl. XIV

— escutcheons, 72, 73, 89, Pl. XV
— origin of, 72-3, 89-90
Hanover, 15, 121, 131
Harden, Dr. D. B., 100, 150
Harness, Body-, 42, 78, 82
— Sam Browne, 78
Harp, 73, Pl. XVIa
Harting, J. E., 154
Harwich, Essex, 106, 111, 112, Fig. 29
Haslingfield, Cambs, 121
Hatley, A. R., 152
Hawkes, Professor C. F. C., 84, 150
Haylett, R. H., 20
Heimskringla, 99
Hele, N. Fenwick, 148
Helmet, 42, 69-70, 135, 136, Pl. X
— Benty Grange, 77, 135
— fittings of bronze, 69, 70, 77
— relief-decorated panels, 70, 134, 136, Pl. XXIIIg, h
Hengist, 116, 117, 119, 120
Henry, Françoise, 90, 150
Heorot, hall of the Danish king, 132
Heraclius I, 85
Historia Brittonum, 119
Hjortspring boat, *see* Ships and Boats
Hodgkin, R. H., 149
Holland, 15, 106, 109
Holme-next-the-Sea, Norfolk, 143
Holmes, T. V., 152
Holstein, 15, 48, 109, Fig. 32
Holywell Row, Suffolk, 121
Hook of Holland, 112, Fig. 29
Horns, Drinking-, *see* Drinking-horns
Horsa, 116, 119, 120
Houtzager, Dr. M. Elisabeth, 20
Humber, river, 15, 103, 105, 109
Humbla, P., 153
Hunstanton, Norfolk, 143, 144, Fig. 2
Hurst, J. G., 152
Hutchinson, J. N. and P., 19, 152
Hutchison, r.n., Lt.-Cdr. J. K. D., 48
Hygelac, king of the Geats, 132, 134

Iceni, 118
— province of, 141
Icklingham, Suffolk, 136

Icknield Way, 127, 129, 146, Fig. 31
Idle river, battle of, 68
Idols destroyed, pagan, 97
Inhumation burials, *see* Burials
Inquest, Coroner's, 46
Interlace ornament, 70, 79, 80, 83, 136
Ipswich, 129, 130, 134, 144, Figs. 2, 31
— Museum, *see* Museums
'Ipswich People', 131
Irish hanging-bowls, 90
— millefiori glass, 89, 90
— monks, 89, 90, 93, 94
— raiders and settlers, 116
Iron, 37
— angon-heads, 41, 71
— axes, *see* Axes
— bucket-mountings, 40, 43, 76
— cauldron collars, 76
— chain-mail, *see* Byrnies
— chainwork and bars, 43, 76
— clench-nails, *see* Ships and Boats
— ferrules, 41, 77
— fragments, 27
— helmet-fragments, 69, 70
— — frame, 77
— 'lamp', 43, 76, 81
— 'lamp-stand', 40 (*see also* Standard)
— plate-support for specimens, 40
— ring, 27
— scramasax blade, 42, 77
— shield-boss, 41, 71
— spear-heads, 41
— standard, *see* Standard
— swords, *see* Swords
Ivory, 27, 40, 80, 83
— games-piece, 27, 40
Ixworth (Suffolk) pendent cross, 146

Jade Bay, Germany, 110, 112
JANKUHN, Dr. H., 20, 153, 154
JESSEN, K., 153
JESSUP, R. F., 83, 151
Jewelled buckles, 42, 83, 144, Pls. XXII, XXIII
— clasps, 42, Pl. XXV
— mounts, 42, Pls. XXII, XXIII
— pin-head, 83

— purse, 42, Frontispiece
— pyramids, *see* Swords
— scabbard-bosses, *see* Swords
— sword-hilts, *see* Swords
Jewellery, 17, 32, 42, 77, 78, 79, 84, 131
JOHANNESSEN, F., 153
JONCKHEERE, E., 153
Juist, Germany, 111
JURMIN of East Anglia, 98, Fig. 28
Jutes, 13, 15, 16, 103, 120, 130, Fig. 1
Jutish continental homeland, 15, Fig. 1
Jutland, 15, 106, 107, 108, 130, 131, Fig. 32

KEABLE, Mr., 60, 63
KENDRICK, T. D. (*afterwards* Sir THOMAS), 16, 17, 69, 78, 80, 84, 85, 86, 87, 89, 148, 150
Kenninghall, Norfolk, 130, 144
'Kenninghall brooch', 130
Kent, 15, 66, 77, 82, 83, 84, 85, 92, 116, 117, 120, 130, 131, 137, 141, 143, 145
— Men of, 16, 120
KENT, Dr. J. P. C., 101
KERSTEN, Professor, 20
KING, JUDITH, 19
King Barrows, Old Uppsala, 85, 134
Kingston brooch, *see* Brooches
KITZINGER, ERNST, 148
KLAEBER, Professor F., 154
Kvalsund boat, *see* Ships and Boats

LACK, Miss M. K., 32, 44
Lackford, Suffolk, 144
Ladle, silver, 40, 75, 76
Lakenheath, Suffolk, 144, 145
LAMBERT, Dr. J. M., 62, 152
'Lamp', iron, 43, 76, 81
'Lamp-stand', iron, 40, 66 (*see also* Standard)
Language-change in East Anglia, 118
LANKESTER, Sir E. RAY, 154
Lapidary-work, 79, 80 (*see also* Jewellery)
Lapis-lazuli, 83
Lark, river, 129, 130, 136, 144, Fig. 2

LAYARD, Miss NINA F., 129, 151
Leather, 37
— arm-strap on shield, 71
— axe-holster, 27
— bags, 38, 40, 77
— cup, 77
— harness with gold and jewelled
    mounts, 42, 78, 82
— shoes, 40, 77
— sword-sheath, 81
LEATHES, H. MUSSENDEN, 60
LEEDS, EDWARD THURLOW, 14, 16, 83, 84,
    88, 107, 120, 130, 131, 150
Leeds, Yorks, 94
Leire, Denmark, 132, Fig. 32
LETHBRIDGE, T. C., 17, 121, 150, 151
Liber Eliensis, see *Ely Chronicle*
Liim Fjord, Denmark, 106, 130, Fig. 32
Lincoln Museum, *see* Museums
Lincolnshire, 117, 120
LINDQVIST, Professor SUNE, 69, 71, 95, 96,
    99, 132, 149
Little Belt, 106
Little Ouse river, 144, 146, Fig. 2
Little Wilbraham, Cambs, 121, 127, 144
Lombards, 116
London, 118, 125, 145
Low Countries, 104
LUCK, KENNETH W., 60
Lympne, Kent, Saxon Shore fort, 114

Mablethorpe, Lincs, 105
MAGOUN, F. P., 149
Mail, Chain-, *see* Byrnies
Making of the Broads, The (1960), 19
Mälar, Lake, Sweden, 136, Fig. 32
Maldon Corporation records, 31
'Man and lions' motif, *see* 'Daniel in the
    Lion's Den'
MARYON, HERBERT, 18, 69, 70, 135, 149
MATHESON, COLIN, 154
MAYNARD, GUY, 24, 25, 29, 56, 148
Mead, 75, 76
Mediterranean Sea, 75, 116
Medway, river, 16
Melton, Suffolk, 144

Mercia, 138, 139, 146-7 (*see also* Mercian
    Angles)
Middle Anglia, 16
Midlands, The English, 94, 107, 146
Mildenhall, Suffolk, 144
— Treasure, 75
Millefiori glass, 72, 80, 81, 89, 90
Monasteries, Fig. 31
— Blythburgh, Suffolk, 94
— Brie, France, 94
— Burgh Castle, Suffolk, 90, 93, 94
— Bury St. Edmunds, Suffolk, 93
— Ely, Cambs, 94
Morston, Norfolk, 143
Mosaic glass, *see* Millefiori glass
Moselle, river, 86
MOTHERSOLE, JESSIE, 152
Mounts, Harness-, 42, 43, 78, 80, 81, 89,
    Pls. XXII, XXIII
Museums,
— Ashmolean, Oxford, 14, 101
— British, 17, 19, 31, 32, 43, 46, 47, 75,
    76, 85, 96, 135
— — (Natural History), 19
— Bury St. Edmunds, 136
— Ipswich, 19, 24, 29, 87
— Kiel, 48
— Lincoln, City and County, 20
— Norwich, Castle, 20, 87
— Oslo, University, 20
— Schleswig, Schleswig-Holstein for Pre-
    history, 20, 48
— Science, 31, 48
— Utrecht, Centraal, 20, 49
MYRES, Dr. J. N. L., 17, 117, 150, 151, 152

Nar, river, 127, Fig. 2
Narrow Seas, The, 104, 106, 111, 112, 131
Needham Market, Suffolk, 144
Nene, river, 146
NENNIUS, 119, 140, 150
NERMAN, Professor BIRGER, 95
NEVILLE, The Hon. R. C., 151
Niello-inlay, 70, 71, 78-9
NIKLASSON, N., 153
Norderney, Germany, 111, Fig. 29
Nordland boats, *see* Ships and Boats

Norfolk, England, 109, 111, 122, 127, 129, 130, 140, 143, 144, 146 (and *passim*)
Normans, 13, 142
Norsemen, 13, Fig. 1
North Sea voyages, 19, 20, 103-13, 120, 130, 131, 137, 142-4, Fig. 29
Northumbria, 66, 67, 68, 94, 97, 139, 141, 147
Norway, 99, 137
Norwich, 122, 127, 130, 140, 141, 142, 144, Fig. 2
— Castle Museum, *see* Museums
Notitia Dignitatum, 114, 115
Nouhuys, J. W. van, 153
Nydam ship, *see* Ships and Boats

Offa, king of the continental Angles, 138, 139
Offa, king of Mercia, 138
Ohtere, *see* Ottarr
Ongentheow, *see* Egil
Onyx intaglio, 100, 101
Origin of the English Nation, 15
Orosius, 15
Oseberg, Norway, 99, Figs. 1, 32
— ship, *see* Ships and Boats
Oslo University Museum, *see* Museums
Oswald, king of Northumbria, 66
Oswy, king of Northumbria, 66, 94
Ottarr Vendelcrow, king of the Swedes, 134
Ouse, river (Great), 146, Fig. 2

Pagan Saxondom, 82
Pakefield, Suffolk, 101
Pattern-welded swords, *see* Swords
Paulinus, 93
Peddar's Way, 127, 140
Pellworm, Germany, 110, Fig. 29
Penda, king of Mercia, 93, 94, 97, 98, 147
Petch, D. F., 151
Pevensey, Sussex, Saxon Shore fort, 114
Phillips, C. W., 18, 19, 31, 32, 33, 37, 42, 44, 45, 46, 48, 148, 153
Picts, 13, 116, 119, 120, Fig. 1

Piggott, Mrs. C. M., 32
— Professor Stuart, 32
Pillow, 77,
Pin, jewelled, 83
Place-name Society, 118
Place-name evidence, 118, 122, Fig. 30
Plenderleith, Dr. H. J., 17
Plummer, J. L., 20
Police-guard, 32
Population distribution-patterns, 127
— size of, 124-6
Portchester, Hants, Saxon Shore fort, 114
Post, L. von, 153
Pottery, Anglian, 15, 119
— Anglo-Frisian urns, 106, 113, 117
— Anglo-Saxon handmade, 26, 28-9, 117
— bottle, wheel-made, 43, Pl. XIIId
— Bronze Age, 28, 30
— cremation urns, 17, 106, 117, 120
— Frankish wheel-made, 145
— history of Anglo-Saxon, 145
— Ipswich ware, 29, 131, 145-6, Fig. 31
— Romano-British, later occurrence of, 122
— Romano-Saxon, 117, 118
— Saxon urns, 107, 119
— Thetford ware, 145, 146
— Tiger ware, 31
Pretty, J.P., Mrs. Edith May, 24, 25, 29, 30, 31, 46, 47
— Colonel Frank, 29
Procopius, 15
Ptolemy, 15
Purse, gold and jewelled, 42, 78, 80, 86, 90, 95, 136, Frontispiece
Pyramids, gold and jewelled, 81, 82, 85, Fig. 23, Pl. XXIVb

Raddatz, Dr., 20
Raedwald, king of East Anglia, 66, 68, 92, 93, 94, 95, 96, 98, 100, 101, 131, 141, Fig. 28
Randall, H. J., 124, 153
Read, Sir Hercules, 151
Reculver, Kent, Saxon Shore fort, 114, 115
Reed's Nautical Almanac, 108-9

REGENHERE, of East Anglia, 68, 100, 101, Fig. 28
Rendlesham, Suffolk, 94, 101, 102, 141
Rhine, river, 15, 64, 104, 132, 143, Fig. 1
— frontier, 116
Rhineland, 15, 16, 72, 84, 88, 116, 117, 118, 120, 125, 135, 145, 146
RICHBERT, 93
Richborough, Kent, 118
— Saxon Shore fort, 114
Ring, finger-, 100, 101
'Ring' from ring-sword, 82-3, 136, Fig. 24
ROBINSON, W., 152
ROEDER, Professor F., 121
Roman Britain becomes Anglo-Saxon England, 114
— — cantonal capital(s), 118-9, 125, 141
— — coloniae, 125
— — Ordnance Survey maps of, 124
— — settlements, 125
— — threatened, 116
— decorative styles, 72, 74, 121
— eagle, 68
— fleet, 63, 115
— forts, *see* Saxon Shore
— merchant ships, *see* Ships and Boats
— roads, 127, 129, 140, 141, 142, 145, Fig. 31
— survivals, 121, 122
Romano-Britons, *see* Britons
Romans, 13
ROSENBERG, G., 153
Rottum, Holland, 111, Fig. 29
RUSKIN, Mr., defines the Ashby Dell ship, 60
RUTLAND, Duke of, 24

Saltfleet, Lincs, 105
Sandlings, The, Suffolk, 101, 127, 129-39, 141, 142, 143, 144, 145
'Sandlings Folk', 131, 132, 138, 139, 140, 144, 145, 146
Saxon continental homeland, 15, 121, Fig. 1
Saxons, 13, 14, 15, 49, 103, 107, 108, 118, 120, Fig. 1
— East, 15, 94

— intermixture with Angles, 13, 107, 109
— South, 15, 66
— West, 13, 15, 66
Saxon Shore, The, 115
— — Count of, 114, 116
— — forts, Bradwell, Essex (*Othona*), 114, 115
— — — Brancaster, Norfolk (*Branodunum*), 114, 143, Fig. 31
— — — Burgh Castle, Suffolk (*Gariannonum*), 114, 117, Fig. 31
— — — Carisbrooke, I.o.W., 115
— — — Dover, Kent (*Dubris*), 114
— — — Lympne, Kent (*Lemanis*), 114
— — — Pevensey, Sussex (*Anderida*), 114
— — — Portchester, Hants (*Portus Adurni*), 114
— — — Reculver, Kent (*Regulbium*), 114, 115
— — — Richborough, Kent (*Rutupiae*), 114
— — — Walton Castle, Suffolk, 115, Fig. 31
Scandinavian Archaeology (1937), 137
Scania, Sweden, 130, Fig. 32
Scharhorn, Germany, 110
Schiermonnikoog, Holland, 111
Schlei Fjord, Schleswig, 106
Schleswig, 15, 48, 62, 103, 104, 105, 106, 108, 109, 110, 120, 130, 140, 141
SCHRAM, Dr. O. K., 122, 140, 153
Science Museum, London, *see* Museums
Scots, 13, Fig. 1
Scramasax, 42, 77
Scunthorpe, Lincs, 89
SCYLD SCEFING, 52, 99
Scylfing dynasty of Sweden, 99, 132, 134, 137, 139
Sea-power, *see* Wuffings
Shell in lapidary-work, 79, 83, 144-5
Sheringham, Norfolk, 106, 111, 112, Fig. 29
SHETELIG, Professor H., 65, 137, 153, 154
Shield, 41-2, 70-1, 134, 135, Pls. XI, XII
— -mounts, 41, 70, 71
Ships and Boats, Anglo-Saxon, 18, 49, 51, 60, 63, 64, 65, 103

Ships and Boats, Ashby Dell, 48, 60-3, Fig. 31
— Beowulf's, 52
— Caister-on-Sea, 48, 54, 57, 59, Fig. 31
— Catfield, 63, Fig. 31
— clench- or clinker-built, 27, 49, 51, 52, 59, 61, 62, 63, 64, 65
— clench-nails, 27, 28, 30, 48, 49, 54, 55, 56, 57, 58, 59, 62, 64, Fig. 14
— curragh, 51
— flat keel-plank, 49-50, 52, 60, 62, 64, 65, Fig. 12
— Galtabäck, 64-5
— Gokstad, Fig. 12, Pl. IIIb
— Halsnøy, 62
— Hjortspring, 62
— Kvalsund, 65, Pl. VIIb
— modern, 49, 58-9, 65, 108
— Nordland, 62
— Nydam, 48, 52, 54, 55, 59, 60, 61, 62, 65, 103, 104, 108, 109, 130, 143, Figs. 12, 15, Pl. IIIa
— Oseberg, 52, Pl. IV
— Roman merchantmen, 64, 104, 115, 118
— rowing, 51, 54, 61, 62, 64, 103-4, 130
— sailing, 51, 52, 64, 65, 130
— square sterns disproved, 18, 57, 58, 64
— Scyld Scefing's funeral ship, 52
— Snape, 18, 30, 48, 55, 57-9, Figs. 12, 17, 18, Fig. 31
— Sutton Hoo No. 1, 52, 59, 60, 64, 99, Figs. 11, 12, 31, Pl. V
— — condition when exposed, 30, 48, 54, 55
— — constructional details, 52, 54, 55, Fig. 13
— — method of deposition in grave, 44-6
— — position in grave, 30
— — repairs to, 55, Pl. VIa
— — survey of, 44, 48
— Sutton Hoo No. 2, 27, 28, 48, 56-7, 60, 64, Figs. 12, 16, 31
— Tholes of claw-shape, 54, 61, 62, Fig. 19, Pl. VIb
— Utrecht, 49, 63-4, Pl. VIIa

— Viking, 20, 49, 50, 51, 52, 60, 63, 64, 65, 103, Fig. 12, Pl. IIIb
— Walthamstow No. 1, 63
— Walthamstow No. 2, 64
— Yarmouth, King Street, 63
Ship-burial, Ashby Dell, 62, 100, Figs. 1, 31
— Caister-on-Sea, 57, 100, Figs. 1, 31
— Snape, 18, 57, 100, 101, 102, 144, Figs. 1, 17, 18, 31
— Suffolk, 57, 99, 101, 134, 137, 145
— Sutton Hoo No. 1, 17, 18, 30, 88, 92, 95, 99, 100, 121, 144, 147, Figs. 1, 31
— Sutton Hoo No. 2, 27, 28, 29, 100, 101, 146, Figs. 1, 31
— Sutton Hoo, perhaps in barrows 7 and 10, 23, 101
— Uppland, Sweden, 95, 99, 134, 135
— Viking, British Isles, 64, 99
— — Denmark, 99
— — Norway, 99
— — Sweden, 99
Shoes, leather, 40, 77
Shoe-buckles, 77
SIDONIUS, 49
SIGEBERHT, king of East Anglia, 93, 94, 100, Fig. 28
Signum, 68
Silver, 17, 32, 37, 46
— bowl, 38, 40, 74-5, Pl. XVIIIc
— brooches, 83
— cup, 40, 75, 76, Pl. XIXa
— dish, 38, 40, 43, 74, 75, Pl. XVII
— drinking-horn mounts, 42-3, 73, Fig. 22
— gourd-cup mounts, 38, 75, Pl. XIIIb c
— handles, 38, 74, Pl. XVIIIc
— helmet-fittings, 69, 70
— ladle, 40, 75, 76, Pl. XIXb
— Mildenhall Treasure, 75
— mounts on leather cup, 77
— nest of bowls, 41, 42, 74, Pl. XVIIIa, b
— patches on hanging-bowl, 72, Pl. XIVc
— ring-sword hilt, see Swords
— rivets in helmet, 77
— Roman vessels as pottery models, 117
— shoe-buckles, 77

Silver spoons, 41, 75, Pl. XIXc
SJØVOLD, THORLEIF, 153
Skaggerrak, 130, Figs. 1, 32
Skaw, The, Denmark, 107, Fig. 32
SMEDLEY, NORMAN, 19
SMITH, CHARLES ROACH, 14
SMITH, REGINALD A., 14, 136, 150, 151
Snape, Suffolk, 129, 142, 144, Figs. 1, 31
— boat, *see* Ships and Boats
Södermanland, Sweden, 136, Fig. 32
SØLVER, CARL V., 153
Southampton Water, 114
Spear-heads, 41, 71, Pl. IIa
SPENCER, H. E. P., 19, 25, 56
Spoons, silver, 41, 75, 95, Pl. XIXc
Spurn Head, Yorks, 105
Stag on standard, 40, 66, 68, Pl. VIII
Standard, 40, 66, 68, 96, Figs. 20, 21
STAUNTON, O.B.E., G. E., 32
STENTON, Sir FRANK, 92, 145, 149
Stiffkey, river, 143
STOLPE, H., 154
Stour, river, 21, 143, 144, Fig. 2
STURLASON, SNORRE, 154
Sub-Roman Britons, *see* Britons
Sudbury, Suffolk, 144, Fig. 2
Suffolk, 21, 32, 77, 101, 122, 127, 129, 131, 136, 137, 141, 145 (and *passim*)
'Sutton Hoo jeweller and workshop', 85, 86, 88, 89, 90, 136
Sutton Hoo ship No. 1, *see* Ships and Boats *also* Burial-chamber
Sutton Hoo treasure presented to the nation, 47
Sutton Mounts (round barrow group), 21, 23, 24, Figs. 3, 4
— — Barrow No. 1, 21, 23, 25, 29-32, 33-47, Figs. 6, 7
— — Barrow No. 2, 21, 25, 27-8, 144, 146
— — Barrow No. 3, 21, 25-7, 37, 134
— — Barrow No. 4, 21, 25, 134
— — excavation of, 24-32, 33-47, 101
— — identity of buried persons, 99-102
— — robbery, 23, 25, 26, 29, 30-1
Sutton, Suffolk, 21
— brooch, 87, 131, Fig. 27
Sutton-on-Sea, Lincs, 105

Swaefe (Swabians), 15, 118, 141
Swaffham, Norfolk and Cambs, 141, Fig. 30
Swavesey, Cambs, 141
Sweden, 130, 132, 135, 136, 137, Fig. 32
Swedes, 132, 134, 138, 143, Fig. 1
Swedish affinities and connexions, 69, 70, 71, 80, 83, 85, 88, 95, 132, 134-7
— royal house, *see* Scylfing dynasty
SWITHHELM, king of the East Saxons, 94
Sword(s), 42, 69, 81, 82, 135, Pl. XXIV
— -belt, *see* Harness
— hilt, 81, 82
— knot, pyramids on, 81, 82, 85, Fig. 23
— pattern-welded, 135
— pommel, 86, 137
— — Swedish, 86, 88, 135, 136
— ring-, 82-3, 136
— scabbard, 42, 81, 82
— — jewelled bosses, 81, 135
— Swedish, 82
— — -type fittings, 82, 136, 144
Sylt, Germany, 110, Fig. 29

TACITUS, 15
Taplow, Bucks, barrow-burial, 74, 135
Tas, river, 127
Teifi, river, 73
Temple, heathen, 92, 93, 98
Terschelling, Holland, 109, Fig. 29
Texel, Holland, 105, 106, 109, 111, 112, Fig. 29
Textiles, 25, 37, 40, 42, 77, 81, 82
Thames, river, 103, 131
Thanet, Isle of, 116, 120
Thegn-status, 77
THEODORIC, king of the Franks, 132
THEODOSIUS, Count, 116
Thet, river, 144, Fig. 2
Thetford, Norfolk, 142, 145, Fig. 2
Tides, Theory of, 109
Tin helmet-decoration, 70
— shield-decoration, 71
TISCHLER, F., 154
Town and Country in Roman Britain, 124
Tray, wooden, 26, 29, 40, 41
Treasure Trove, definition of, 46

Tribal Hidage, 147
Trier brooch, 86, 88
'True-born Englishman, The', 13
Tufa, 68
Tune, Norway, 99, Figs. 1, 32
TYTTLA, king of East Anglia, 100, Fig. 28

Ulltuna, Sweden, 71
Uppland, Sweden, 70, 71, 82, 131, 134, 135, 136, Fig. 32
Uppsala, Sweden, 85, 132, Figs. 1, 32
Urus, *see* Aurochs
Utrecht boat, *see* Ships and Boats
— Museum, *see* Museums

Vallstenarum, Sweden, 71
Valsgärde, Sweden, 71, 83, 99, Figs. 1, 32
VAN DER WIJK, Hr., 153
Varberg, Sweden, 64, Fig. 32
Vecht, river, 64
Vendel, Sweden, 71, 80, 99, 134, 136, Figs. 1, 32
Vexillum, 68
Viking period, 27, 63, 99, 131, 146
— ships, *see* Ships and Boats
Vlieland, Holland, 111
VORTIGERN, 119, 120

WAGSTAFF, Miss B., 32, 44
Walcheren, Holland, 112
Waldringfield, Suffolk, 129
WALKER, J. W., 149
Walsingham, Norfolk, 143, Fig. 2
Walthamstow boats, *see* Ships and Boats
Walton Castle, Suffolk, Saxon Shore fort, 115, Fig. 31
Wangeroog, Germany, 110, 111, Fig. 29
WARBURG, H. D., 109
WARD, Dr. GORDON, 149
Warsaw, Poland, 74
Wash, The, 103, 105, 107, 109, 111, 114, 140, 143, Figs. 1, 2
Waveney, river, 21, 129, 140, 142, Fig. 2
WEHHA, king of East Anglia, 100, 132, 134, 137, 140, 142, Fig. 28
WELLS, Dr. CALVIN, 19
Wells, Norfolk, 143, Fig. 2
Wener, lake, Sweden, 132, Figs. 1, 32

Wensum, river, 127, 140, 142, 143, Fig. 2
WEOHSTAN, 132, 134
WERNER, Dr. A. E., 17
Weser, river, 110, 112, 121, 141, Fig. 1
Wessex, 94
WEST, S. E., 152
Westfold, Norway, 99
WHEELER, R. E. M. (*later* Sir MORTIMER), 124, 152, 153
Whetstone(s), masked, 68-9, 96, Pl. IX
Whisky, primitive, 75
WHITE, DONALD A., 152
Whitehall, London, 146
WHITELOCK, Professor D., 77, 138, 154
Wight, Isle of, 15
WIGLAF, prince of the Scylfings, 132, 134, 138, 139
WILSON, D. M., 149
Wilton (Norfolk) pendent cross, 85-6, 88, 146
Winwaed, river, battle of, 94, 98
Woodbridge, Suffolk, 21, 144, Figs. 2, 3
— brooch, *see* Sutton brooch
WOODHOUSE, D., J. and J., 20
Works, Ministry of (*formerly* Office of), 20, 31
Woven fabric, *see* Textiles
WRENN, Professor C. L., 154
WUFFA, king of East Anglia, 92, 100, 132, 134, 137, 139, 140, 142, 143, Fig. 28
Wuffing dynasty of East Anglia, 17, 92, 94, 95, 96, 100-1, 102, 131, 137, 140, 141, 142, 145, 146, 147, Fig. 28
— sea power, 141, 145

Yare, river, 127, 142, 146, Fig. 2
Yarmouth, Norfolk, 117, 142, Fig. 2
— (King Street) boat, *see* Ships and Boats
Yeavering, Northumberland, 141
Ymuiden, Holland, 112, Fig. 29
Yngling kings of Norway, 99
York, 68, 125, 141

ZEUNER, Professor F. E., 32
Zoomorphic ornament, *see* Animal ornament